W9-ABZ-529

WITHDRAWN

FOUNDATIONS OF MODERN PSYCHOLOGY SERIES

Richard S. Lazarus, Editor

The Psychological Development of the Child,   Paul H. Mussen

Tests and Measurements,   Leona E. Tyler

Motivation and Emotion,   Edward J. Murray

Personality,   Richard S. Lazarus

Clinical Psychology,   Julian B. Rotter

Sensory Psychology,   Conrad G. Mueller

Perception,   Julian E. Hochberg

Learning,   Sarnoff A. Mednick

Language and Thought,   John B. Carroll

Social Psychology,   William W. Lambert and Wallace E. Lambert

Physiological Psychology,   Philip Teitelbaum

Educational Psychology,   Donald Ross Green

The Nature of Psychological Inquiry,   Ray Hyman

Organizational Psychology,   Edgar H. Schein

RICHARD S. LAZARUS

Professor of Psychology
University of California, Berkeley

second edition

Personality

PRENTICE-HALL, INC., ENGLEWOOD CLIFFS, NEW JERSEY

Current Printing (last digit)
10   9   8   7   6   5   4   3   2   1

Prentice-Hall International, Inc., London

Prentice-Hall of Australia, Pty. Ltd., Sydney

Prentice-Hall of Canada, Ltd., Toronto

Prentice-Hall of India Private Limited, New Delhi

Prentice-Hall of Japan, Inc., Tokyo

To my dear children, David and Nancy

Contents

THREE
The Development of Personality   *46*

FREUD'S PSYCHOSEXUAL THEORY

PIAGET'S THEORY OF COGNITIVE DEVELOPMENT

CONTRASTS AND OVERLAPS BETWEEN FREUD AND PIAGET

FOUR
Personality Dynamics   *60*

THE TENSION-REDUCTION MODEL

APPROACHES SUPPLEMENTING THE TENSION-REDUCTION MODEL: EFFECTANCE

THE FORCE-FOR-GROWTH MODEL

IMPLICATIONS OF THE THREE MOTIVATIONAL MODELS

OTHER ISSUES OF PERSONALITY DYNAMICS

FIVE
Personality Determinants — Biological Factors   *92*

BIOLOGICAL AND CULTURAL EVOLUTION

GENETIC INFLUENCES

PHYSIOLOGICAL INFLUENCES

SIX
Personality Determinants — Social Factors   *122*

CONTEMPORANEOUS SOCIAL INFLUENCE

DEVELOPMENTAL SOCIAL INFLUENCE

THE MECHANISMS OF SOCIAL INFLUENCES ON PERSONALITY

BIOLOGICAL VERSUS SOCIAL DETERMINANTS: THE PRINCIPLES OF INTERACTION 145

SEVEN

Foundations of Modern Psychology Series

The tremendous growth and vitality of psychology and its increasing fusion with the social and biological sciences demand a search for new approaches to teaching at the introductory level. We can no longer feel content with the traditional basic course, geared as it usually is to a single text that tries to skim everything, that sacrifices depth for breadth. Psychology has become too diverse for any one man, or few men, to write about with complete authority. The alternative, a book that ignores many essential areas in order to present more comprehensively and effectively a particular aspect or view of psychology, is also insufficient, for in this solution many key areas are simply not communicated to the student at all.

The Foundations of Modern Psychology Series was the first in what has become a growing trend in psychology toward groups of short texts dealing with various basic subjects, each written by an active authority. It was conceived with the idea of providing greater flexibility for instructors teaching general courses than was ordinarily available in the large, encyclopedic textbooks, and greater depth of presentation for individual topics not typically given much space in introductory textbooks.

The earliest volumes appeared in 1963, the lastest not until 1967. Well over one and a quarter million copies, collectively, have been sold, attesting to the widespread use of these books in the teaching of psychology. Individual volumes have been used as supplementary texts, or as *the* text, in various undergraduate courses in psychology, education, public health, and sociology, and clusters of volumes have served as the text in beginning undergraduate courses in general psychology. Groups of volumes have been translated into eight languages, including Dutch, Hebrew, Italian, Japanese, Polish, Portuguese, Spanish, and Swedish.

With wide variation in publication date and type of content, some of the volumes need revision, while others do not. We have left this decision to the individual author who best knows his book in relation to the state of the field. Some will remain unchanged, some will be modestly changed, and still others completely rewritten. In the new series edition, we have also opted for some variation in the length and style of individual books, to reflect the different ways in which they have been used as texts.

There has never been stronger interest in good teaching in our colleges and universities than there is now; and for this the availability of high quality, well-written, and stimulating text materials highlighting the exciting and continuing search for knowledge is a prime prerequisite. This is especially the case in undergraduate courses where large numbers of students must have access to suitable readings. The Foundations of Modern Psychology Series represents our ongoing attempt to provide college teachers with the best textbook materials we can create.

Preface

The earlier edition of this text, entitled *Personality and Adjustment,* has been completely rewritten to deal exclusively with personality. Although the field has enormous scope, a text on personality must provide a thorough introduction to the most influential ideas and a reasonable sample of its research. In spite of the book's modest size, I have tried to give the beginning student a sophisticated and complete overview, sacrificing only some detail and direct contact with primary source material.

Personality is set off from other topics in psychology by its emphasis on the complex organization within the person of what general psychology treats as individual psychological functions, such as perception, learning, thinking, motivation and emotion, and on individual differences in adaptive functioning. Indeed, the concept of personality focuses on the whole man and on differences among men, studied systematically by empirical research employing many diverse methods of inquiry.

The major topics of this volume include: *1,* the nature of personality as a field of inquiry; *2,* personality theories and the manner in which they overlap and diverge; *3,* typical examples of empirical research on the issues posed by theory; and *4,* the assessment of personality. The book is issue-centered, and the issues organized around what I have called the four D's of personality, *description, development, dynamics* and *determinants,* each of which is treated in a separate chapter.

In arranging the topics, I have endeavored to create an orderly structure for thinking about personality, so that the student can readily assimilate additional reading and experience. In a field where coherence is not obvious, and where students tend to be confused by the welter of seemingly unrelated ideas and observations, such a structure is a valuable asset in learning. I hope I have succeeded through this book in providing the student with a useful outline for thinking about and understanding personality.

RICHARD S. LAZARUS

Personality

The Nature of Personality

When the layman thinks about personality, he is likely to view it as the impression one makes on others; he is likely to be concerned with such things as having a "good" or "effective" personality, one that permits him to accomplish the things he wants in the social world. Thus, he buys books and reads articles about how to do something or other with his personality, to cultivate it in such a way as to "win friends" or "be successful." When the psychologist thinks about personality, however, he sees it as the study of the stable psychological structures and processes that organize human experience and shape a person's actions and reactions to his environment. The latter is what this book is all about.

The primary domain of personality psychology is substantially different from the scope of general psychology, although there is of course considerable overlap. There are three main differences. 1. In general psychology the emphasis is usually on people in general, rather than on individual variation. A psychologist studying memory, for example, properly seeks rules about the conditions that influence memory. He may discover that memory is better for meaningful materials, such as stories or poems, than it is for meaningless and unrelated material, such as the connection between names and dates. The rule would apply to all people, more or less, and if it applied differently to some individuals than to others, such variations might be regarded as deviations or errors in the applicability of the general psychological rule. It is known, for example, that the difference in memory for meaningful and meaningless materials is less for the bright individual than for the dull individual.

More than other branches of psychology, personality tends to emphasize variations among individuals in psychological functions such as emotion, motivation, perception, learning, memory, language, thought, etc. This does not mean that individual differences are the sole concern of personality, but rather that they represent a primary emphasis. Personality psychologists are also interested in those aspects or rules of personality that apply to all mankind. We all share many features of personality in common. For example, the capacity for inhibition of action increases from the early stages of life to later periods; for all persons there are motivational and regulatory functions which operate according to certain general rules; for all persons there is an increase in the complexity of psychological processes from birth to maturity; we are all influenced by experience according to some common rules and by the biological properties we share with other animal species. The search for such "general laws" is just as characteristic of personality theory and research as of any other scientific discipline or any other segment of psychology. But the psychology of personality tends to be distinguished from these other segments by its great concern with psychological variation as well as commonality.

2. In general psychology, the focus is placed on individual psychological processes in people and infra-human animals, for example, motivation, emotion, perception, learning, memory, thought. Each of these functions or processes is usually treated as a separate chapter or subchapter in the typical general psychology text. However, in personality psychology, the person is more likely to be seen as an "integrated whole," a synthesis of all of the individual part-processes of which he is comprised. In other words, the functions or processes are seen as parts of an integrated system, and it is this system which is being studied as the subject matter of personality. The person engages in all of the individual functions; however, it is the distinctive manner in which these functions are organized in a given person that comprises what we call his personality. If we are to describe a person as a personality we must state the way in which these functions combine in his adjustments to the physical and social world. The personality psychologist is thus ultimately concerned with the "whole" man as distinguished from the various part-functions in which the man engages.

3. In general psychology, most of the emphasis is placed on external stimuli as determinants of immediate behavior. In contrast, personality psychology gives much of its attention to the stable attributes inside the

person, so to speak, which as traits or dispositions, guide his actions or reactions.

No one challenges the idea that we react to stimuli in the environment. Whether physical, as in the case of a speeding automobile that crosses our path, or social, as in the case of the known expectations of our friends or family, such stimuli represent powerful determinants of our thoughts, feelings, and actions. However, reference to environmental influences is insufficient to explain fully our behavior. Even as we acknowledge the dependency of our behavior and feelings on outside stimuli, we recognize another major class of determinants, one which resides within us, and which gains particular importance in the human animal as it develops from infancy. Even newborn children show major variations in reaction before there has been much opportunity for different kinds of experience. Each person comes into the world with different attributes that influence how he will behave, but after life has proceeded for a while, he develops a unique psychological structures that will make him react somewhat differently from every other person in the same situation. Therefore, along with the environmental stimuli to which people are exposed, their varying psychological structures must be recognized as a major determinant of how they behave. It is at this point that we enter the realm of personality psychology, which is the disciplined effort to pinpoint the nature of and variation in these structures.

Many common-sense examples of the role of personality variables as determinants of a person's reactions can be thought of, but one will suffice to illustrate the point. We observe that the same limited quantity of alcohol given to different people can produce loss of control in one individual, but scarcely noticeable effects in another. Some of this variation may, of course, be explained by differences in the momentary social and physical conditions. For instance, when the social circumstances of drinking are friendly and benign, people are less guarded and more inclined to permit themselves to get drunk than when the situation is hostile or dangerous. Moreover, the amount and type of food in the stomach before and during drinking also determine the effect of the alcohol by influencing its rate of absorption into the bloodstream. These are not really personality determinants, since they refer to external social and physiological conditions. However, some of the variation in the effects of alcohol result from stable personality characteristics which are often or usually operative. Consistent variations in reaction among people may be found even when the external situation is held constant. For example, some people are consistently more hostile in the same social contexts in which others are nonhostile: some are more tense, some are more outgoing, some are more cautious, some are more alert, some are more dependent. The same point applies to any item within a large catalogue of behavioral traits on which people can be compared.

The Structures and Processes of Personality

To describe personality, psychologists use the concepts of structure and process, as do scientists in other fields. Structures refer to the more or less stable arrangement or patterning of parts in a system, whereas processes have to do with the functions carried out by the parts, that is, what they do, and how they interact and change (in psychology, this is often called "dynamics"). The geological patterns of the countryside about us are *structures* because the individual parts—hills, river beds, even the foliage —are relatively stable or semi-permanent fixtures of the area, recognized by us as familiar objects and patterns. Similarly, in describing personality we endeavor to identify the structures of the psychological system which remain recognizable over time, perhaps even a very short time. Naturally, too, the concepts used to describe psychological structures will be different in content from those related to physical landscape and will reflect notions relevant to human behavior and experience.

Geology again provides a useful analogy to help us comprehend what is meant by *process* or dynamics. Mountains and valleys came into being through gigantic upheavals of the earth's surface, as a result of many processes, including the force of heat deep below the surface, slipping earth faults, and so on. Once formed, the topography in turn has an influence on the direction of wind striking the ground, the direction and rate of water flowing down the river beds from the mountain watersheds, the movements of storms, etc. Moreover, natural activities, such as the flow of water and the blast of wind, produce continuing changes in the structures themselves. For example, the wind wears down and polishes the mountain rock; botanical and zoological activities deposit layers of organic matter; the rains flowing down the mountain slopes become rivers that erode the ground and produce river valleys and canyons, or carry soil and deposit it elsewhere. These activities and the changes involving the interplay of natural environmental forces are *processes*. As can be seen above, structure and process are very closely interrelated.

One must not take the geological analogy too literally, because it tends to provide a too concrete image of visible, stationary things as structures, and of moving, changing things as processes. Actually, something can be a structure and at the same time involve dynamics. For example, a river in one sense represents a dynamic force which erodes the earth on which it flows, thus changing the topography. However, from another standpoint, the river also has the features of a structure, for example, forcing us to detour around it or over it if we want to get to the other side, or determining the life patterns of fish and other organisms living in it. Structures are merely parts in a system, parts which require that the system operate in particular ways, thus influencing dynamics. They may operate in this way for only an instant, or for long periods of time. And conversely, processes determine how the parts of the system operate.

The mechanically minded reader might think of an internal combustion engine as another example that effectively illustrates the interplay of structure and dynamics. The automobile engine consists of a variety of parts, all connected into a system in particular ways that determine how energy is transformed from its latent form as gasoline to the synchronous turning of the wheels. The pistons, valves, driveshaft, differential, and thousands of other elements or parts comprise the structures; the explosion of the gas and air mixture, intake and expulsion of gases, movement of the pistons, all comprise processes. Note that the movement of the pistons depends on the shape and alignment of the cylinders and, in turn, the pistons and cylinder walls eventually change their structure (wear out) as a function of that movement. Structures and processes are in continual interplay, mutually influencing each other and sometimes even changing their function in the course of the operation of the system.

Any system can be described by the scientist in terms of structures and processes. Thus, we can speak of social structures (for instance, our cultural institutions) and social processes (for instance, the interaction among individuals in a group, or between groups, or the effects of social institutions on human activity); we can also speak of biological structures (tissue or organ systems) and biological processes (metabolism, or cell death and replacement). Psychological systems are no exceptions; thus we can speak of personality structures, as when a person is said to be intelligent or have a strong ego, and personality dynamics, as when a person is said to be solving a problem or engaging in a self-deception.

Personality as Inference about Structure and Process

Unlike the most obvious geological structures and processes, such as mountains and riverbeds (structures), and erosion of the land or the movement of winds (processes), many of the structures and processes in the physical, biological, and social sciences are not directly observable and must be constructed logically by theoretical effort. For example, the oxidation of food or metals is a process we cannot see, but we know about it from observing the regular changes that occur when these substances are exposed to oxygen under given conditions of heat. The atom is a theoretical structure with parts or substructures which have never been seen directly, yet which interact with each other in ways that are known from carefully controlled observations of the conditions under which they occur and the effects they produce.

Psychological structures and processes too are theoretically conceived events that cannot be observed directly, though we can learn about them by inference from their causal conditions and effects. Mental abilities are one example of psychological structures which are not observable, although their effects are. Other things being equal, the person who has much ability will solve problems better or display more information than someone with less ability. We cannot observe this ability directly, since ability is an inferred property, but we can know about it from its effects as assessed by tests of information and problem solving. Similarly, when we speak of a person as having the motive, say to achieve or to be liked by others, we are attributing to him certain qualities which cannot be directly observed, but which can be known by observing behavior in social contexts that arouse that behavior. The reasoning is quite the same as when we speak about people being hungry or thirsty. What are hunger and thirst? We cannot see them. Yet we know they exist. It is a reasonable inference that a man will be hungry if he has been made to do without food for a number of hours—this is one of the arousing conditions of hunger—and we will not be surprised to discover that when such a man is brought before a plate of appetizing food, he will eat it with relish—such behavior is one of the observable effects of hunger.

Applied to personality the same argument holds. We don't see a personality, as we see an action or a physical object. Nor do a person's behaviors constitute what we mean by personality. Personality refers to a theoretical inference which is made by observing psychological reactions, and by conceiving logically what might be the underlying system (of structures and processes) which would explain the behavior. Except that since the personality is a complex system comprising many structures and processes, a very extensive set of inferences is called for, rather than a single one about hunger, or thirst, or ability. Moreover, it must deal with those properties of the person that are stable or consistent over time and from situation to situation, remembering that a large percentage of our actions and feelings are also shaped by the stimulus situation, as well as by personality.

THE BASES OF INFERENCE

It was said earlier that concepts of personality structure and process were inferences because only the visible actions and reactions of the person were ever observed directly. These observable actions and reactions, taking place in some situational context, are, therefore, the basic data on which a science of personality is based. There are three fundamental categories of observable events from which inferences about personality are made: movements or actions, verbal reports, and physiological changes which accompany psychological activity, as in emotion.

Actions. This of course refers to what people or infra-human animals do.

Two qualities of action can be distinguished, that which might be called "goal-oriented" or instrumental, and that called "style." The former quality refers to its intended result, some goal which the person seeks. The action is instrumental in achieving the result. The quality of style has little or perhaps even nothing to do with the intended results of the action. It reflects mainly the characteristic manner in which the act is carried out. Remember that the same act can and usually does have both goal-oriented and stylistic aspects. Sometimes one or the other is more evident and hence emphasized by the observer making inferences about its meaning for the person.

The *goal-oriented aspect of actions* communicates to an observer something about a person's motives, intentions, and interests even without the observer's asking the person about these things. Consider two students, for example: One spends the bulk of his time studying, whereas the other passes his time in social activities. Their respective choices among behavioral alternatives can lead us to infer that the first student is motivated or oriented principally toward academic achievement and that the second has strong needs for affiliation (the wish to be liked and accepted by others).

The thoughtful reader might see some difficulties with the above inferences from the goal-directed aspect of an action. It is probably much too simple. For example, the first student might really prefer to associate with others but be very shy and socially awkward. He regards the possibility of affiliation with others as closed to him and, hence, commits himself to study. Correspondingly, the second student might prefer achievement but considers himself incapable and therefore spends little time in study. Thus we see that motivation can be expressed directly in a person's actions, or also—whether because of internal conflict or external constraints—in the blocking of such behavioral expression and the consequent selection of substitute activities which conceal the fundamental motive or goal. Such complicated instances are especially interesting to the personality psychologist and provide the greatest challenge to his understanding.

If the latter argument is correct, then we can never really be very confident about the validity of inferences derived from a single source of information, such as the goal-oriented aspect of action. Although action may provide very important information about motivation, inferences from it will always be incomplete and should be supplemented by other behavioral evidence, such as the stylistic aspect of the action, or verbal reports from the person. Such additional information may force us to revise our original, sometimes over-simple inference, and to introduce complicating concepts such as inhibition and defense.

Turning now to the *stylistic aspect of an action,* every intentional act can be performed in a variety of ways without altering its efficiency in achieving the intended goal. We can walk with a rapid or slow pace, make gestures which are expansive or inhibited, take up much or little room on a page, write with weak or strong pressure, use simple language or elaborate sentence structure with much qualification, and so on. Such stylistic variation can be highly consistent for a given individual, although the specific acts involved will vary with their goals and the stimulus demands. These styles are often easily recognized as marking a particular person, as in the case of a public figure who is frequently mimicked, and whose recognition by the audience provokes amusement. The person being imitated is instantly recognized from the manner of speech, as well as from certain characteristic contents of that speech, gestures, body movements, and facial expressions.

The importance of such stylistic qualities for personality lies not in the fact that mimics can entertain us with them, or that they can sometimes be used by police detectives in tracking down a thief by his *modus operandi* (style of working) from one crime to another. Much more significant is that styles may communicate certain things about the person over and above that which is learned from goal-oriented action. For example, under certain circumstances at least, facial expressions may communicate an emotional state that the individual does not wish to make public. Other styles of action, such as expansiveness or constrictedness in drawing, writing, or gesturing, may communicate unrecognized attitudes toward oneself and others. In such usage, styles are treated as expressive of some inner motivational state. Charles Darwin (1873) looked at the way animals acted when they experienced emotion in this way, that is, as expressive of that emotion. The angry cat hisses and arches its back, and the angry dog snarls and bares its teeth; however, when frightened, these animals will display a very different bodily conformation than when they are angry. The pattern or style of motor activity is thus sometimes expressive of an inner mental state, and may then be used to make inferences about that state.

There are two fundamental issues underlying the use of stylistic aspects of action in making inferences about processes of personality. One concerns whether such styles are consistent for the same individual across different situations. Years ago Allport and Vernon (1933) did some classic research on this issue, discovering some consistency in characteristics such as tempo and expansiveness, characteristics which they referred to as "expressive movements." The consistency was greater when the two acts were performed close together in time, or in comparatively similar situations, but in any case a small degree of consistency in such styles was demonstrated. Allport and Vernon's research supported the idea that action styles could be personality traits.

The second issue is more complicated. It concerns whether styles of action are really *expressive* of personality characteristics or inner psychological states (and if so, which ones), or mainly reflect the goals or intended results of an action (i.e., are *instrumental* as opposed to expressive). If facial expressions, for example, reveal emotions (disgust or anger) which the individual may not wish to communicate, this is an expressive function. Ekman and Friesen (1967) have referred to this as the "leakage" of information. It is likely that facial and bodily movements do both, that is, reveal emotional states whose communication was not intended, and also serve as instrumental acts, revealing in part what the person wishes to communicate.

A good example of research which adopts an expressive interpretation of a style of action is a recent study by Wallach, Green, Lipsett, and Minehart (1962). These researchers assumed that among individuals who were socially outgoing in behavior, some would, in reality, prefer social isolation, while others would be genuinely desirous of social interaction. On the other hand, among those who were socially withdrawn, some actually would have strong wishes for social contact, while others would be genuinely desirous of maximum social interaction. In such a case of contradictory "overt" and "covert" tendencies, the individual's social motivation could certainly not be accurately inferred from overt social action alone. Some other tendency would have to be revealed in order to make an accurate inference about motivation.

To assess social motivation more accurately, Wallach *et al.* added a stylistic variable that might be expressive of the underlying disposition. This was a measure of graphic constriction as opposed to graphic expansiveness, which presumably tapped the subject's "covert" wishes about establishing social ties. They requested drawings from the subjects, and then paid attention to the extent to which the drawings were either expansive (e.g., using up most of the page) or constrictive (e.g., using up very little space). They assumed that constricted drawings would be made by those who, regardless of extensive *actual* social interaction, preferred social withdrawal, and that expansive drawings would be made by those who desired extensive social contact, even though the usual behavioral evidence of such desire was absent.

In addition, by means of a questionnaire, Wallach *et al.* measured defensiveness, that is, the tendency to conceal ones wishes, especially conflictful ones. The questionnaire assessed the willingness or unwillingness of the subjects to admit to the occurrence of occasional disagreeable but common feelings and experiences. For example, a subject might be considered defensive if he denied such things as "occasionally feeling unhappy or scared" (1962, p. 5).

Wallach *et al.* found that defensive subjects who were "overtly" active socially tended to show highly constricted drawings, implying to the authors that such subjects had the "covert" wish to be socially withdrawn. Similarly, defensive subjects who were "overtly" socially withdrawn made highly expansive drawings. This sort of contradictory pattern was not found in the case of the nondefensive subjects. Illustrative examples of each of the patterns observed by Wallach *et al.* may be found in Figure 1.

The study by Wallach *et al.* illustrates the theoretical treatment of styles of action as forms of expression, that is, as communicators of internal personality dispositions. The empirical case for the measurement of covert social tendencies in this study depends on the uncertain assumption that graphic constriction does, indeed, relate to the wish to withdraw, and graphic expansiveness to the wish to have social ties. Such wishes are assumed, with some logical consistency, to be "covert" when they occur in a person who is demonstrated to be defensive, that is, unwilling to admit to disagreeable traits. But the covert impulse itself has not been demonstrated, only the defensiveness of the subjects, although this allows the authors ingeniously to interpret certain contradictory tendencies in a logically consistent way. More research is needed before we can have strong confidence in the interpretation. Nevertheless, the study illustrates very well the widely held assumption that action styles are often expressive of internal psychological structures and processes having considerable significance for the person's psychological functioning.

Some styles of action seem to be more the result of an intended effort to have some effect on another person. They have, in effect, instrumental value. This is well illustrated by the research of Rosenfeld (1966). Female students were instructed to seek the other person's approval in a social interchange, and their gestures were compared with those of other female

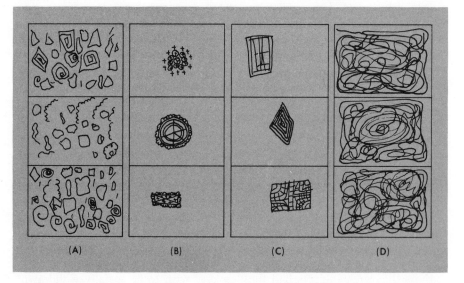

FIGURE 1. Illustrative drawings by a (*A*) nondefensive subject with extensive social ties; (*B*) defensive subject with extensive social ties; (*C*) nondefensive subject who is socially isolated; and (*D*) defensive subject who is socially isolated. (First to third drawings are arranged from top to bottom, respectively.)

students who were instructed to avoid approval. The approval-seekers were observed to use more smiling and gesticulation (noticeable movements of the arm, hand, or finger) than the approval-avoiders. Such a finding suggests that action styles may sometimes have goal-oriented or instrumental significance, being used to produce some given result. Actors are certainly skillful at simulating such action styles in order to convince the audience that the character being portrayed is feeling a certain emotion, or is a certain type of person. Whether the actor necessarily feels that emotion as a result of his "role playing" is not at all clear. One must conclude that styles of action are, indeed, a source of information about the personality, but that the conditions under which they unintentionally "express" an inner state or are instrumental or goal-oriented are not well-established. Styles of action and thinking offer fascinating possibilities for the study of personality traits and are the subject of much research in the field. However, as with the goal-oriented aspect of actions, their simplistic use without confirmatory evidence from other sources makes questionable the validity and usefulness of the inferences drawn from them.

Verbal reports. Inferences about personality structure and process can also be derived from verbally reported introspections. People can describe and label their inner experiences, and report them to an observer. In contrast with infra-human animals, man can thus provide a valuable clue to psychological events through verbalization.

There are really two basic kinds of introspection. In one, which might be termed "empathic introspection," an observer places himself in the shoes of another to whom some event is happening and, by a kind of psychological sharing of the experience, judges empathically what is happening in the other person. The success of this kind of inference process depends on similarities among people, and to the extent there are fundamental individual differences in reactions to comparable stimuli, it is vulnerable to error. One person may experience primarily grief in the same situation in which another experiences gratification and guilt, and a third, relative indifference. For this reason, empathic introspection is not very confidently accepted as a source of inference about personality among scientifically oriented psychologists. Yet it is commonly employed informally in our social living and by writers, and it does have considerable value as a source of hypotheses which might be tested in other ways.

The second, more usual kind of introspection, is widely employed in personality research. It makes use of the subject's own analysis of his reactions, rather than an analysis by an observer. The subject may tell us about what he is thinking, feeling, and wishing, and what has characterized his attitudes in other situations of the past and present. Psychotherapy is a prime example of this sort of data collection in which the therapist learns about the person mainly from what the person reports in the therapy sessions. Since the therapist cannot hover over the patient outside of the therapy context, he cannot be present at the events being discussed in order to observe them at first hand. He is heavily dependent on verbal reports about these events from the patient whom he is trying to understand.

Special problems arise in using verbal reports to make inferences about personality structure and process. The main problem is that words can be used to dissimulate as well as to communicate. That is, a person may express what he wishes another person to believe rather than what is actually true. Furthermore, what is said may arise in large measure from ignorance about oneself and one's reactions, without any intent to dissimulate. Thus, if we take introspection at face value, it is easy to interpret the person quite inaccurately. As was noted earlier, precisely the same problem exists in using styles of action as the basis of inference about personality, since although facial expressions, gestures, and other movements are sometimes expressive of inner dynamics, they may also be deliberately manipulated to produce intended effects. This problem of the accuracy of the source has been much more emphasized with respect to self-report than with any other source of information about personality. At the same time introspection is one of the richest sources of data in personality research.

There have been two basic solutions proposed for dealing with the problem of dissimulation in verbal report. One, advocated by writers such as Carl Rogers (1942; Rogers and Roethlisberger, 1952), involves reducing the motivation on the part of the person to dissimulate by creating an atmosphere of permissiveness and acceptance. If a primary reason for dissimulation is the desire on the part of the person to present himself favorably, or in a way consonant with his own self-evaluation, then a permissive and nonevaluative attitude on the part of the investigator in which the person is accepted regardless of what he says should go a long way toward minimizing the distortion in his self-reports. Permissiveness removes some of the motivation to distort the truth as one understands it. Such an approach is particularly appropriate in the therapeutic context where the therapist-investigator can, over a considerable period of time, adequately assure the person that it is perfectly safe to reveal himself. The process of self-revelation is the very task of "insight therapy." The aim is to discover hidden aspects of the self which, presumably, lie at the root of his psychological troubles.

The difficulty with this solution is twofold: first, personality investigation cannot always adopt the time-consuming process of psychotherapy, nor is such investigation limited to a context where, as in therapy, the person necessarily accepts an arrangement designed to reveal himself; second, in all probability, only some of the inaccuracy of verbal report stems from willful or even unconscious deception. Some of it may be based on defects in language with which one labels and communicates about his inner life, or lack of self-comprehension on the part of the reporter. Thus, the above solution of acceptance and permissiveness is a partial one at best.

The second solution is to treat what the person says about himself as behavior to be observed, rather than as fact about his inner life. At the turn of the century, introspection was employed by the structuralist school of psychology under Titchener, a student of Wundt (see Boring, 1950) as the basic method of investigation of psychological experience. Titchener used trained introspectionists in attempting to study the structure of psychological experience, thus treating the person being studied as a colloborator-observer-scientist. In psychology today, the person being studied is treated differently, even when he provides introspective self-reports. What he says is regarded and observed as behavior to be understood. In this way, the investigator can disregard some of the things that are reported and accept others in making inferences about personality. Even in therapy, the observer can continually check the inferences derived from self-report against other behavioral or physiological evidence. As he listens to what is said, he also observes such motor acts as gestures, facial expressions, and physiological evidence of distress, such as those communicated by facial pallor or flushing, tremulousness, etc. If the person says he felt no distress but gives other behavioral evidence of disturbance, the contents of the verbal report can be qualified by this evidence. The rules for doing this remain fragmentary as yet, and the problem of what to regard as a valid inference is still a fundamental one in personality research.

The above solution of checking one source of inference against another depends on knowledge of the correlates of inaccuracies in verbal report, as known, for example, from the discrepancies which may be observed between the verbal report and other behavioral or physiological signs. Weinstein, Averill, Opton, and Lazarus (1968) recently reviewed six experiments, all performed in their laboratory, in which two types of response measures of stress reaction were obtained while subjects were watching a disturbing movie. In each of the experiments, one measure of stress reaction was a report by the subject about how distressed he was, and the other was a physiological measure known to be affected in emotional states. Often these two response measures were in disagreement; that is, some subjects reported being much more distressed than appeared evident from the physiological measure; other subjects reported being much less distressed than was evident from the physiological measure. Data from personality questionnaires like those employed by Wallach *et al.* (1962), previously described, to measure defensiveness, showed the subjects to vary in the tendency to deny unfavorable and unpleasant things about themselves; some showed this tendency very strongly, others very little or not at all. It was found that those who had the tendency to deny, also showed comparatively higher physiological indicators of stress reactions than they had reported in the experiments.

In short, by identifying one of the correlates of inaccurate self-reports, in this case the tendency to deny distressing things about oneself, Weinstein *et al.* were able to improve somewhat the accuracy of the inference about inner states derived from self-reports. To do this it was necessary to assume that the physiological reaction was a sound indicator of emotional distress, an assumption which itself is open to some argument. In any case, if most or all of the sources of inaccuracy in self-reports could be discovered and assessed, theoretically speaking this information could be used to increase greatly the validity of such reports as a basis of inference about personality structure and process.

Physiological measurements. Physiological changes, particularly those associated with emotion, can thus be used as indicated above as a source of information about internal events and, hence, personality structure and process. The existence of physiological concomitants of emotion has been known for a long time. Many of these can be observed without technically advanced instrumentation, for example, flushing and paling of the face, breaking out in perspiration, and trembling. Such reactions are the result of activity of the autonomic nervous system and the secretion of hormones that affect the visceral organs whose activity can be easily detected. Nowadays electronic instruments are readily available that are capable of measuring fairly minute changes of this sort. An example of such measurement as used in experimental research in stress and emotion is shown in Figure 2.

In the experiment from which the graph in Figure 2 was obtained, volunteer subjects were required individually to watch a film portraying three bloody accidents in a woodworking shop. While subjects watched the film, the electrical resistance of the skin was recorded continuously by means of a psychogalvanometer. Three different experimental treatments were provided: One group was told before the film started that the accidents were all staged very cleverly to look as though injuries and bleeding occurred, but that they really didn't happen (denial). Another group was given a statement focusing in a detached, intellectual fashion, on the social relationships among the various characters in the story (intellectualization). A control group was given only a very brief introductory statement that they were to watch some accidents. Two things may be noted in Figure 2. First, the high peaks of the skin conductance (actually lowered electrical resistance as a result of autonomic nervous system activity) clearly occurred during the accident scenes, while troughs (indicating relaxation) appeared in benign periods between the emotionally relevant events. Second, both forms of prophylactic orientation (denial and intellectualization) given to the subjects before watching the film succeeded in

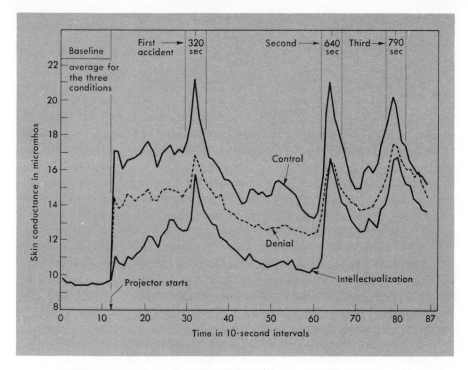

FIGURE 2. Effects of the experimental treatment (denial and intellectualization statements) on skin conductance measured while subjects watched a film showing stressful accidents. From Lazarus, Opton, Nomikos, and Rankin (1965).

lowering the level of skin conductance below that produced under the control conditions. In effect, the emotional disturbance normally produced by the film was reduced by the treatments. In any case, we see that stress or emotional reactions can be measured by recordings of certain physiological changes, and the level of emotional response under different conditions compared.

The above research illustrates the growing use of physiological measures in the study of emotional states. One particular virtue of physiological measures is that they can sometimes be used as in the Weinstein *et al.* (1968) study cited earlier to check other response indicators of emotional processes, such as self-reports. However, the reader should not assume from this that physiological measures or any other behavioral responses are necessarily more scientific or accurate than self-report. Physiological arousal can also be produced by conditions which are irrelevant to emotional states, such as temperature changes or physical movement and exertion. All response measures from which personality inferences are made, especially when used alone and without reference to other sources of information, are vulnerable to many kinds of error. The point is that inferences about personality structure and process are usually sounder when based on multiple evidence. Each type of response evidence supplements the other in providing grist for an interpretation about the personality.

SURFACE AND DEPTH IN PERSONALITY

The idea of depth seems to have two meanings. In Freudian theory where it is given great emphasis, depth refers to forces or mechanisms which are inaccessible to the person, hence unconscious. In Freud's concept of defense mechanism, for example, the person is said not to recognize certain features of his inner mental life. Unacceptable and hence threatening impulses and feelings are particularly salient examples. Freud regarded these as being repressed and unconscious, although presumably they continue actively to influence the person, guiding his behavior in all major life contexts. Not only is the person unconscious of much of his mental life, but to a considerable degree he keeps it unconscious by a censoring or inhibiting process called "repression." In an era (often called the Age of Reason) when man was thought to make decisions on conscious, rational bases, Freud's idea that unconscious, irrational forces controlled most of man's actions was, indeed, a highly disturbing one.

In suggesting that unconscious forces dominated man's life adjustments, Freud invented a colorful metaphor about the mind, likening it to an iceberg (see Figure 3). An iceberg reveals on the surface of the water only a small portion of its total mass, the rest being sunk beneath the sea and being ordinarily invisible. What a vivid way this was of dramatizing the idea that most of the mental life is deep below the surface, so to speak, and inaccessible! Thus, the first meaning of depth, the one emphasized by Freud, is that the *person himself is unconscious* of the dominant aspects of his mental life.

The second meaning of depth refers to the *accessibility* of personality structure and process *to the observer,* who must conceive of it by inference since he cannot observe it directly. The latter meaning of depth says simply that personality is a theoretically based inference, and it implies nothing about the person's awareness of his own mental life.

The former meaning of depth is more controv ial among psychologists than the latter, although it has continued to h e considerable influence on thought in personality and clinical psychology, and in recent years in the lay world as well where the idea is widely accepted today. One reason for the controversy among professionals is that foolproof methods for assessing awareness cannot be found, since they all depend on what the individual reports about his thoughts, and such reports are always in some measure suspect. Some writers argue that the concept of awareness should be expunged from psychology as a useless and untestable idea. But so pervasive and important is the concept that the reader cannot proceed effectively through the study of personality as a field without confronting it repeatedly.

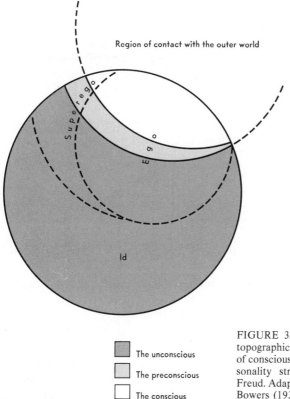

Region of contact with the outer world

■ The unconscious

▨ The preconscious

□ The conscious

FIGURE 3. Sketch suggesting the topographical relationship between levels of consciousness and the elements of personality structure, as elaborated from Freud. Adapted from Healy, Bronner, and Bowers (1930, p. 656).

Two Strategies of Research on Personality

Throughout the modern history of personality, tastes about how to expose it to study have differed and have taken the form of two styles or strategies: the *nomothetic* approach and the *idiographic* approach. The main distinction between them is one of emphasis. Should it be placed on the intensive study of single persons (idiographic) in order that generalizations can be made about that person in a variety of life contexts? Or should the emphasis be on particular personality traits studied in many persons (nomothetic) in order to make generalizations about how such traits determine behavior of people in general? In the nomothetic strategy, it is important to establish that some given trait or traits guide behavior in a particular way, and that this influence, observed in a given sample of persons, is repeatable with other samples. The nomothetic search clearly is directed toward the establishment of general principles of personality functioning. In contrast, the idiographic strategy makes a detailed examination of a single individual in a variety of respects, situations, or times of his life. This approach is often called "ipsative," referring to the iterative examination of the same person in a variety of settings or times.

A second distinction is that nomothetic research in personality tends to isolate for study one or several properties of personality rather than attempting to gain directly a sense of the whole personality as a functioning system. In contrast, idiographic personality research aims primarily at capturing the essence of this "whole" as an organized system. Although this distinction is logically quite independent from the other, that is, idiographic research can be analytic about a specific trait in the individual studied and nomothetic research can study more than one property or trait and the organization of these traits as well, the different approaches tend to be correlated in actual practice. For example, nomothetic studies are typically concerned both with generalizations across persons *and* with single, or at most a few, isolated personality traits; and idiographic studies are usually concerned more with generalizations about the single person currently under study *and* with the accurate portrayal or description of the "whole" personality.

The nomothetic approach represents an attempt to adapt for personality research the analytic and methodological traditions of the major experimental sciences. In these sciences, a complex event is studied by breaking it down into its component parts or variables, isolating each variable for separate study, making precise measurements under conditions as controlled as possible, and seeking to show that the resulting generalizations are repeatable. Those who model their personality research after the physical and biological sciences are apt to see this approach as best for the creation of a genuine science of personality.

In nomothetic research, some trait, say aggressiveness, is varied by selecting subjects who differ with respect to it (or by using a correlational analysis to relate the variation in aggressiveness to other variables), thus producing two or more populations for study, one highly aggressive and one lacking or lower in that quality (a middle group may also be used). It doesn't matter (at least for the purposes of that study) that the subjects within each group differ greatly from one another in other respects—at least they share that one trait, i. e., aggressiveness, in common.

EXAMPLES OF NOMOTHETIC AND
IDIOGRAPHIC RESEARCH

There are countless concrete illustrations that illustrate these two research strategies. A study by Hetherington and Wray (1964) illustrates a relatively complex type of nomothetic study using two personality variables and two situational contexts. Two personality traits were assessed by means of different questionnaires. One of these questionnaires required the subject to state his feelings and actions in certain types of situations which often elicit aggression. Some subjects reported strong feelings of aggression, and others did not. In another questionnaire, the desire for approval or social acceptance was similarly measured. On the basis of the questionnaire data, the authors selected four types of subjects; one type was high in aggression and high in desire for social approval; a second was high in aggression but low in desire for social approval; a third was low in aggression but high in desire for social approval; and the fourth group was low in aggression and low in desire for social approval.

Next, each subject was given a series of photographed cartoons to evaluate on a scale from extremely funny to extremely unfunny. The cartoons expressed aggression. It was assumed that if they were thought to be funny, the subject was accepting the aggressive implication comfortably, while if they were judged as unfunny, aggression was disapproved or perhaps a touchy subject. These ratings were made under two conditions; in one, half the subjects were given an alcoholic drink; the other half was tested without having drunk anything alcoholic. The purpose of this was to study the disinhibiting effects of alcohol on the acceptance and expression of aggression through the ratings of the humorousness of the aggressive cartoons.

The results of Hetherington and Wray's study are complex but most interesting. Under nonalcoholic conditions, highly aggressive subjects who also had a high need for social approval were more disturbed by the cartoons and thus rated them much less funny than did both subjects who were low in aggression and those who were high in aggression but low in desire for social approval. However, the alcohol resulted in the increase in ratings of funnyness by the subjects who were high in aggression and had a strong desire for social approval. In effect, the alcohol disinhibited those with strong desires for social approval, thus allowing them to enjoy the aggressive humor which otherwise would be disturbing. The subjects high in aggression but low in the desire for social approval showed no change between drinking and nondrinking conditions.

Hetherington and Wray suggested interpretively that subjects with low aggressive needs apparently do not have much impulse to express aggression either when drinking or not. However, those high in aggression and also high in desire for social approval have strong aggressive impulses, but they inhibit these because of the strong desire for social approval. It is not clear whether the effect of alcohol results from its tendency to reduce the fear of social censure for an aggressive impulse, or because social approval ceases to be as important under the influence of alcohol.

We need not dwell on the details or defects in the study by Hetherington and Wray to make clear the nature of the nomothetic strategy of personality research. The most striking nomothetic feature is the isolation and examination of two traits or dispositions of personality, in this case, aggressiveness and desire for social approval. The study sought to generalize across persons about the role of these personality traits in determining behavioral reactions. The emphasis was not placed on a single person, observed in a variety of contexts, but on persons in general (as reflected in a particular sample) who happened to have high or low amounts of the traits in question. Although these two traits were isolated from all of the other possibly relevant qualities of personality, this study is an advance over the simplest version of nomothetic research in which the behavioral effects of only a single trait are examined, and only in one situation. In Hetherington and Wray's case, it was possible to study the interplay of both traits by examining how each influenced the other in determining aggressive behavior. In this way nomothetic research attempts to get a little closer to the ideal of studying the whole personality, including as it does multitudes of traits, each of which presumably influences the behavioral outcome in given situational contexts.

The idiographic study of personality is perhaps best illustrated by the case study. Here a single individual is examined from the point of view of his past and present functioning in a variety of life contexts. There are numerous examples of case studies in the literature of psychology and other related disciplines, such as psychiatry and social work. There have been several books which attempt to teach abnormal psychology through outstanding literary examples, for example, Gogol's *Diary of a Madman,* and Nabokov's *Pnin* see Stone and Stone, 1966).

Idiographic case studies have had considerable influence on psychological thought. One of the great exponents of this approach was Gordon Allport (1965), who published a set of 301 letters written over a period of more than 11 years by a woman with the pseudonym of "Jenny" about her relationship with her son. Allport compiled the letters and from them constructed a portrait of "Jenny's" personality from the point of view of several different theoretical systems. Other examples include the six case studies published by Freud. These, along with Freud's psychological analyses, have continued to influence strongly the thinking of clinical and personality psychologists. In the Schreber case (1933), for example, Freud studied an autobiographical account of a paranoid patient, and set forth the principle that paranoia was based on homosexual urges which had been transformed into attack and projected onto another person. In little Hans (1933) Freud illustrated clinically his theory of infant sexuality, and of the Oedipus complex and castration anxiety.

ADVANTAGES AND LIMITATIONS
OF THE NOMOTHETIC AND IDIOGRAPHIC
RESEARCH STRATEGIES

In nomothetic research, the focus is on traits and their function, and the repeatability of the established relationships across persons. This provides the advantage of making possible generalizations across people who share the trait or traits in question. Because of the requirement of repeatability, control, and careful measurement, what one says about a given sample of subjects can then be generalized to others, making possible the establishment of general principles of personality structure and dynamics. However the advantage also brings with it a serious liability in that no actual individual is studied as a "whole" person. Thus, in nomothetic research we never see characterized an actual personality. Concepts of such a personality must be reconstructed or synthesized, so to speak, from a more or less piecemeal manipulation of isolated traits whose role in influencing behavior has been the focus of nomothetic study. As nomothetic research becomes more ambitious by considering more and more individual traits and their interaction, and by studying these traits in a variety of situations, it also becomes more cumbersome, and less possible to perform.

Idiographic research with its emphasis on intensive studies of individual cases preserves better the sense of wholeness and uniqueness of the personality system and its functioning under a variety of life conditions. In case studies, the person is not a collection of separate traits, but an integrated unit, reacting as a total entity or system to whatever situations he may face, and with a continuity between the past, present, and future. These facets are undoubtedly great advantages, however they are bought at a serious price, that of generalization to other persons. Idiographic generalization is oriented to a single personality, that is, to statements about how the individual will function in many contexts. It is weak in permitting statements about people in general. This could be overcome, of course, by studying many individuals, but such extension would be extremely costly and is not typically pursued systematically.

Although it is always hazardous to make generalizations across persons from a single or even a few cases, there are occasions when such generalization can be successful. As Dukes (1965) has shown so well, single cases have been used in the history of psychology to establish important principles. This happens when little important variation in some process is found across different cases, and where the investigator has successfully identified the regularizing principle. One example is the classic study by Morton Prince (1920) of a case of multiple personality, a modern version of which is Thigpen and Kleckley's (1957) book, *The three faces of Eve*. Prince identified the major characteristics of this fascinating disorder so well, and the pattern observed in such cases appears to be so typical that, although both studies were published several decades apart they have much in common. Nevertheless, a single case cannot establish broad generalizations about a phenomenon unless there are other cases to compare it with, and the successful use of such a case to establish a valid principle is certainly the exception rather than the rule.

Moreover, although it need not be so, case studies tend to be somewhat global and impressionistic, rather than precise and carefully oriented to measurement. Furthermore, it is difficult to establish with idiographic study the variables that are important or not important in accounting for the person's functioning. In practice, most idiographic study is highly intuitive and descriptive and does not usually satisfy the criteria set forth by the more science-centered personality researcher.

THE NECESSITY OF HAVING BOTH STRATEGIES

In traditional debates about the comparative virtues of the idiographic and nomothetic strategies of personality study, the two approaches have typically been placed in opposition. This is well illustrated in a published interchange between Gordon Allport (1962) and Robert Holt (1962) in which Allport espoused the idiographic position and Holt the nomothetic. Holt argued, for example, that the idiographic idea is a product of the romantic tradition in which the highest value is placed on understanding life on its own terms, rather than the attempt to explain it. Idiographic personology, says Holt, is devoted to the creation of portraits of uniqueness in which the thrill of recognition is the major source of gratification. This, says Holt, is not science, but art. Furthermore, uniqueness is just as likely to be trivial as important. Holt notes that each planet in the solar system is unique. There may not be another Saturn in all of creation, yet astronomers do not respond by having a different science of astronomy for each individual planet, or for the planets as opposed to other heavenly bodies. There is only one science of astronomy, just as there is only one science of psychology.

Allport has responded by arguing that personality psychologists have invested precious little effort in describing particular persons, committing most of their effort to the study of people in general. Yet describing particular persons is a fundamental part of the overall task of psychology. Allport argued too that Holt underemphasized the amount of effort given to idiographic concerns in sciences such as astronomy. Although universal laws for the entire universe are sought, much effort is given to describing objects in the solar system to which visits may some day be made. For example, as many place-names have been given to features of the moon's surface as the reader himself might be able to think of in his home town. Comparable effort, said Allport, cannot be found in psychology. The idiographic study of the whole individual remains a relatively undeveloped territory in the psychology of personality and he advocates more of it.

The point is that neither the idiographic nor nomothetic strategy of research is fully sufficient by itself. One provides a crucial supplement to the other. It would be quite difficult, for example, to imagine an adequate science of personality built solely around the idiographic approach. As typically used, it is too global, and fails most critically in the most precious values of science, that is, controlled observation, precision of measurement, and repeatability. However, this is not a necessary feature of idiographic research, since it too could be and has been done with careful measurement at least. Still, control and repeatability are difficult to achieve in the ipsative study of the single case, making the creation of valid general principles exceedingly unlikely. Similarly, a science of personality that was entirely nomothetic would also fail because of the distortions of nature resulting from analysis, its study of parts in isolation, and its failure to examine the full range of reactions to a variety of life contexts. Without our being able to draw on the holistic and naturalistic perspective of the idiographic strategy, the errors of analysis could not be readily overcome. The idiographic and nomothetic strategies tend to be pursued by different investigators because different interests and skills are involved in each other. Nevertheless, their mutually supplementary use is required in the creation of a viable science of personality.

Personality Theory

The discussion of personality has thus far been rather general, and it is appropriate now to get more specific about the elements that define it. We need to ask a series of broad but specific questions about personality, namely, how personality is *described,* how it *develops,* its *dynamics* (that is, how it works), and its *determinants* (that is, the forces that shape it). These are the "four D's" of personality, around which most of the remainder of this book is organized. The answers to these four general questions depend on the theory of personality which one espouses. That is, there is not one answer to each question, but many.

It is often distressing to the beginning student to discover how many diverse ways there are of conceptualizing personality. The myriad of theoretical systems is confusing, and it frustrates the desire to have simple authoritative statements about structure and process. The multiplicity of theories reflects two realities—first, the great richness and complexity of the subject matter of personality, and second, the early stage of knowledge at which the science of personality remains at present.

With respect to the early stage of our knowledge, the science of personality, like psychology as a whole, is very new, having had its modern beginnings shortly before the turn of the century. Of course, learned men had speculated about such matters for thousands of years, and their ideas make up part of the philosophical background for the modern theoretical systems. Among the speculators were the Greek philosophers, Aristotle and Plato, and the Greek physician, Hippocrates, who introduced a personality typology based on the idea that temperament depends on the distribution in the body of certain fluids. Although the details of this idea have long been discarded, the general point bears a striking resemblance to the current concept that temperamental characteristics are greatly influenced by the distribution of bodily hormones.

In any case, scientific, empirically oriented approaches to personality are relatively recent developments, and knowledge has not yet advanced far enough to consolidate the diverse theoretical systems into a single, generally accepted system of thought. If we knew enough and had a sufficiently comprehensive and detailed framework of thought, theories which could be shown to be inadequate would be discarded, and whatever was valuable in them incorporated into one single, widely accepted system of thought. But the presence of so many systems claiming our serious consideration suggests inadequacies in each of their formulations, and in the available evidence with which to evaluate them. In spite of many similarities among them, each of the theories remains influential because it contributes some valuable element which the others do not, and which cannot yet be discarded or incorporated satisfactorily into another.

Neither the student nor the expert can "know" the field of personality unless he is familiar with the most important of the theoretical systems designed to conceptualize it. Reviewing such theories is itself a large task, and is impossible to do thoroughly in this book. Books that do so, such as that of Hall and Lindzey (1957), can be confusing to students because they provide summaries of each system of thought, without analyses of how they are similar and on what points they differ. The latter has been attempted by Maddi (1968), but is written at too high a level for the relative beginner. Yet some review of personality theory must be attempted because the very substance of personality, including its definition, depends on the theoretical system for viewing it.

Each personality tends to belong to a larger class of theories of which there are a number of specific variants, too many to cover here. The main classes of theory differ from each other in their fundamental tenets or assumptions about the nature of man. Whatever their terminology, the important thing is to understand these assumptions, which in effect are central issues in the conceptualization of personality. We have chosen to pick one individual instance to represent each of the main classes of theory, and to illustrate that point of view by pointing to central issues on which the classes of theory differ. These issues fall within the four main rubrics of personality: description, development, dynamics, and determinants. The six subsequent chapters of this book are devoted to each of these rubrics, contrasting the selected systems of thought in their response to the issues, and providing examples of research on them. The reader should consider supplementing this skeletal account with additional primary and secondary sources such as those listed at the end of each chapter and which more elaborately spell out the particular theoretical positions.

The Description of Personality

chapter two

A fundamental task of personality theory is to describe the structures of the system with which it is dealing. At the very least a descriptive language is required, one that makes possible the creation of a psychological portrait of people in general, and of a given person in particular. Although personality theory must do more than this, our concern in this chapter is with description alone.

How the basic structures of personality might be set forth can be illustrated by reviewing the way it was done by Freud (1949, 1961) in one of the most influential modern systems of thought, psychoanalysis. Freud conceived of personality as a tripartite arrangement, consisting of three sets of subsystems the "id," "ego," and "superego," each with its own special characteristics. Somewhat oversimplified, the id comprises the drive or motive forces within man, the ego has to do with controlling and adaptive properties, and the superego is concerned with the moral values and ideals which are internalized from culture and family—in effect, conscience. All the psychological functions performed by the personality system are expressed in these three subsystems.

Freud's conception of the structures of personality has become perhaps the most widely utilized way of thinking about the various "parts" of the system. This is not because everyone who uses these terms adopts the

Freudian view in every detail, but because included in this system are all the general components of personality that people recognize as important, that is, drives or motives, controlling and adaptive structures, and the internalized moral values which are the product of socialization. Used in such a general way, the terms ego, id, and superego become neutralized, so to speak, from the specific ways in which Freud used them in his theory of dynamics and development. When used as originally intended by Freud, each of these subsystems contains the theoretical assumptions of Freudian theory, including the particular drives, controlling tendencies, and moral ideals, the functions of each substructure, its manner of development, and the rules about how the substructures interact. However, to most psychologists and laymen and outside the specific Freudian context, id, ego, and superego have become merely an eclectic, shorthand way of referring to fundamental structures and functions of personality. Since many theoretical systems employ these words without necessarily implying all that Freud meant by them, if one hears the word id, ego, or superego, it may be necessary to ask whether or not it is being used in the Freudian sense, or in some other way.

A good example of the confusing use of the same term to connote something different may be found in Carl Jung's personality theory which overlaps with that of Freud but is also quite different in important ways. Jung was one of the early group of innovators around Freud who later quarrelled with Freud and went his separate theoretical way. He used the term "ego" to refer to processes that were entirely conscious, while Freud emphasized that the ego's activities were unconscious. By sometimes using the same terms having such different meanings, and sometimes using different terms having the same meaning, personality theorists have done the student of personality considerable disservice, inasmuch as such practices have contributed to widespread confusion among laymen and professionals alike.

Many personality theories have discarded the tripartite concept of the structure of personality altogether. Jung (1916) kept it but began to emphasize the concept of the "self" as the structure which harmonizes the animal instincts of man with his spiritual and social heritage. The concept of *self* is today found in a number of theories as the central unit of personality, for example, those of Carl Rogers (1951), Abraham Maslow (1954), and Kurt Goldstein (1940), each of whom has presented overlapping and influential theories of personality. In these theories, the person is described and understood in terms of how he conceives of himself, that is, on the basis of his "self-concept," which causes him to act and react as he does. Still a different picture of personality structure was offered by Otto Rank (1952), who, like Jung, was one of the original group of thinkers about Freud in the early days of psychoanalysis. Like Jung, Rank also left the Freudian movement to establish a system of his own. He totally abandoned the tripartite division of personality and substituted the elements of *will* and *counterwill,* which were in perpetual conflict, mobilized by man's fear of separation and the opposing fear of loss of identity. The outcome of this struggle was expressed in the emergence of a personality fitting one of three types: the "average man," "neurotic," and "artist."

It is evident that a considerable variety of ways exist by which the personality structure is described, each arising from some particular conception of the nature of man. The above examples by no means exhaust the possibilities which have been tried. And it will take little imagination to foresee that each version will result in practice in quite different concrete descriptions of a person. Moreover, within each broad category of structure—id, ego, superego, self, self-concept, or will—is a variety of more specific attributes which must be considered to fill out the bare bones of the system with the flesh of drives, adaptive tendencies, and conceptions about oneself. To do this one finds in use two basic kinds of language, the language of traits and the language of types.

The Language of Traits

The simplest and most traditional way of describing a person in specific terms is to identify patterns of behavior characterizing him and to label them with trait names. "Traits" are dispositional concepts, that is, they refer to tendencies to act or react in certain ways. Psychological dispositions are presumably carried around by the person from situation to situation, and they imply a certain likelihood of his behaving in some given way. Traits must be distinguished from "state" concepts, which refer to a reaction which is now taking place. For example, a person may experience the state of anxiety in a certain situation. However, having the trait of anxiety means that he will respond with the state of anxiety under given circumstances, although he may not be experiencing anxiety just now. Having the trait does not imply that the person will always be anxious, but only that he is disposed to react with anxiety in given situations.

Speaking in terms of their contents there are many possible kinds of traits. The range of such contents include motive traits referring to the kinds of goals to which behavior is directed; ability traits referring to general and specific capacities and skills; temperamental traits, such as tendencies toward optimism, depression, energy, etc.; and stylistic traits involving gestures, styles of behaving, and thinking not functionally related to the goals of that behavior. Traits theorists have approached the task of defining trait categories quite differently. For example, although Cattell (1950) included motives within the category of traits, Murray

(1938) and McClelland (1951) distinguished between traits and motives, traits involving characteristic means by which goals are attained.

Every language contains large numbers of words that define personality traits. People are described as shy, aggressive, submissive, lazy, melancholy, easy-going, ambitious, and so on. Traits may refer to surface manifestations such as aggressiveness, or to deeper or more inferential qualities such as beliefs, or capacities to control the expression of impulse. In any case, the descriptive aspects of personality theory depend on a language of traits or dispositions, and each theory sets up its own terms with which to picture a specific person or people in general.

Some theoretical systems are more explicit than others in setting forth the various traits which make up the personality. Kurt Lewin (1935), for example, believed that it was a fruitless task to try to list all of the motives that impel people to action, or all the concepts that they might have about various recourses to action. The result has been that Lewin's system of personality theory has never led to extensive clinical application, a major task of which is the diagnosis and description of patients suffering from various emotional and adjustive difficulties. By contrast, Henry Murray (1938) went to great pains to list and describe the basic human tendencies. Among the social motives, he listed need for achievement, for dominance, autonomy, aggression, affiliation, nurturance, etc. As a result, those concerned with personality description, in both the clinical and the research context, were given a useful vocabulary with which to differentiate one person from another. Hence Murray's analysis stimulated the popularization among professionals of a list of traits which could be employed in personality description. The same thing occurred with respect to Freud's ideas about psychosexual stages (oral, anal, and genital), and his concepts of ego-defense mechanisms. The existence of a rich vocabulary of traits makes it easier for personality researchers and clinical psychologists to differentiate descriptively between one person and another.

The dean of personality trait psychology unquestionably has been Gordon Allport (1937, 1961). Allport regarded the trait as the natural unit of description of personality, and he and Odbert (1936) examined an unabridged English dictionary locating 17,953 words designating personal forms of behavior out of a total of 400,000. This was too many to use effectively. So dropping all those which dealt with temporary mood states, those which were primarily evaluative rather than descriptive, and those which designated mainly physical rather than psychological qualities, Allport and Odbert narrowed down the list of trait names to 4,541. These were thought to make a good starting point for the study of personality. Allport then set about formalizing in theory what is part of the common-sense, intuitive approach to personality used by the layman when the latter attempts to describe someone, as in a letter of recommendation.

Allport emphasized the idea that traits are integral properties of a person, not merely part of the imagination of the beholder. That is, they referred to actual neuropsychic characteristics which shaped how the individual behaved; they could be known only by observation, and by inference about what was central and essential about the person, and what was peripheral and unimportant. He also emphasized the uniqueness of every person, not only in each individual trait, but in the organization of these traits into an integrated whole. Allport also differentiated between cardinal, central, and secondary traits. Some people are dominated by a single focus of behavior, and they may become known for this focus; this focus, when it exists, exemplifies the "cardinal" trait. One example might be the legendary Don Juan, whose life style was presumably expressed in terms of heterosexual conquest. Allport also believed that about five to ten trait terms would usually cover the main characteristics which distinguish one individual from another, and he called these "central" traits. "Secondary" traits are attributes which are either peripheral or weak, and hence relatively unimportant in characterizing the person and his life style.

Two other significant features of Allport's view of traits should also be mentioned. One has already been considered in Chapter 1, and has to do with Allport's tendency to champion an idiographic approach to the study of personality, as opposed to the nomothetic approach. This is consistent with his emphasis on the uniqueness of a person's traits and of personality in general. The other feature is Allport's view that traits are not independent entities within a person, but an interdependent set of attributes which combine to produce behavioral effects. Thus, a single complex act cannot be blamed on a single trait, but is always the product of a set of interdependent traits, each trait contributing to some aspect of the behavior. Thus, for example, when a person tells a story in a social gathering, many traits contribute to this series of acts. Not only are motivational traits involved, having to do, say, with entertaining others, showing off, or avoiding offense, but stylistic traits relevant to the manner in which the story is told, say, bashfully, boringly, or expansively, play a role too. Thus, the traits of a person combine to form a coherent cluster, an interrelated way of life, an organized whole. This structure is contained in the single concept of the self, or "proprium" as Allport referred to it.

The proprium (1955) concerns all the particular characteristics belonging to the person, including one's body image, one's sense of self-identity, self-esteem, self-extension, rational thinking, and knowing, etc. These individual functions develop over the life span of the individual. The proprium or self, in Allport's analysis of personality, is used adjectivally, as a concept which acknowledges the importance of qualities such as self-esteem and self-concept, without reifying these qualities into a "little man within the man" which governs him. Such a "man within the man" is often implied in personality theory, seeming to be an explanation for behavior, when in reality it is an example of the circular device of naming instead of explaining. Such circular explanations beg the further question, "Who or what tells the little man within the man what to do?" The concept of self or proprium as Allport used it, is not an entity governing behavior and separate from everything else, but a term for a group of important intimate functions which make the person distinctive from other persons.

If Allport was the dean of trait theorists, then Raymond Cattell is, in a sense, one of its main architects and engineers, because Cattell's (1950) main effort has been directed toward systematically reducing the list of personality traits to a manageably small number by means of a statistical method called "factor analysis." This method analyzes the intercorrelations among personality-relevant behaviors elicited by a wide variety of observational and test methods, determining which such personality test measures go together and which do not, and serving as the basis of inferences about the factors which underlie the observed pattern of covariation.

Cattell illustrates the approach with a pattern of measures we can easily understand. Suppose, for example, we measure the ability of a group of college men to do four things, use calculus, understand the subject of physics, play football, and ice skate. As we might expect, when these four abilities are correlated with each other, those who do well in calculus are found also to do well in physics, and those who do well on the football field also skate well; but performance on the academic subjects turns out to bear little or no relationship to performance in the physical sports. Factor analysis would reveal two factors or source traits underlying this matrix of intercorrelations, one which might be called "mathematical and science ability," the other "ability in sports." Naturally, in the case cited, the existence of the two factors which sum up the intercorrelations of the four variables or trait elements is so obvious that the computation of factor analysis would hardly be necessary. However, if the correlation matrix contained many variables, comprising dozens of personality tests, then the statistical computations of factor analysis would be necessary to analyze effectively the pattern of relationships and reveal the various factors that could explain it.

Cattell (1965) has pointed out that if one takes a few hundred young men or women and arranges to have them rated by people who know them well on 60 different trait elements, from about 12 to 20 independent factors or source traits can be identified by factor analysis. Tests can then be devised to assess such factors. Cattell has developed a questionnaire for this purpose which he calls the 16 P.F. because it is designed to measure the 16 source traits which he thinks can account for the most important surface trait elements. Table 1 illustrates 10 such variables or trait elements, with brief descriptions of the qualities involved in each,

Table 1

1. Adaptable: flexible; accepts changes of plan easily; satisfied with compromises; is not upset, surprised, baffled, or irritated if things are different from what he expected. *vs.* Rigid: insists that things be done the way he has always done them; does not adapt his habits and ways of thinking to those of the group; nonplussed if his routine is upset.

2. Emotional: excitable; cries a lot (children), laughs a lot, shows affection, anger, all emotions, to excess. *vs.* Calm: stable, shows few signs of emotional excitement of any kind; remains calm, even underreacts in dispute, danger, social hilarity, etc.

3. Conscientious: honest; knows what is right and generally does it, even if no one is watching him; does not tell lies or attempt to deceive others; respects others' property. *vs.* Unconscientious: somewhat unscrupulous; not too careful about standards of right and wrong where personal desires are concerned; tells lies and is given to little deceits; does not respect others' property.

4. Conventional: conforms to accepted standards, ways of acting, thinking, dressing, etc.; does the "proper" thing; seems distressed if he finds he is being different. *vs.* Unconventional, eccentric: acts differently from others: not concerned about wearing the same clothes or doing the same things as others; has somewhat eccentric interests, attitudes, and ways of behaving; goes his own rather peculiar way.

5. Prone to jealousy: begrudges the achievement of others; upset when others get attention, and demands more for himself; resentful when attention is given to others. *vs.* Not jealous: likes people even if they do better than he does; is not upset when others get attention, but joins in praise.

6. Considerate, polite: deferential to needs of others; considers others' feelings; allows them before him in line, gives them the biggest share, etc. *vs.* Inconsiderate, rude: insolent, defiant, and "saucy" to elders (in children); ignores feelings of others; gives impression that he goes out of his way to be rude.

7. Quitting: gives up before he has thoroughly finished a job; slipshod; works in fits and starts; easily distracted, led away from main purposes by stray impulses or external difficulties. *vs.* Determined, persevering: sees a job through in spite of difficulties or temptations; strong-willed; painstaking and thorough; sticks at anything until he achieves his goal.

8. Tender: governed by sentiment; intuitive, empathetic, sympathetic; sensitive to the feelings of others; cannot do things if they offend his feelings. *vs.* Tough, hard: governed by fact and necessity rather than sentiment; unsympathetic; does not mind upsetting others if that is what has to be done.

9. Self-effacing: blames himself (or nobody) if things go wrong; reluctant to take credit for achievements; does not seem to think of himself as very important or worthwhile. *vs.* Egotistical: blames others whenever there is conflict or things go wrong; often brags; quick to take credit when things go right; has a very good opinion of himself.

10. Languid, fatigued, slow: lacks vigour; vague and slow in speech; dawdles, is slow in getting things done, *vs.* Energetic, alert, active: quick, forceful, active, decisive, full of pep, vigorous, spirited.

From Cattell (1965, p. 63-64).

and Table 2 illustrates the 16 factors or source traits. They are presented here to suggest the substantive content of the most important source traits of personality as seen by one distinguished researcher in this field.

The methods involved in this statistical process, and the issues revolving about its use need not concern us here. Suffice it to say that factor analysis as employed by Cattell and others is one method of attempting to determine the basic trait sources of personality variation. Such analysis can then be used in personality description and the evolution of personality theory. Cattell's approach to personality description and his working

Table 2

Sixteen Factors or Source Traits from Cattell

Factor A.	*Cyclothymia vs. Schizothymia* Liking for people vs. stubborn, rejecting withdrawal from people
Factor B	*General Intelligence vs. Mental Defect*
Factor C	*Emotional Stability or Ego Strength vs Dissatisfied Emotionality* Capability for immediate integration and control of emotional impulses and bodily reactions vs. incapability
Factor E	*Dominance or Ascendance vs. Submission*
Factor F	*Surgency vs. Desurgency, or Depressive Anxiety* Happy-go-lucky cheerfulness vs. restraint and worry resulting from inhibition consequent to exposure to punishment and deprivation
Factor G	*Character or Super-ego Strength vs. Lack of Internal Standards* Positive injunctions against idleness, neglect or responsibility, etc., vs. frivolity, emotional dependency and general spinelessness
Factor H	*Adventurous Autonomic Resilience vs. Inherent, Withdrawn Schizothymia (Parmia vs. Threctia)* Parasympathetic immunity to threat (hence casualness) vs. threat reactivity (associated with lower thresholds)
Factor I	*Emotional Sensitivity vs. Tough Maturity (Premsia vs. Harria)*
Factor L	*Paranoid Schizothymia vs. Trustful Altruism (Protension vs. Inner Relaxation)* Paranoid projection and tension vs. absence of projecting tendencies and tension
Factor M	*Hysteric Unconcern (or "Bohemianism") vs. Practical Concernedness (Autia vs. Praxernia)* Autonomous, self-absorbed relaxation (attention to ideational over sensory stimulation) vs. incapacity to dissociate feelings of inadequacy
Factor N	*Sophistication vs. Rough Simplicity (Shrewdness vs. Näiveté)* Quick, competent, realistic vs. vague, sentimental, incontinent
Factor O	*Anxious Insecurity vs. Placid Self-Confidence (Guilt Proneness vs. Confidence)* Formerly called free-floating anxiety; timid, inadequate and self-abasing at positive pole
Factor O_1	*Radicalism vs. Conservatism*
Factor O_2	*Independent Self-sufficiency vs. Lack of Resolution*
Factor O_3	*Will Control and Character Stability*
Factor O_4	*Nervous Tension*

Factor descriptions from life record or behavioral ratings in Cattell (1957).

assumptions about personality turn out to be quite different from those of Allport. Although both use the language of traits, they each conceive of the personality quite differently.

The Language of Types

The type approach is an extension of the reasoning used in the trait approach. Whereas a variety of traits can be assigned to a single person, and we say he has this or that trait or pattern of traits, in the "type" approach a broader, more unifying scheme, that of classification or pigeonholing, is adopted. A person is classified as belonging to a *type* by the pattern of traits he displays. If he shares a trait pattern with a large group of other individuals, then in common with the members of that group he belongs to a type, thus simplifying description immensely, since each shared trait need not be listed separately for each individual. For example, if naiveté is observed to go with certain other qualities, such as the tendency to great lability of affect, blocking, amnesia, and so on, then this collection of traits might be referred to simply by the single inclusive category called "repression" as a defensive style. An opposing type can also be identified called "isolation" or "intellectualization." Having isolated these two opposing defensive categories, each made up of clusters of traits that are found together, one can now say that because the person has one or the other set of traits, he is a member of one or the other type. Types are, therefore, usually made up of complex systems of opposing traits that have been simplified into a few main categories.

As in the case of traits, a vocabulary of types has existed for thousands of years. As noted in Chapter 1, the best known typology in ancient Greece was that of Hippocrates in the fifth century B.C. Theorizing that the body contained four fluids or humors—yellow bile, black bile, phlegm, and blood—Hippocrates speculated that personality depended on which of these humors predominated in the person. Thus, yellow bile went with a "choleric" or irascible temperament; black bile with "melancholy"; phlegm with the sluggish, apathetic, or "phlegmatic" person; and blood with the cheerful, active, or "sanguine" person.

Among the best-known modern typologies of personality is that of Carl Jung (1933). Jung's typology includes two broad categories—the *extrovert,* who is oriented primarily toward others and the external world, and the *introvert,* who is more preoccupied with himself and his subjective world. Extroversion and introversion are expressed in a variety of functions, thinking, feeling, sensing, and intuiting, so that in actuality Jung's typology is far more complex than people usually realize. One could be, for example, a thinking extrovert, but an introvert in the intuitive function.

In one important respect the typology of introvert-extrovert is not an ideal example of the concept of typology because introverts and extroverts are frequently thought of as falling along a continuum rather than representing a dichotomy. In modern typological thinking (e.g. Cattell, 1965; and Eysenck, 1952), types are distinguished from each other by being qualitatively different rather than being merely different in degree. This is illustrated in Figure 4, in which Distribution A shows a normal statistical distribution (bell-shaped curve) of people who are high or low on a particular trait such as intelligence or ego-control, with most people falling in the middle range; on the other hand, Distribution B shows two distinct groupings, one at the low end and one at the high end. Distribution B more nearly represents what is meant by types than does A. There is little point in using type classifications in the case of Distribution A. It would be like calling tall people different in type from short people, when in actuality, there is a continuum with most people falling somewhere in the middle range. The concept of typology is more suitably used when the types are separated and display qualitively different properties, as in the case of breeds of dogs, types of animal species, or people who prefer to use different forms of defense mechanisms such as denial vs. projection. Freud's typology of oral, anal, and genital types, discussed below, would be an example of a typology that more nearly reflected such qualitative differences.

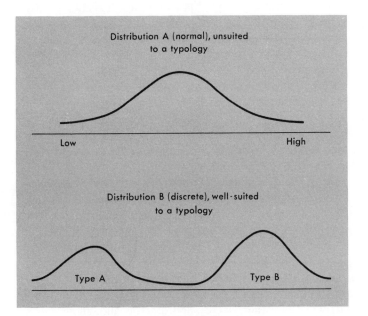

FIGURE 4. A normal distribution or continuum, and a discrete distribution on which typological thinking is founded.

Freud's (1933) typological categories arise readily out of the theory of psychosexual development. As will be seen in more detail later, in this theory everyone is said to pass through three infantile psychosexual stages which are distinguished according to the primary means of sexual gratification characteristic in each. In the oral stage, erotic activity centers around the lips and mouth, in the anal stage on stimulation of the anus, and in the phallic stage on the genital organs. In the course of psychosexual development, some individuals fail to progress normally to the next stage. Although they ultimately reach chronological adulthood, the primitive psychosexual tendencies characteristic of the respective immature stage persist, and these govern the personality and produce the characteristic psychological traits connected with that stage.

Freud identified three types of personality based on the "fixation" of psychosexual or libidinal energy at one given immature stage of development. The *oral* type is characterized by passive dependent attitudes toward others, in which the person continues to seek sustenance (as in feeding) from others. Depending on when during the oral stage fixation occurred, the oral type is either optimistic, immature, and trusting, or pessimistic, suspicious, and sarcastic about the prospects of gaining and retaining the needed sustenance. The *anal* type also has two substages, the first identified with outbursts of aggression, sloppiness, and petulance, the second with obstinacy, orderliness, and parsimoniousness. The *phallic* type is characterized by adolescent immaturity, with heterosexual conflicts stemming from an unresolved Oedipus complex. Psychologically, the phallic period (and type) is apt to be stormy, with sharp emotional swings and preoccupation with the choice of a love object.

Three other points should be emphasized in connection with trait systems and typologies such as the above. First, as we have said, in reasoning typologies are closely interdependent with trait analyses. There are a number of traits which one must possess if he is to be assigned to a given type, say the anal personality. If one shows the trait combination of obstinacy, orderliness, and parsimoniousness, he closely fits the anal type. Thus, trait and type analyses represent a common, interdependent style of thinking and speaking about personality structure.

Second, trait analyses and, if they are carried further, typologies usually are based on certain theoretical propositions about personality structure and process, of which the typological categories are illustrative. The author of a typology usually has some explicit or implicit principles in mind about the way personality works. Thus, Hippocrates thought of the mental life as dominated by fluids or humors, and his typology was a reflection of this concept. Jung expounded the idea that some psychological functions were emphasized in the person's life style (he called them "superior functions"), while others were subordinated and unconscious ("inferior functions") although the latter were, nonetheless, important forces in the personality. His typology, involving always a polarity such as extroversion-introversion, reflected this notion. Similarly, Freud was trying to articulate concepts about psychosexual development and dynamics in his typology of oral, anal, and phallic personalities.

Third, typological thinking in personality seems to be more congenial to an idiographic research approach and a more global view of the personality, while trait thinking appears more congenial to the nomothetic approach and the measurement of individual attributes. If people can be categorized into a limited number of types or pigeonholes, then one is encouraged to select a given individual as an ideal example of each type, and to study each one intensively; the individual is studied as a representative of a whole class of persons who share some property in common. And since typologies in personality tend to be built around major qualities, such as an entire "life style," rather than discrete and minor variations, the approach lends itself readily to global analysis. In contrast, trait analysis implies the existence of many individual personality attributes, each of which appears in varying amounts in different persons. These traits, and the task of generalizing about their functions in people in general, become major focuses of interest, rather than the individual person as an organized whole. Thus, there seems to be an ideological link between typologies and the idiographic research strategy, and between trait analysis and the nomethetic research strategy.

There are other personality typologies, just as there are other theoretical models of personality. Each makes use of somewhat different ways of describing the personality structure, that is, each identifies different units of description which fit the theoretical assumptions of the system. Most theories make use of a language of traits and types, since this makes it possible to concretize the structure of personality in the terms of that particular theory. Such a language is fundamental to personality description.

The Unit of Analysis in Personality Description

A number of issues can be found which illustrate divergences in the way personality structure is conceived and described among different personality theories. However, there is one issue which stands out as particularly important, not only in personality theory, but in all of psychology, and the remainder of this chapter is about it. The issue has to do with the unit of analysis that is used to describe the person. There are two main alternatives. First, the *person in the situation* can be the primary unit of analysis, with the emphasis placed on the situation or the stimulus as physical reality, to which the person must respond in accordance with its objective qualities. This sort of view of personality is an interactive one in which behavior is the outcome of the interplay of two sets of variables: a person's characteristics, (his needs, motives, habits of perception and thought, etc.) and the situation in which he is placed. Second, the *person himself* can be the primary unit of analysis, with the emphasis placed not on the situation as objective reality, but on the perceptions the person has of the situation, that is, as it is subjectively apprehended by him. Let us examine each of these philosophical outlooks, with our attention centered in each instance on the role of the stimulus or situation.

THE STIMULUS AS OBJECTIVE REALITY

One of the striking things about animal and human behavior is that it is highly adaptive, that is, actions and reactions are well attuned to the stimulus world. We respond to sounds, sights, touch, and so on, in ways predictable from a knowledge of the physical characteristics of such stimuli. When we reach out to pick up an object, we do not usually overreach or underreach, but our fingers accurately extend the right distance to it. As we pass one another in the street, we do not bump, because our senses seem to take in accurately the realities of the stimulus world and permit us to respond in appropriate fashion. We also get accurate feedback from our actions allowing us to adjust them as necessary.

Personality theories that have emphasized this adaptive sensitivity of the organism to the physical world have tended to be associated with an interest in the mechanisms of *learning*. The focus of their attention is directed at how we learn appropriately to react in one way or another to the stimuli to which we are exposed. Such reactions are then seen as arising from stimuli whose basic elements are light waves, sound waves, shape, weight, size, distance, pressures on the tissues, or chemicals that reach sensory receptors. In other words, we respond to objective physical stimulus events arising in the outer environment, as well as to those arising in the inner environments of our bodies. From this point of view, all behavioral responses are made to objective physical stimuli, and by virtue of the processes of learning, they became established as habits of adjustment to them.

Although many psychologists of this persuasion were earlier concerned only with the principles of learning, some of them also came to recognize that such propositions about learning might have application to behavior in general and to personality. Therefore, theories of learning tended to become theories about the whole of human psychological functioning. Perhaps the best known instance of such a general behavior theory was that of Clark Hull (1943), whose views have had great influence on psychology over the past several decades. But the explicit extension of this form of thought to personality is best represented by the writings of John

Dollard and Neal Miller (1950). From their point of view personality essentially consists of the habits of reaction a person acquires in response to physical stimuli through learning. The fundamental principle is that an association or bond is formed between such stimuli and the reactions that are elicited in their presence. The emphasis is on the objective, physical stimulus as the event which elicits the response, and which can be defined without reference to the organism responding. Description of the person will then be made in terms of such learned systems of habits of response. The basic ingredient of individual differences in personality consists of divergent habit patterns, whether these habits are simple skills, or complex emotions, motives, beliefs, defenses, or neurotic symptoms. The person's behavior is understood by reference to two separate but interacting sets of variables, the person on the one hand, and the situation on the other, that is, *the person in the situation.*

THE STIMULUS AS APPREHENDED BY THE PERSON

In sharp contrast with the above view of personality is a class of personality theories identified as "phenomenological" in point of view. These latter theories derive from an emphasis on perception and cognition, rather than learning. For such a theorist, defining a stimulus physically and objectively poses an insoluble problem, namely, that our perception of objects is not necessarily identical with the objects themselves. Our senses do not directly transmit physical objects. Rather we respond to representations of objects, that is, objects as mediated by our perceptual apparatuses and by our individual interpretations. The phenomenologist argues that physical objects themselves do not determine our responses. Rather, the intervening structures and processes within a person that mediate the physical stimuli do. From this point of view the causes of action must be reconstructed through inferences about these mediators or psychological representations of external stimuli.

Thus, instead of focusing on the objective physical stimulus, *phenomenological* theories of personality emphasize mediating cognitive processes, such as perceptions and conceptions about events, that is the "phenomenal" rather than the objective world of events. They argue, moreover, that the cause of action is the world as a person apprehends it privately, and this private world can, of course, be quite different from objective reality. And their descriptions of the personality are descriptions of those mediating cognitive processes which distinguish one individual from another and presumably cause his behavior. In short, the unit of analysis is the *person,* since within him are to be found the key constructs on which his behavior is to be built. We cannot know him by reference to the situation, since this operates only through the subjective-cognitive processes lying inside the person.

There are two main forms which phenomenological theories of personality have taken, one that is built around the concept of the "self," and another that refers in general to cognitions about the world. The first class includes the personality systems of such writers as Carl Rogers (1947, 1951), Abraham Maslow (1954), Kurt Goldstein (1940), and some features of Henry Murray's (1938) account of personality, among the most influential. The second class includes Kurt Lewin's (1935) field theory and George Kelly's (1955) theory of personal constructs among the best exemplars. Space does not permit elaboration of each of these approaches to personality description. The main forms can be illustrated by brief discussion, first, of Lewin's field theory and then of Rogers self-concept theory.

LEWIN'S APPROACH

For Lewin the psychological representations of the world, referred to as the "life space," consists of the person's needs and the available potentialities of action as he apprehends them. Every aspect of a person's physical environment that is not part of the *life space* and to which he does not directly respond is the "foreign hull" of the life space. To understand a person's behavior at any moment we must reconstruct and describe the life space at that moment, which means that we must understand the psychological forces then in operation.

These forces are usually described by Lewin graphically in topological diagrams that include: goal regions (shown as enclosed places); positive and negative valences (designated by plus or minus signs), and which identify desirable or undesirable aspects of the life space; vectors (arrows), which point out the directions to which a person is pulled; and barriers (lines separating the person from positive goals), which block or slow down the approach to any goal region. Many forces may affect the life space, and the person's behavior at any time is a resultant of them. The Lewinian diagram of the life space presented in Figure 5 is interpreted as follows.

> ... a child passes a candy store, looks in the window, and wishes he had some candy. The sight of the candy arouses a need, and this need does three things. It releases energy and thereby arouses tension in an inner-personal region (the candy-wanting system). It confers a positive valence upon the region in which the candy is located. It creates a force which pushes the child in the direction of the candy.
>
> Let us say that the child has to enter the store and buy the candy. This situation can be represented by Figure A. Suppose, however, that the child does not have any money; then the boundary between him and the candy will be an impassable barrier. He will move as close to the candy as possible, perhaps putting his nose against the window, without being able to reach it (Figure B.).

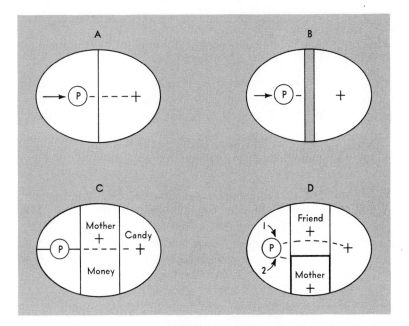

FIGURE 5.   Lewinian diagram representing the changing life space of a child in a specific psychological transaction with his environment.

He may say to himself, "If I had some money, I could buy some candy. Maybe mother will give me some money." In other words, a new need or quasi need, the intention to get some money from his mother, is created. This intention in turn, arouses a tension, a vector, and a valence which are represented in Figure C. A thin boundary has been drawn between the child and the mother on the assumption that he has to go home, find his mother, and ask her for money. Another thin boundary has been drawn between the mother and the candy to represent the effort required to return to the store and make a purchase. The child moves to the candy by way of the mother.

If the mother refuses to give the child any money, he may think of borrowing it from a friend. In this case, the region containing the mother is surrounded by an impenetrable barrier, and a new path through the region containing the friend to the candy is transcribed (Figure D).

This topological representation could be endlessly complicated by introducing additional environmental regions and boundaries of varying degrees of firmness, and additional needs with their coordinated tension systems, valences, and vectors. (From Hall and Lindzey, 1957, pp. 230-31.)

The important elements in the Lewinian system are these: Psychological events are considered in terms of the construct of life space, which involves subjective definitions of the environment. Inferences about the life space are always derived from systematic observation of the person's behavior in the environment. Yet the terms of the analysis of behavior and setting are not static traits and stationary objects, but the person's own subjective apprehension of his environment and his relationship to it.

ROGERS' APPROACH

The self-theory of Rogers is also phenomenological, and its concepts are also couched in the language of subjective experience (for example, what we want and how we think and feel). The Rogerian concept that is analogous to Lewin's life space is the "phenomenal field," and the core (or most important aspect) of that field is the "self-concept," that is, a person's notion of who he is in relation to his environment. It is this *self-concept* which determines his behavior. This phenomenal self is, for a person himself, reality. One does not respond to the objective environment but to what he perceives it to be, regardless of how distorted or personalized his perception may be. These subjective realities are tentative hypotheses that a person entertains about environmental situations.

Thus, one person will conceive of himself as a reformer with the mission of correcting certain worldly ills and helping others to "see the light." Another will view himself as a "realist," able to accept gracefully, and even benefit from, the weaknesses of human nature and man's social institutions. Self-concepts are complex and variable, and they determine how persons will react to and deal with a wide variety of situations. These conceptions of who and what one is not only comprise central values and belief systems, but also include images of oneself as physically strong or weak, attractive or unattractive, popular or unpopular, and so on, based partly on the reflected appraisals of other people with whom one has had contact. According to self theorists, this differentiated portion of the phenomenal field, the self-concept, determines all behavior. And most behavior, indeed, is organized around efforts to preserve and enhance this phenomenal self.

While Lewin goes about the task of reconstructing a person's life space, with its multiplicity of psychological forces, by observing how that person acts in different situations, Rogers identifies the *self-concept* largely from introspection. That is, a Rogerian learns about someone's self-system by listening to his introspective verbal report about himself and his conceptions of himself and the world, usually in the context of psychotherapy. Lewin, in contrast, systematically observed behavior in various naturalistic and experimental situations.

FURTHER COMPARISONS

The two viewpoints about how to regard the stimulus are not as far apart in reality as they look, and to state these positions without some qualification is a gross oversimplification. Remember that both points of view must contend with two kinds of events, 1. those where man's behavior is highly adaptive and seems responsive to the environment, and 2.

those where the behavior is maladaptive and seems to be based on faulty perceptions of or judgments about the environment. Obviously, personality theories must be used to deal with both kinds of events, and to the extent that they are used successfully, the points of view will not be as far apart as first appears. Moreover, while the stimulus may be defined independently of the responder in the *person in the situation* perspective, theorists of this persuasion still acknowledge that its effect will depend on the present state of the individual, his previous experience, and genetic constitution. There is danger that the differences in point of view may be painted too strongly.

The issue of the nature of the stimulus deals with philosophical arguments which are quite old. For example, the frames of reference of idealism, materialism, realism, and naive realism in philosophy reflect this issue. Materialism—the view that the material world exists regardless of our perception of it, and that it determines our perceptions—tends to be a popular outlook associated with Bertrand Russell, and with modern Soviet psychology. In its extreme form idealism—the viewpoint that the material world does not exist except as it is perceived—has little influence on contemporary psychological thought. It was associated particularly with the British philosopher Bishop Berkeley, and also with Hegel. Realism, stating that ideas themselves are real, was the viewpoint adopted by Plato. And naive realism, that things are literally as they are perceived and that our senses mirror this reality, may be found implicit in much of the work of perception psychologists, past (e.g. Wundt) and present.

The philosophical differences between the two main viewpoints toward the stimulus outlined above also extend to other issues about the manner in which man ought to be conceived and studied. Learning theorists, for example, are strongly behavioristic, tending to be suspicious of easy speculation about private inner experience, and of excessive reference to constructs which cannot be directly observed; they prefer to link their ideas about man and his personality more closely to observable behavior. Their preference for a science of man is one that emphasizes the analysis of behavior into its basic elements. They assume that even the most complex patterns of behavior can be reduced to more simple elements and, in fact, that only in this way can personality be understood. Thus, they tend to be nomothetic rather than idiographic in orientation. Moreover, they are interested in reductive analysis of complex events to the common properties on which the behavior of all organisms depends, not only that of infra-human animals, but even of the rat, worm, and cockroach, all of whom are assumed to learn by means of forming associations between stimuli and responses. Man is thought of merely as a more complex instance of such a basic process.

In contrast, the phenomenologically oriented theorist assumes that the organized system that we call personality cannot be synthesized readily from a molecular analysis of its component elements. A positive value is placed on such terms as system, integration, organization; in short, the phenomenologist is "holistic" and "molar," rather than "analytic" and "molecular." His units of analysis are apt to be complex and to include goals as well as the means by which goals are achieved. And perhaps most important of all, the phenomenological theorist freely speculates about inner, mediating, cognitive processes, such as the self-concept or the life space, which he takes to be the real determinants of man's actions and feelings.

The philosophical distinction between the molar and molecular (or atomistic) approach can be found also in modern research and theory in perception. Sensory psychologists have traditionally thought of perceptions as being built up of numerous minute sensory impressions when physical stimuli impinge on the sense organs, such as the eyes and ears. The nervous system is thought to respond in ways parallel to the physical stimuli which strike the sense organs, collating and organizing these impressions deep within the brain. Such a view is molecular in emphasis. In contrast, Gibson (1966) has viewed perception in a molar fashion as the active process of seeking information about the environment. As he put it, "The eyes, ears, nose, mouth, and skin can orient, explore, and investigate. When thus active they are neither passive senses nor channels of sensory quality, but ways of paying attention to whatever is constant in changing stimulation. In exploratory looking, tasting, and touching, the sense impressions are incidental symptoms of the exploration, and what gets isolated is information about the object looked at, tasted, or touched. . . ."(p. 4).

Personality may also be looked at as passive accumulation of associations between stimuli and responses, that is, as a complex collection of simple and discrete conditioned reactions, or as an organized unit (system) actively searching the environment for relevant cues about the requirements of adapting. Such a philosophical difference is important in characterizing the thinking styles and assumptions of the various personality theories about the nature of man and how he should be studied. It may be found in every field of psychological study, but is most evident in personality because personality is a field that attempts to integrate the many psychological functions of the person into a comprehensive framework.

Where do the Freudian and neo-Freudian approaches to personality fall in this analysis? The answer is not clear and will depend somewhat on which of the various psychoanalytic viewpoints one is talking about, for example, that of Freud, Jung, Rank, Adler, etc., and which aspects of theory one is considering. It seems to me that Freudian theory is somewhat in-between in its treatments of the stimulus, although probably emphasizing the stimulus as objective reality more than as subjectively apprehended. Thus, for example, Freud sought to understand the individual on the basis of his actual (objective) life experiences, and the patterns of healthy or neurotic reaction (mostly the latter) which resulted from such experiences. The sources of trauma in the life of the person were treated as real events. Misperceptions and idiosyncratic forms of adjustment were understood in terms of the acquisition of the neurotic defense mechanisms. Such a position could readily be accommodated within the association-learning framework of Dollard and Miller (1950). In fact, the main personality-relevant work of these authors, *Personality and Psychotherapy,* was primarily a translation of large portions of psychoanalytic theory into association-learning terms, and the translation was not very difficult to make. This suggests that Freudian theory and association-learning theory must have much in common, including their basic approach to the stimulus as an objective event.

But there are phenomenological leanings in Freud too. For example, Freud was not very reductionistic, and there was much speculation about inner mediating processes which were, supposedly, hidden from view. Also, he focussed more on the distortions of reality (as in defense mechanisms) which were mediated by the not-so-healthy ego of the neurotic, than on effective adaptation. Neo-Freudians such as Jung introduced mediating, organizing concepts such as the self. Moreover, all psychoanalytic writers have relied more heavily on introspection as the source of information about personality structure and process than on observing behavior, although both were used. That is, the psychoanalytic therapist was always on the lookout for behavioral evidence which contradicted the verbal introspection of the person, and inferences about the personality from such introspection were always qualified by reference to behavioral signs of conflict and defense.

To sum up and conclude, it should be clear by now that the varying descriptive units employed by different theories derive from divergent assumptions about the nature of man and how he should be studied. Whether one adopts the Freudian framework of ego, id, and superego, the association learning framework of learned habits of response to physical, objective stimuli, or the phenomenological framework of life space or self-concept, certain philosophical predilections for thinking about man are revealed by the choice. The differences in descriptive units are not merely terminological, but go to the heart of the conceived nature of man. Yet, in the last analysis, whatever descriptive language is used, the facts of man's behavior and of the individual differences in that behavior provide the constant reality against which to evaluate the adequacy and fruitfulness of that language and its conceptual underpinnings. Man is the same, only the systems for conceiving and describing him vary.

It must be clear too that issues concerning the units employed for describing personality are more trivial than the more fundamental questions of how it develops, how it works (dynamics), and what influenced it (determinants). We turn now to these further questions. The development of personality is the theme of our discussion in Chapter 3.

The Development of Personality

chapter three

The developmental approach provides a time-oriented perspective to personality theory, since it is concerned with the universal sequences or stages through which personality evolves from its earliest beginnings in infancy.

Formal theories of development must first be differentiated from the effort to identify the biological and social conditions, which by facilitating, retarding, shaping, or distorting the "normal" course, influence development. In this book, the latter focus will be taken up later under the heading of determinants of personality (Chapters 5 and 6). Our concerns in this chapter are solely with formal development, that is, with the task of describing and cataloguing the *sequence* of psychological changes through which all persons typically pass in the progression from infancy to adulthood.

The perspective of *formal* developmental theory in psychology is analogous to that of embryology in tracing the stages through which human and infra-human embryos pass from conception to birth. By investigating babies born prematurely at various intra-uterine periods, embryologists have demonstrated that the human fetus proceeds through definite stages in its response to local stimulation of the face by a stiff hair or other object (e.g. Hooker, 1943). At a very early stage the embryo reacts with a diffuse, total-body response to the stimulation. Later, as the embryo grows into a fetus, the response becomes more and more differentiated, so that ultimately, as the fetus approaches full maturity preparatory to being a newborn infant, the response becomes highly localized and specific; that is, only the immediate part of the body touched reacts to the stimulation. Thus, fetal development demonstrably includes a progression through certain neuromuscular stages. This progression constitutes a universal biological law—it applies virtually to all cases, and other species. The task of cataloguing and understanding the stages of psychological development is of course far more complicated than in the above illustration which deals with a relatively limited neurological form of organization. Nevertheless, the illustration portrays how, in the *formal* analysis of development, attention is directed at the universal stages through which certain structures and processes pass, rather than at the factors which account for development.

Since the structures and processes of personality cannot be observed directly, but require inferences from the observed pattern of reaction in a given situational context, it will come as no surprise that the stages of personality development have been variously conceived by different writers. For example, in his analysis of psychological development, Freud emphasized the evolution of drives and emotions, particularly during the first three years of life. Other developmentally oriented writers, such as Piaget and Werner, were totally unconcerned with the evolution of drives or emotional patterns and gave their attention entirely to cognition or adaptive thought. Still others, such as Erikson, retained the basic outlook entailed in Freud's analysis, but made modifications and extensions of the scheme to later periods of life. Thus, some of the differences among theories of development arise from varying developmental phenomena, and other differences concern the periods of life which are emphasized.

As in the case of the description of personality, our brief treatment cannot cover all the important theoretical variations. Comparison of different approaches will be restricted here mainly to two of the most influential systems of thought, that of Freud (including some of the additions and modifications by Erikson) and that of Piaget.

Freud's Psychosexual Theory

We have already touched upon this aspect of Freud's (1933, 1949) theory in Chapter 2 where reference was made to oral, anal, and phallic personality types. That discussion need not be repeated here; however, some additional detail could profitably be given in connection with the *phallic* and *genital* stages. The person is said to pass through three main stages —the oral, the anal, and the phallic—finally reaching the mature adult, genital stage. Freud treated the phallic period as just preliminary to that of mature adulthood, starting at pubescence when the person begins to arrive at physical maturity. To pass successfully through the phallic period in reaching genital maturity, the person must resolve the Oedipus complex (in girls, the Electra complex), which is the key psychosexual problem of the phallic stage. It is simpler first to discuss this problem in the case of the boy.

The boy's first love object is his mother, or someone who plays that role, and he seeks total access to her affection. However, such possession is thwarted by the competing presence of the father. The attachment of the boy to the mother and the competition of the father constitute the family love triangle, or the "family romance," as Robert White (1956) has whimsically referred to it. The natural response of the boy to this situation is to develop hostile feelings toward the father. But the boy also realistically perceives the father as far more powerful than he, and likely to retaliate for the boy's hostile wishes by hostility of his own. And it is not uncommon for the attachment between the boy and his mother to be reacted to by the father with some annoyance, especially if the father himself feels insecure about his relationship to his wife. This could add a reality basis to the boy's impression of danger from the father. The retaliation by the father that is feared by the Oedipal boy was conceived by Freud to be "castration," that is, the destruction, literally or symbolically, of the offending organ, the penis, which expresses his maleness. The girl is already missing the penis, a fact which the boy believes to be her punishment for similar transgressions. In any event, the boy experiences "castration anxiety" in proportion to the strength of his sexual urge toward the mother and its attendant degree of hostility toward the father.

The girl's problem, often referred to as the Electra complex, is parallel to that of the boy. As with the boy it begins with attachment to the mother in early infancy, but this attachment must shift later to the father. How and why this shift occurs is not at all clear, theoretically (see for example, Helene Deutsch, 1944, for one account of this). However, when the girl "cathects" the father as a love object, she now faces competition from the mother in a fashion parallel with the case of the boy and his father. She also perceives the absence of a penis in herself, envies its possession by the boy, and blames her mother for its loss.

During the period from about six years of age until adolescence, the family romance tends to go underground. What happens is that as a solution to the unbearable tension produced by the danger of castration in the boy (or the consequences of its past occurrence in the case of the girl), the erotic and hostile urges of the family triangle are defended against. The child goes into what is often called the "latency period," in which he or she represses the erotic feelings toward the opposite sexed parent. And by the mechanism of "identification with the aggressor," the child takes on the moral and behavior values of the like-sexed parent. Freud believed that it was mainly during this period that the superego was formed, through the defensive process of identification. Here again the case of the boy is simple and easier to use as an illustration. The boy's castration anxiety is reduced by the repressive defense, since it eliminates his awareness of the erotic and hostile feelings; and by making himself like the father through identification, he gains the father's approval and thus does not have anything to fear from him.

The emotional struggles which are part of the family romance are held in abeyance during the latency period until adolescence, when the upsurge of erotic urges breaks through the defensive armor, and the Oedipus and Electra complexes now reappear in full force. The healthy boy and girl ultimately resolve these complexes by giving up the opposite-sexed parent as an erotic love object, and by selecting a sex partner outside the immediate family. The boy and girl are now free to establish nonerotic friendships with the opposite-sexed parent, and in so doing they pass into the mature genital stage of psychosexual development. Only the neurotic individual remains stuck, so to speak, at a pregenital level, either oral, anal, or phallic.

ERIKSON'S CONTRIBUTIONS TO
FREUDIAN PSYCHOSEXUAL THEORY

Erik Erikson (1959, 1963) has modified the Freudian theory of psychosexual development in two main ways, first, by emphasizing even more than Freud the interplay of the social context with the biologically given stages, and second, by expanding the stages from four (oral, anal, phallic, and genital) to eight. Let us examine these two contributions briefly.

1. Erikson stressed the point that each psychosexual stage has its characteristic mode of social interaction. Thus, for example, the biological impulses connected with early orality involve stimulating the mucus membrane of the mouth with food and other objects which are taken into the oral cavity. At this period, "taking in" is thus the basic modality for interpersonal relations. The mother feeds the child, and the child depends on this nurturance and develops certain expectations about its social environment, for example, that the environment can be trusted to provide the necessary sustenance, or that it is unresponsive to his needs. Similarly, in the anal stage, efforts are made to control and discipline the child's bowel and other activities. There develops an interpersonal struggle related to "letting go" (of feces) versus "holding onto," a struggle relevant to the psychological development of the personality trait of autonomy as opposed to those of shame and doubt. Erikson writes about this interpenetration of the biological and social as follows:

Muscular maturation sets the stage for experimentation with two simultaneous sets of social modalities: holding on and letting go. As is the case with all of these modalities, their basic conflicts can lead in the end to either hostile or benign expectations and attitudes. Thus, to hold can become a destructive and cruel retaining or restraining, and it can become a pattern of care: to have and to hold. To let go, too, can turn into an inimical letting loose, of destructive forces, or it can become a relaxed 'to let pass' and 'to let be' (1963, p. 251).

In short, Erikson draws a parallel between social or interpersonal attitudes and the biological processes called for at the different psychosexual stages, pointing to the interdependence of each. The basic mode of response is set by the biological process characteristic of the particular stage, and its physical as well as social expression is further influenced by the interpersonal circumstances in which the child finds himself. In his analysis Erikson, much more than Freud, pointed toward the interpersonal features of each psychosexual stage.

2. In Erikson's expansion of the psychosexual theory into additional stages, the best known addition is expressed by the term "ego-identity," which is the outcome of the struggle at puberty to resolve the Oedipus and Electra complexes of the phallic stage. In emphasizing the effort to discover one's place in the world, and successfully to find one's unique nature, that is, to achieve ego-identity, Erikson gave more importance to the period of late adolescence and early adulthood than was found in Freud's writing. Much influenced by Erikson, one of the more recent writers about the younger generation of social protestors, Kenneth Kenniston (1965, 1968), refers to a new stage of "youth" in which the relations between oneself and the world are the primary concern of the young adult struggling with political and social systems which he often finds alien to his view of himself.

RESEARCH ON THE PSYCHOSEXUAL STAGES

The psychosexual theory has had enormous influence on psychological thought, particularly in clinical psychology where many forms of psychopathology have been viewed as based on disturbances of psychosexual development. Anthropological and sociological analyses have also been greatly influenced by this theory. For example, examination of weaning and toilet training practices in different cultures and subcultures derives from an interest in the basic premises of Freud's psychosexual theory. Variations in such practices are studied to determine their influence on the typical personality found in that culture.

There is no portion of Freudian theory that is more controversial than the conception of psychosexual development. Although everyone agrees that experiences in early childhood are of vital importance for personality development, many writers (e.g. Horney, 1937) have questioned the almost exclusive emphasis given by Freud to sexual drives. The stages of psychosexual development were viewed by Freud as reflections of a universal, biological law. He gave little attention to the manner in which the culture might have contributed to each stage. The possibility exists, for example, that the Oedipus complex can be better understood in terms of the social relations within the family rather than in sexual terms. The boy might come to fear the father not because he literally expects castration, or because of sexual urges toward the mother, but because the father controls power within the family, particularly in Viennese society of the late 1800's. Similarly, the girl might envy the boy, not literally for his penis, but because in most societies, girls are usually subordinate to boys. The penis may only symbolize masculine social power to the child, not the organ of love. These questions, however, fall within the rubric of personality determinants, and they must be deferred until later chapters.

Some fascinating experimental research has been performed to test whether the relationships postulated in the psychosexual theory actually hold. A recent experiment by Timmons and Noblin (1963) is an excellent example. Timmons and Noblin used an ingenious assessment tool called the *Blacky Test* which was devised by a psychoanalytically oriented psychologist, Gerald Blum (1950). It consists of a series of cartoons portraying twelve situations theoretically representing the typical conflicts of each pregenital psychosexual stage. The main character in the cartoons, Blacky, is a dog. The rest of the cast of characters includes Blacky's Mama, Papa, and Tippy, who is Blacky's sibling. One assumes that the person taking the test will identify with Blacky. One of the cartoons shows Blacky nursing on the mother dog, a theme suggesting oral eroticism. Others deal with sibling rivalry, Oedipal urges, anal impulses, and so on. The subject's task is to write a vivid story about each cartoon, to indicate which he likes best, and to give the reasons for the choice. This material is then examined clinically to evaluate the psychosexual characteristics (e.g., fixations, psychosexual conflicts, anxieties, and psychosexual type, i.e. oral, anal, phallic, genital) of the subject.

Timmons and Noblin gave the Blacky Test to 90 undergraduate students, from which 15 were then selected on the basis of their test protocols as representing "oral" types, and fifteen as "anal." Then a series of 120 cards were shown to each subject individually. At the top of each card were two pronouns, one in the first person ("I," or "we") and the other in the third person ("he," "she," or "they"). On the bottom of the card was a fragment of a sentence. The task was to complete the sentence with one of the pronouns. After 30 trials without any attempt to influence the subject, the experimenter began to "reinforce" the subject's response by making mildly affirmatory utterances, such as "Um-hum," "That's fine," "Ok," and "Good," whenever the subject made use of a pronoun in the first person.

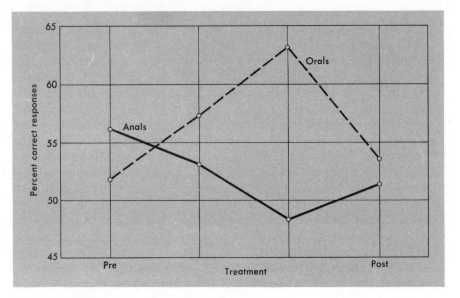

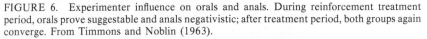

FIGURE 6. Experimenter influence on orals and anals. During reinforcement treatment period, orals prove suggestable and anals negativistic; after treatment period, both groups again converge. From Timmons and Noblin (1963).

The psychological issue tackled via this procedure was whether the orals and anals would be differently influenced by the experimenter's subtle encouragement to use first person pronouns. Remember that according to the psychosexual theory oral personalities are supposed to be dependent and oriented toward nurturance, while anals should be obstinate and resistant to authority. Thus, in the present experimental situation, orals are expected to be positively influenced by the experimenter's suggestions, while anals should resist them. This is precisely what was found. Shortly after the reinforcement by the experimenter began, orals began to show a marked tendency to choose the first person pronoun, while anals showed a decline in its use. Later, after the experimenter ceased to comment suggestively, the two groups again returned to about the same baseline (in their use of the first-person singular pronoun) as when they began. In effect, the two groups ceased to be differentiated, showing that the divergence had been a reaction to the experimenter's suggestions. These findings are graphically portrayed in Figure 6.

Experiments such as the above provide empirical support for the idea that people can indeed be differentiated on the basis of the psychological characteristics imputed to each pregenital stage of psychosexual development. This does not, however, prove that such characteristics were acquired in the manner proposed by the theory. In any case, the theory has been quite fruitful in generating personality research, and it has had perhaps its greatest impact on clinical diagnosis and psychopathology. It is a formal developmental theory because its main emphasis is on universal psychological sequences through which a person passes on his way from infancy to adulthood.

Piaget's Theory of Cognitive Development

As in the case of Freud, Jean Piaget (1952; see also Flavell, 1963, Langer, 1969, and Inhelder and Piaget, 1958) has also been concerned with the universal stages through which Langer, 1969, he person passes during the early years of his life. Therefore, his too is a formal theory of development. However, unlike Freud who emphasized the development of motivational and emotional processes (e.g. sexual drives and the affects connected with them), Piaget focused exclusively on cognitive development, that is, the intellectual processes marking the progression from infancy to adulthood. By the same token, the observations available to Freud and Piaget were also different, as were their conceptions of research. For example, Freud studied childhood development mainly by having adults describe their emotional life during childhood while undergoing psychotherapy; in contrast, Piaget studied cognitive development by giving children problems to solve and examining the ways they went about this at different chronological ages. Like Freud's, Piaget's point of view is consistent with the Darwinian approach to adaptation. He conceived of behavior as an adaptive life process by means of which the person maintains a state of equilibrium between himself and his environment. Changes in the environment continually disturb this equilibrium, and adaptation could take place only through a person's changing himself ("accommodation" to the environment) or manipulating the environment ("assimilation"). Intelligent thought develops out of this continuing adaptive interchange between the person and the environment.

As is necessary in any formal developmental theory, Piaget sought to identify and describe the stages through which intelligent thought evolved. He proposed two main stages, the *sensori-motor* and the *conceptual*, within which there are a number of definable subperiods. He also used great ingenuity in setting up intellectual tasks for children that showed the observer the processes of solution of which the child was capable at various chronological ages. Most of Piaget's research observations were drawn from his own children, and although the sample was very small and of doubtful representativeness, the overall analysis has proved remarkably fruitful in describing the progression of thought in the growing child.

The sensori-motor stage extends roughly from birth to the age of two.

During this time the child acquires his first knowledge of the objects of his environment. There are six subperiods within the sensori-motor stage, covering the first eighteen months of life. In the first subperiod from birth to about one month, the infant engages mainly in "innate reflexes," such as sucking. Next is the subperiod of "primary circular reactions," extending from one to four months, in which simple acts such as opening and closing the fists or fingering a blanket are repeated for their own sake. During later subperiods, activities are more intentional. For example, in the third subperiod going from four to six months, and referred to as "secondary circular reactions," the child repeats actions that produce interesting changes in the environment. The fourth subperiod from seven to ten months of age involves the "coordination of secondary reactions"; the child begins to solve simple problems through the use of previously mastered responses. In subperiod five, consisting of what Piaget called "tertiary circular reactions," and taking place from eleven to eighteen months of age, the child engages in trial-and-error experimentation on the environment, and several alternative methods may now be tried to attain a goal. The child understands that he can have an effect on the world of objects, and now recognizes these objects as separate from himself. Finally, in the sixth sensori-motor subperiod from eighteen months on, the child makes use of "mental combinations," and appears to think foresightfully about the effects he creates. At this point, thought has begun to shift from a purely sensori-motor to a conceptual level.

The second major stage of cognitive development, the conceptual stage, begins with the emergence of thinking somewhat independently of the explicit presence of objects. Before this, symbols and language had not been used extensively. The conceptual stage is divided into four subperiods. The "preconceptual" subperiod begins at about two years of age and proceeds until about four. Objects begin to take on symbolic meaning in that they can be used to stand for or represent other objects or events. A doll or plastic figure can be reacted to as though it were a parent or sibling. The concept of class or category is emerging. The subperiod of "intuitive thought," from about four to seven years of age, involves the construction of more complex images. But thought is still intuitive in that it is based heavily on simple sense characteristics, and the concept of the object has not yet become divorced from the concrete perceptual experience. For example, if two squat jars of the same shape and size are presented to the child and filled with beads, the child understands that they contain an equal number of beads. If the contents of one are poured into a tall thin jar, the four-year old is likely to report that the tall thin jar now contains more beads, since he observes that the beads go higher up than they do in the squat jar. The concept of amount is rigidly tied to the perceptual quality of height. Thus, the height of the jar is intuitively equated with the quantity it holds. Somewhere between five and seven years of age, the child enters the subperiod of "concrete operations," becoming aware that the amount of beads is the same, although the two jars differ in shape. During this subperiod he discovers that width compensates for height, and he develops a sense of constancy concerning the concepts of amount, size, weight, and height regardless of the perceptual context. Finally, beginning at about age eleven, the last subperiod of the conceptual stage arrives, that of "formal operations," during which thought becomes virtually completely freed of the manipulation of concrete objects. Events can now be imagined, manipulated symbolically, reasoned about, evaluated, and planned for, without direct contact with the physical features of these events. That is, an object can be apprehended without its being seen or touched, resulting in thought which is abstract and highly adaptive.

Contrasts and Overlaps Between Freud and Piaget

The reader may have wondered about the direct relevance to personality of Piaget's analysis of the development of adaptive thought. Freud was quite explicit about the connections with personality of his psychosexual stages. For example, Freud viewed adult personality as often characterized by "hangovers" from pregenital struggles, as in the cases of the oral, anal, or phallic personality types. Even the "normal" individual was said to have some psychological residuals of the pregenital stages, as in the pattern of sexual foreplay prior to coitus. Kissing exemplifies such a residual (of oral sexuality) as does "latrinalia" (see, for example, Dundes, 1966), the phenomenon of writing on toilet walls in which oral and anal sex jokes predominate. Morover, in the emphasis Freud gave to the psychosexual stages, he also presented a kind of implicit blueprint for childrearing, in which overindulgence or underindulgence at any given stage were conceived of as traumatic, and likely to produce abnormal fixations which impeded advancement to the next stage.

Piaget, on the other hand, never made explicit, nor did he express any interest in, the links between developmental stages and adult personality, although links are there implicitly. There are two lines of reasoning linking cognitive developmental theory to personality. First, one could argue that the truly fundamental features of adaptive behavior, and hence of personality, are the person's intellectual capacities and modes of thought. It is thus reasonable to argue that the motivational, emotional, and social life of the individual are determined by what and how he thinks about himself and the world in which he lives. In short, the cognitive processes which the person has developed are the warp and woof of everything else in his life, including the emotional, motivational, and social experiences of healthy and disturbed people. Nevertheless, Piaget did not make the connections clear or express any real interest in them. This remains mainly to be done by those who follow.

The second line of reasoning is based on the idea of individual differences in the stage of cognitive development which the person attains in his life, and hence, in the developmentally determined manner in which the tasks of life are managed. This can be seen in Freud's concepts of fixation and regression, and in his treatment of oral, anal, and phallic types. In effect, some individuals remain at pregenital levels, or under traumatic conditions later in life regress to an immature level of functioning. Schizophrenia, for example, was thought of by Freud as a regression to a very early oral level, paranoia to an early anal level, and neuroses to late anal or phallic psychosexual levels. The highest developmental level attained thus determines the motivational and emotional life, and probably the pattern of social relations of the person too.

This reasoning is nicely illustrated by the work of some students of Heinz Werner (1954), who presented a theory of cognitive development which parallels and overlaps Piaget's in many ways, although it has not been as influential. Werner argued that cognitive development always proceeds from an initially "global, diffuse stage," to increased "differentiation" or specialization of function, ultimately perhaps reaching the highest level, that of "hierarchical integration." Many kinds of behavior exemplify such a universal, biological law. For example, Werner, like Piaget, observed that a very young child is unable to differentiate objects in his environment such as furniture and other people from one another and from himself. Only gradually does he recognize persons as distinct from things. Eventually, of course, he differentiates and identifies individuals and their various moods, and ultimately he comes to conceive of himself as physically and psychologically distinct from others about him. This conception of psychological development has influenced two kinds of research, a sophisticated approach to individual differences in "psychological integration" developed by Witkin and his associates (1962), and some studies by Werner's own students on psychopathology and development. We shall illustrate briefly from the latter.

One of the ways Werner's students set about to test some of these ideas was to make use of the Rorschach inkblot test, a projective device for personality assessment that will be discussed more fully in Chapter 7. An inkblot is a rather ambiguous stimulus, and when the person is asked to tell what it looks like to him, he must organize the stimulus perceptually in some way. He may give a *global* response, an instantaneous impression of the whole blot ("It's a cloud or a blob"), or he may select some small segment of the blot and interpret that detail ("This part is the head of a man"). The latter process illustrates *differentiation* of percepts.

At the most advanced level of perceptual organization, *hierarchical integration,* he may differentiate certain details, that is, identify inkblot segments which appear like parts of a body, say a head, arms, legs, and then organize them into a complex, integrated percept which is made up of the parts, for example, a whole person or animal. In Werner's view, perceptual development always proceeded from diffuse processes to more differentiated and ultimately integrated ones at the most advanced developmental stage. Such a sequence was indeed supported by cross-sectional research (e.g. as reviewed by Hemmendinger, 1960) with children of different ages. It is illustrated in Figure 7 in which the percentage of detail responses (differentiated percepts) on the Rorschach test is shown as an increasing function of age.

Werner's students also were able to show that mental patients had regressed in the developmental level at which they organized their perceptions of the inkblots as a result of their disorder; the more severely disturbed psychotic patients showed patterns of perception which were similar in form (not similar in content) to those of immature, young children, while the less severely maladjusted neurotic patients displayed perceptual functioning which was more similar to that of normal adults. This is graphically illustrated in Figure 8, in which the percentage of developmentally advanced whole responses to the inkblots is plotted as a function of age and degree of psychopathology (i.e., comparing schizophrenics, paranoids, neurotics, and normals, from the most to least disturbed).

To this point, very few personality characteristics have been related in this way to variations in cognitive developmental level. However, it is not difficult to imagine how a variety of personality traits, including motivational, emotional, and social ones, could ultimately be linked to the level of cognitive development which the person has reached.

An illustration of research on the links between cognitive development and social functioning can be found in a recent study by Adelson and O'Neil (1966). These social scientists were interested in the manner in which socio-political ideas emerged and expressed themselves in adolescence. They conducted intensive interviews with 120 young people, 30 in each age group studied (ages eleven, thirteen, fifteen, and eighteen) to investigate how the adolescents felt about community issues as a function of age. Before thirteen, the social consequences of political actions could not be readily imagined by the youngsters, their analysis of these actions being restricted to the stereotyped, concrete polar opposites which were found within the community. Before the age of fifteen, they had difficulty conceiving of the community as a whole, and they thought of government mainly in respect to specific, tangible services which it performed. Moreover, the younger adolescents were particularly insensitive to concepts of individual liberties; they usually opted for authoritarian solutions to politi-

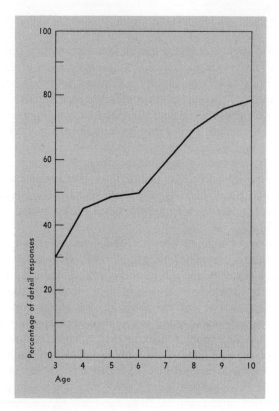

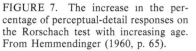

FIGURE 7. The increase in the percentage of perceptual-detail responses on the Rorschach test with increasing age. From Hemmendinger (1960, p. 65).

FIGURE 8. (*below*). Median percent developmentally—high whole responses of all whole responses: child and adult groups. From Hemmendinger (1960, p. 67).

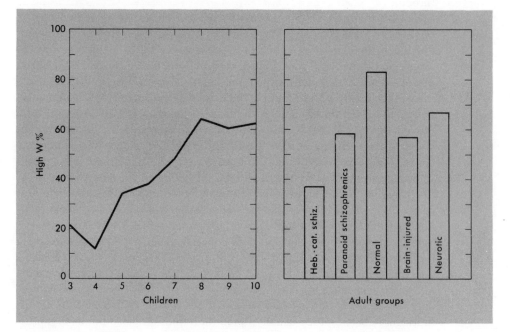

cal problems, but could not grasp legitimate claims of the community on the citizen. It was only the older subjects who had a clear sense of future and took into account the long range effects of political action. With increasing age there was increasing reference to philosophical principles in the determination of their political attitudes. Adelson and O'Neil's findings suggest that the contents of attitudes, and surely, therefore, motivational, emotional, and social behavior, are governed by some of the same rules of cognitive development that Piaget formulated concerning the child's progression from the concrete, sensori-motor to the abstract and conceptual.

Although Freud did not emphasize cognitive processes in his theory of psychosexual development, he did not altogether leave out reference to them. Some attention was given to ego development and ego defenses at different psychosexual stages. For example, the mechanism of projection, in which one attributes to another unacceptable urges within oneself, was linked theoretically to the early anal stage and considered to be the prime mode of coping used by the paranoid. Similarly, isolation and undoing, considered characteristic of the obsessive-compulsive neurotic, were thought to arise in the late anal period, while repression was viewed as having its origins in the phallic period as a defense against threatening Oedipal urges. Thus, in Freudian theory a connection is assumed between stage of psychosexual development, type of urge or drive (e.g. oral versus anal), and the adaptive or defensive mode of thought by which the drive is managed. Moreover, for Freud the energy for the emergence of adaptive thought came mainly from the sexual drives or instincts. For Piaget, the cognitive structures themselves contained all the necessary energy for their emergence and development. Recent innovations in psychoanalysis, for example, the "ego-psychology" movement (cf. Rapaport, 1967; Hartmann, 1964) have turned renewed attention to the cognitive, adaptive processes of the ego. This suggests the possibility of rapprochement between the two orientations to formal development, those of Piaget and Freud. Attempts to examine the bases for such a rapprochement have recently been made by P. H. Wolff (1960).

Obviously, exclusive focus on cognitive development leaves out essential elements of the personality which are contained in the rubrics of motivation and emotion, or in social behavior. Similarly, exclusive preoccupation with the development of motivation, emotional, and social processes leaves out what is perhaps an underlying theme of greatest importance in these processes, that is, cognitive activity. What is needed is a system of thought that preserves the most useful elements of both interdependent themes and unites them into a single system that integrates all of the essential features of personality within a developmental framework.

Personality Dynamics

chapter four

A most significant task of a personality theory is to describe the function of the personality as a system, that is, the mechanisms or processes of its operation and how they are reflected in observable behavioral events. As the reader might recall from Chapter 1, in geology, dynamics might involve the action of wind and water on rock and earth as the most obvious examples. Dynamics in an automobile engine would include the intake of fuel and its explosion in the cylinders, the escape of exhaust, and the conversion of the resulting energy into turning the drive shaft and wheels. In investigating personality dynamics, we must look to psychological processes rather than physical ones.

As with personality description and development, the dynamics of personality are variously conceived. Although theories diverge on many issues relevant to dynamics, the one on which this chapter concentrates concerns the nature of human motivation. This has to do with the forces that are assumed to energize and direct human behavior, the organization of these forces within the person, and the manner in which they are set in motion and controlled. The major theories of personality each adopt certain positions on the nature of man's motivation. Our account will be concerned less with the details of motivation and more with broad lines of thought, that is, with the basic assumptions. Other books are available that deal with the substance of motivation, for example, with types of motives, the arousal of motives, the relations between motives and cognition, and the conflict of motives.

The motivational assumptions of the most influential theories of personality fall within three main types, which may be referred to as tension-reduction, those supplementing tension-reduction with additional principles such as effectance, and force-for-growth. The tension-reduction point of view is best represented by Freud and some of the neo-Freudians, as well as by the association-learning approach of Dollard and Miller. The effectance model has been outlined most fully by Robert White. Although strictly speaking he does not have a full-scale personality theory, White speaks eloquently for any such theory which would base its conception of dynamics on the principle of effectance. The force-for-growth point of view includes the personality theories of Rogers and Maslow, to name its most influential protagonists.

The Tension-reduction Model

The fundamental principle of this position is a simple and elegant one, that all behavior (in man as well as in infra-human animals) can be understood as an effort to reduce tension. This principle has had a close connection with two other modern themes. The first is Darwin's (1859) theory of evolution, which emphasized "natural selection" as the process by which those species or biological attributes less well-adapted to their environments were weeded out while well-adapted ones survived. This Darwinian theme encouraged psychology to adopt a general biological orientation to man, and focused interest specifically on adaptive behavior. Not only was survival important, but so was the achievement of an ideal state of balance in the inner environment of man. This could be achieved by adaptive activities which prevented hunger, thirst, excessively lowered body temperature, etc. Such a view was also encouraged by the work of the great physiologist, Claude Bernard, a contemporary of Darwin who did the pioneering work on the concept of "homeostasis," i.e., the maintenance of balance in the internal environment. Man's adaptive activities could contribute to homeostasis because his behavior was governed by the principle of tension-reduction. The absence of the ideal homeostatic steady-state resulted in painful tension (as when one is hungry or thirsty), and thus led to behavior, such as eating, which reduced the tension.

The second theme stemmed from the evident need to find a principle whereby tension-reduction could be achieved, that is, so that animals and man could learn to engage in the behavior that preserved homeostasis. This was the principle of "association" which had its origins in the writings of certain philosophers of the eighteenth century, for example, David Hartley (1705–1737) and James Mill (1773–1836). It stated that one idea becomes connected to another by means of association in time or space. Complex mental life and adaptive behaviors could be viewed as built up from such associations. Thus, learning to reduce tension could be achieved successfully in higher organisms by the association of adaptive behavior with the appropriate cues; we eat in the presence of cues of hunger and drink when thirsty. The reader should not assume that all theories of learning adopt a tension-reduction or associationistic frame-work; there are others. However, the tension-reduction and association principles have been most important ones in the history of psychology.

All theories espousing the principle of tension-reduction postulate two kinds of drive forces, those which are primary and largely innately given, and those which are secondary or social, and the product of learning. Let us examine two prominent versions of this form of analysis in personality theory, that of "association-learning through reinforcement," and "Freudian Psychoanalysis."

ASSOCIATION-LEARNING THROUGH REINFORCEMENT

The principle of reinforcement states that an association will be estab-lished between any stimulus and response when there has been gratifica-tion of a drive, that is, when the response to a stimulus succeeds in reducing the tension created by an unsatisfied drive. Not all association-learning theories are based on this reinforcement principle. Nevertheless, the reinforcement concept has probably been the most influential one in association-learning theory, and certainly the one which has been most used in the application of learning theory to personality. This is not the place to discuss the alternative principles or their histories. Suffice it to say that John Dollard and Neal Miller (1950) have become the most articulate spokesmen for the association-learning through reinforcement view of personality.

Dollard and Miller identify four concepts of prime importance in the learning process: "drive," "response," "cue," and "reinforcement." *Drive* is what initiates responses. This primary basis of human motivation stems from unsatisfied tissue needs. We must, for example, take nourishment, replenish water, get sleep, and prevent excessive variation in body temper-ature, to mention some of the most important examples of what are called tissue "deficits." Their presence creates tension or discomfort. This ten-sion serves as a drive stimulus to behavior, until responses are made which succeed in eliminating the deficit *(reinforcement),* after which the drive subsides. In effect, we learn the behavior *(responses)* that enables us to gratify tissue needs and reduce their related drive tensions. Because such drives arise from the way animals are inherently built biologically, and survival depends on satisfying them, they are often referred to as "primary drives."

Secondary, or *social drives* do not arise directly from inherited tissue needs, but are learned through social experiences because certain responses are associated with the reduction of primary drive tensions. For example, in the young child the affectional responses of the mother become associated with the elimination or reinforcement of the tension of hunger when she feeds him. Therefore, the child comes to want such affectional responses from the mother and from others, just as he wants the innately given satisfaction of filling his stomach. Through the process of feeding he has acquired an association between affection and subsidence of hunger and a new or secondary drive for affection has been created. Such associations or connections are formed between responses and certain *cues,* or stimuli, in the environment. Thus, if the reinforcing response is eating, a person must identify those stimuli to which the response is appropriate. These situations may involve the presence of food or environmental circumstances under which food may be found—for instance, a refrigerator can be an appropriate cue for obtaining food. In sum, under conditions of drive, and in the presence of cues or stimuli, a person makes responses that reduce the drive; those responses that reinforce are learned so that later the appropriate cues will elicit them.

In addition to these fundamental elements of association-learning through reinforcement, Dollard and Miller specified certain other characteristics of learning. For example, the strengthening of connections between certain cues and drive-reinforcing responses also implies the converse, that is, the weakening of other connections and the elimination of inappropriate responses that may have been tried before. This elimination of previously learned responses is called "extinction." This process is essential to learning, because learning could not take place unless unwanted acts were *extinguished* along with the establishment and strengthening of desired acts.

According to still another principle, "stimulus generalization," responses that have been learned in association with one specific cue may be transferred to other similar cues or situations. If we have learned to be afraid of speaking up in one particular social situation, the response of fear is then likely to be induced by other social situations. The greater the similarity between the situations, the greater the likelihood that a response learned to one will generalize to the other; and conversely, the less the similarity, the less the likelihood of such generalization. No two cues or situations are ever precisely the same; therefore consistency of behavior would never occur without *stimulus generalization.* Since we can respond to stimuli as similar on the basis of many physical and subjective dimensions, specification of the qualities that determine psychological similarity among situations remains one of the most perplexing problems in learning theory. The basis on which a person responds or fails to respond to stimuli as similar is difficult, if not impossible, to predict without a knowledge of internal psychological events.

Stimulus generalization is very important, but if responses learned to one stimulus tended to generalize indiscriminately to others, learning could not occur since the same response could then be made to all stimuli. For adaptive behavior to develop, a person must learn also to distinguish among stimuli so that he makes drive reinforcing responses to the correct one. To give a concrete example, we must learn to differentiate a refrigerator that contains food from a cabinet that contains material incapable of reducing our hunger drive. The process by which we differentiate appropriate from inappropriate cues is called "discrimination." Just as stimulus generalization is required in order for a given response to spread to all members of a class of appropriate cues, so *discrimination* is required to permit us to select the proper class of cues that will produce drive reduction.

Finally, through "anticipation" we identify the probable consequences of a stimulus or response before it happens, and thereby we can learn to perform actions that will reduce a drive in the future and to avoid those that will have painful or dangerous consequences. *Anticipation* helps the individual react appropriately to an impending danger or benefit about which he has been alerted.

Complex social motives, such as the desire to achieve or to be liked, are assumed to be learned in the same way as simpler responses, such as tying a shoe or hitting a typewriter key. Rewards can also be learned. Thus, we learn to accept expressions of approval as rewards because the approval has become associated in childhood with the reinforcement (by parents or other adults) of primary drives such as hunger and thirst. In other words, we learn that approval is connected with desirable consequences even though such approval itself may have had no intrinsic biological value.

According to the principles of learning briefly sketched above, we can learn any complex pattern of response in this way, including neurotic symptoms such as phobias and hysterical paralyses and the defense mechanisms connected with these disorders. The source of such maladaptive responses is the emotional drive of fear, which is said to be reduced by the neurotic symptom or the defensive activity. Clearly then from this point of view, any characteristic of personality—motives, inhibitions, defense mechanisms, and so on—may be learned according to the same set of laws of association-learning by reinforcement.

Dollard and Miller offer many illustrations of the application of the principles of learning they espouse to the learning of pathological symptoms, such as phobias, compulsions, alcoholism, and defense mechanisms such as regression, displacement, rationalization, and projection. A case of phobia which they describe offers an excellent illustration:

The essential points are illustrated by a case of a pilot who was interviewed by one of the authors. This officer had not shown any abnormal fear of airplanes before being sent on a particularly difficult mission to bomb distant and well-defended oil refineries. His squadron was under heavy attack on the way to the target. In the confusion of flying exceedingly low over the target against strong defensive fire, a few of the preceding planes made a wrong turn and dropped their bombs on the section that had been assigned to the pilot's formation. Since not enough bombs were dropped to destroy the installations, the pilot's formation had to follow them to complete the job. As they came in above the rooftops, bombs and oil tanks were exploding. The pilot's plane was tossed violently about and damaged while nearby planes disappeared in a wall of fire. Since this pilot's damaged plane could not regain altitude, he had to fly back alone at reduced speed and was subject to repeated violent fighter attack which killed several crew members and repeatedly threatened to destroy them all. When they finally reached the Mediterranean, they were low on gas and had to ditch the airplane in the open sea. The survivors drifted on a life raft and eventually were rescued.

Many times during this mission the pilot was exposed to intensely fear-provoking stimuli such as violent explosions and the sight of other planes going down and comrades being killed. It is known that intense fear-provoking stimuli of this kind act to reinforce fear as a response to other cues present at the same time. In this case, the other cues were those from the airplane, its sight and sound, and thoughts about flying. We would therefore expect the strong drive of intense fear to be learned as a response to all of these cues.

When a strong fear has been learned as a response to a given set of cues, it tends to generalize to other similar ones. Thus one would expect the fear of this airplane and of thoughts about flying to generalize to the similar sight and sound of other airplanes and thoughts about flying in them. This is exactly what happened; the pilot felt strongly frightened whenever he approached, looked at, or even thought about flying in any airplane.

Because he had already learned to avoid objects that he feared, he had a strong tendency to look away and walk away from all airplanes. Whenever he did this, he removed the cues eliciting the fear and hence felt much less frightened. But ... a reduction in any strong drive such as fear serves to reinforce the immediately preceding responses. Therefore, we would expect any response that produced successful avoidance to be learned as a strong habit. This is what occurred; the pilot developed a strong phobia of airplanes and everything connected with them.

Similarly, he felt anxious when thinking or talking about airplanes and less anxious when he stopped thinking or talking about them. The reduction in anxiety reinforced the stopping of thinking or of talking about airplanes;

he became reluctant to think about or discuss his experience.

To summarize, under traumatic conditions of combat the intense drive of fear was learned as a response to the airplane and everything connected with it. The fear generalized from the cues of this airplane to the similar ones of other airplanes. This intense fear motivated responses of avoiding airplanes, and whenever any one of these responses was successful, it was reinforced by a reduction in the strength of the fear. When all of the circumstances are understood, as in this case, there is no mystery about the phobia. In fact, such things as the avoidance of touching hot stoves or stepping in front of speeding cars usually are not called 'phobias' because the conditions reinforcing the avoidance are understood. Our contention is that the laws of learning are exactly the same, although the conditions are often different and much more obscure, especially when the fear is elicited by the internal cues of thoughts or drives (1950, pp. 157–59).

Some such learning-oriented view of the acquisition of symptoms underlies the modern approach to psychotherapy of "behavior therapists," who seek to extinguish unwanted symptoms and behaviors by producing the conditions of unlearning or extinction. Their premise, like that of Dollard and Miller, is that "the laws of learning are exactly the same" for the acquisition of any habit, be it pathological (symptom) or desirable. As we shall see shortly, the Freudian conception of the acquisition of a symptom is quite different. It might be asked, for example, why this particular pilot developed a "phobia" for airplanes while other pilots subjected to the same stress did not. Furthermore, strong fear reactions of this sort do not usually persist long after the experience has ended, and only when they do should the symptom suggest a genuine phobia. The Freudian would assume that in such cases, and perhaps even in the case of the pilot cited by Dollard and Miller, there was some connection between this current adult event and an unremembered one from childhood. Only such a connection would dispose this particular pilot to develop his symptoms. Perhaps the events of the bombing mission aroused forbidden or unacceptable impulses which reinstated earlier guilt or fear. Although this is not mentioned by Dollard and Miller, it is common for airmen in such situations to feel great guilt over their own survival and the death of their buddies. Thus, although the extreme personal danger to the pilot seems to be the outstanding feature of the mission, the total event is actually pregnant with all sorts of dynamic complications stemming from the pilot's relations with the other men with whom he shared the danger. Precisely this sort of issue currently divides psychotherapists who adopt views similar to those of Dollard and Miller or other learning theorists, and those who see pathological symptoms in Freudian terms as expressions of more subtle, usually hidden or unconscious forces, which are apt to have had their origin in early childhood, and perhaps were reactivated by some current event.

FREUD'S PSYCHOANALYSIS

Freud (1925) too acknowledged two classes of drives, those which are biologically inherent in man, and those which evolve from life experiences. However Freud, unlike Dollard and Miller, did not place much emphasis on the manner in which the latter were learned. For Freud the primary drives or instincts consisted of two categories, the "life instincts" which contributed to the survival of the person and of the species, and the "death instincts," involving self-destructive forces which could be turned outward toward others and which produced aggression and war. Freud's entire theory of personality was built around the transformations taking place in the sexual and aggressive drives, the fruits of living in a social world.

The behavior of the human infant as seen by Freud is organized around the "pleasure principle," which has the flavor of a minimum tension or tension-reduction concept. Everything that the infant does reflects the tendency to seek immediate pleasure by means of the direct discharge of instinctual energy. Thus, for example, libidinal (sexual) drives must be instantly discharged to avoid painful tension, and this discharge could sometimes occur through various automatic motor reflex actions. The requirements for discharge also differ depending on the psychosexual stage of the child. That is, oral forms of discharge are at first appropriate, but later the erogenous zone of the body on which the sexual drive is focused (and hence, the pattern of discharge) shifts, first to the anal, and then to the phallic region (see discussion of Freuds' psychosexual stages in Chapter 3).

In certain spheres, reflex actions are not always applicable. They are sometimes proscribed or limited by the culture, as in sexual climax involving masturbation or defecation. In other cases an object is necessary to produce the discharge; one cannot, for example, eat unless there is food. In such instances, the person must locate a suitable object for gratification by means of a realistic search of the environment. Such a search is facilitated by another mechanism through which discharge is made possible, that is, the "primary process," by means of which a person forms an image or hallucination of the appropriate object. Such an image is often referred to as a "wish-fulfillment." Although it does presumably permit some discharge of tension, such discharge is insufficient, and the main function of the primary process is that it ultimately facilitates the search for the suitable object.

It is not altogether clear whether Freud assumed that the person learns through experience about suitable objects, or has inherently-given images that are part of the species or both. Research by Tinbergen (1951) with lower animals, such as fish and fowl, suggests that they are constructed with built-in "releaser" mechanisms which automatically result in specific adaptive responses when they are provoked by the appropriate stimulus. For example, the male stickleback fish even without previous experience will engage in sexual activity merely on viewing the red underbelly of the ready female, and a complex pattern of sexual response is automatically elicited in the male when that stimulus is present. In fact, the male responds in essentially the same way even to a poor cardboard drawing of a fish, as long as the bottom portion is the appropriate red. It is conceivable that even in higher organisms suitable releasers of action could stem in part from inherited neurological mechanisms, although these releaser mechanisms would not be so rigid or automatized in operation as in lower animals. The latter possibility has never been adequately demonstrated for humans, and so we tend to emphasize learning rather than biological inheritance when considering Freud's concept of the primary process wish-fulfillment.

A research example of what might loosely be called wish-fulfillment in human adults, probably accentuated because of the extreme deprivation to which they were exposed, comes from observation of the fantasy behavior of men participating during World War II in militarily sponsored experiments on the effects of semi-starvation (Keys *et al.*, 1950). For many weeks volunteers engaged in full-time physical labor while being fed a diet severely reduced in caloric value. Some rather interesting personality effects of this semi-starvation were noted, including tremendous preoccupation with food, the placing on the walls of the barracks food "pin-ups" showing juicy steaks and other appetizing dishes, and frequently expressed determination to change vocations in favor of food-oriented occupations, such as cook or restauranteur. We might well regard these activities as examples of primary-process wish-fulfillment: The chronic and powerful craving for food led the men to search for images of food objects ordinarily capable of reducing hunger-induced tension. Hallucinations in mentally disturbed patients, as well as distortions of perception in normal people, can be thought of as instances of this primary-process conjuring up of images of satisfying objects.

The trouble with the primary process is that often we cannot discharge libido directly and immediately, either due to social inhibition (as in toilet discipline in the young child), or the unavailability of the actual object required to produce discharge (as in food or a sex partner). Thus, delay or thwarting of gratification takes place, and from this thwarting there emerges the "secondary process," which operates according to the "reality principle." It must do two things. First, it must protect the person against external dangers, and second, it must simultaneously make possible the discharge of tension by gratification of the instincts. The environmental situation must be evaluated to determine whether instinct-discharge is possible and safe, and the necessary objects to permit such discharge must be located. The *secondary process* is the way Freudians conceptualize the development of adaptive behavior in the child. It is another way of speaking about the emergence and growth of the "ego." Ego development involves the same thing as is implied in the development of the *secondary process;* when we refer to the former we are speaking in terms of one of the major structures or subdivisions of the personality, that is, the *ego,* which operates in accordance with the rules of secondary process.

The ego must be capable of inhibiting the expression of instincts until a safe, satisfying object is found. The *reality principle* therefore requires the postponement of immediate gratification, and this is likely to produce pain in order to yield later gratification more safely. Freud regarded all complicated mental activities such as learning, perception, memory, and reasoning as functions of the ego. In fact, he considered all secondary process mental activity to be based on the adaptive requirements posed by the postponement or frustration of immediate drive discharge. Such postponement and frustration are, to all intents and purposes, inevitable for the developing child. By following the reality principle and utilizing the secondary process, the ego inhibits direct instinctual discharge and finds substitute or transformed methods of gratification.

Many examples may be cited of the operation of the secondary process and its inhibition of direct and immediate discharge of tension. The socialized toilet behavior which evolves from infancy to later childhood and lasts throughout life is one. Defecation must be withheld until the appropriate time and place even though the bodily impulse calls for immediate discharge. Such withholding requires the capability to control the anal sphincter muscles and the cognitive processes necessary to recognize social pressures about the "proper" thing to do. Similarly, anger and the impulse to attack must be inhibited and either diverted to safe objects and situations, or transformed into more socially accepted impulses. The parent who cannot control rage toward his child when the child's behavior leads to frustration may wind up beating the child so severely as to cause serious injury or even death. Such cases are continually occurring in our society and evidence a failure of secondary process activity in a disturbed adult who is unable to control impulses and perhaps even to foresee the consequences of his actions (reality principle). Without these constraints against immediate gratification, it is difficult to see how any society could exist, for without them people could hardly live together in reasonable harmony and safety.

Freud thus subscribed to the division of motives into those that are inborn and physiological (primary drives) and those that are acquired (social motives). Sex provides an example of an inborn physiological force (the id), while learning, perception, and engaging in a wide range of socialized behavior represent the Freudian versions of secondary, or social, motives. The latter ego motives arise only because the *pleasure prin-*

ciple cannot always operate. A person is born into a society that interferes with the direct gratification of the instincts through social regulations aimed at channeling human instincts into socially acceptable paths. This results in the creation of new forms of drive discharge, which are in a sense similar to the secondary motives emphasized in association-learning through reinforcement theory.

OVERVIEW OF THE FREUDIAN AND ASSOCIATION-
LEARNING VERSIONS OF TENSION-REDUCTION

It should be clear that Freud and Dollard and Miller subscribe to a tension-reduction point of view about man. In both systems, drive tensions activate behavior through which adaptive behavioral solutions to the tension are found. These views were much influenced by the assumptions about mental life of the British associationistic philosophers, and by Darwin's (1859) thinking about evolution and natural selection. Furthermore, Freud's analysis came first, and Dollard and Miller explicitly set out to translate it into the language and format of association-learning theory which, they believed, was more susceptible to scientific verification. Although not all that is essential in Freud was incorporated into this translation, the fact that both outlooks contain in common many fundamental assumptions about man is illustrated by the ease with which such a translation could be accomplished.

Nevertheless, in spite of fundamental similarities between Freud's theory and association-learning reinforcement theory, there are four very significant differences in the way they view motivation. One difference is in the use of the term "discharge" in Freudian theory, as opposed to "deficit" in Dollard and Miller's. In the latter, the elimination of tissue deficit is the reinforcement or reward which stamps in the adaptive behavior. The model relies on the concept of a need which must be filled. In Freud, however, the model is one of mounting, undischarged energy. The analogy is that of a steam boiler in which the level of pressure rises until released by discharge through exit valves or by explosion. In short, in the deficit theory gaps or deficits need to be filled in, while in Freud's discharge theory, pressure needs to be released.

A second difference stems from the nature of the connection between the original tissue drive and the secondary or social motive which it creates. In association-learning theory, the connection between the primary drive, say hunger or thirst, and the secondary or social motive is purely accidental. For example, when affiliative behavior is displayed toward the child by the mother, it tends merely by chance to become associated with the reduction of a primary drive tension, such as hunger; that is, these two events are connected or associated because they occur together adventitiously in time or place, not because there is any biological link between them. In contrast, Freudian theory postulates a more biologically meaningful connection between the life instincts and social motives. The latter are viewed as derivatives of the former, that is, as substitute (sublimated) versions of the former. Thus, for example, altruistic affection is viewed as a desexualized or neutralized form of libidinal energy. The sexual drive can be modified to permit discharge in some other, perhaps more acceptable, manner. The new or modified forms of discharge are not quite as adequate as the original, but nonetheless, they do allow the sexual energy to be drained off, so to speak. The closer the form of the sublimated outlet to the original drive, the more satisfactory the discharge of tension is assumed to be.

Both systems of thought have some difficulty in dealing with the high degree of autonomy which the social motives seem to have in adult life. These motives eventually seem to depend no longer on their original connections with the primary drives. Thus, although working for income may have its origins in the need for food and other forms of sustenance, long after the individual has more than enough income, work seems to have a strong motive power of its own. As Gordon Allport (1937b) put it, it has become "functionally autonomous" of its primary drive origins. Staying closer to the Freudian scheme, modern ego psychologists such as Hartmann (1964) and Rapaport (1967) have dealt with this difficulty by introducing the concepts of "neutralization" of sexual drives, and "ego autonomy." These are quite similar in scope and design to Allport's principle of *functional autonomy.*

Although the principle of functional autonomy makes intuitive sense, at least descriptively, its mechanisms or rules of operation have not been made clear. Thus, the conditions under which a social motive will or will not become an independent motive force in its own right have not been established. This remains an unresolved problem in the theoretical analysis of the relationships between primary or biological drives and secondary or social motives.

A third difference lies in the nature of the primary drives emphasized by the two systems of thought. Dollard and Miller make no special point about the particular drive contents which might be central or peripheral in personality development. All the survival drives on whose gratification life tends to depend are alluded to, and hunger and thirst are treated as prototypical of all primary drives. Although Freud did not reject the idea that such drives played an important role in adaptation, he saw them as having little significance for the personality. As Freud saw it, the biologically critical drives of hunger and thirst are not surrounded by social conflicts and taboos, as are sex and aggression. Since the management of the former is not a major source of guilt and anxiety, those drives are not likely to result in psychopathological outcomes, except perhaps in rather extraordinary circumstances. In contrast, sex and aggression assume great importance in Freudian thought because they are major sources of conflict in human life, and since they are often linked to guilt and anxiety, they play a crucial role in personality development. Moreover, hunger and thirst are peremptory in that they cannot be postponed or repressed without endangering life, while sex and aggression as drives are capable of repression without such danger and hence likely to be associated with neurotic problems. Notice too that sex and aggression as drives are not too compatible with the deficit model of Dollard and Miller in which some substance, such as a nutritive element, is absent and must be replaced, but they are quite compatible with the discharge model of Freud. Thus, in a review of the differences between the two tension-reduction theories, there is an interesting connection between points one and three.

A fourth and final difference concerns the way in which unconscious processes are seen. Dollard and Miller accepted the notion of unconsciousness, but gave to it a rather special meaning. In their view, unconsciousness arises from the failure of the person adequately to label verbally the components of his experience, or from the active process of extinguishing (repressing) a label. Our language fails to label adequately all our drives and reactions, the nuances concerning them, and the features of the physical and social environment in which we live. In some societies, for example, there are abundant terms for colors which are of particular importance in that ecology; in other societies, such verbal distinctions may not even exist. These gaps in language are particularly important in early childhood, before the person has acquired the means to label and verbalize psychological events. Impulses (drives and motives) and experiences occurring at such times of life may, therefore, never be labeled at all. Thus, according to Dollard and Miller, they are experienced without awareness, because of this failure of labeling, or because of the blocking of a *verbal label*. However, for Freud it is the blocking of impulses from awareness through the defense mechanisms of the ego that in large measure accounts for unconscious mental activity.

In spite of these differences, both Freudian and association-learning theory (at least the reinforcement version of it popularized by Dollard and Miller) share the basic principle of tension-reduction in their conceptions of human behavior and its motivation. Whether expressed by the term, "pleasure principle" or "principle of reinforcement," all behavior without exception is said by both to be a means of reducing tension, even behavior which seems on the surface to produce more tension than it reduces. In the Freudian view of such seemingly contradictory instances, for example, as when people or infra-human animals seem to choose painful rather than benign behavioral alternatives and variously make trouble for themselves, the tension-reduction principle is not regarded as violated, but rather as being suspended in the interests of learning more effective means of overcoming obstacles to tension-reduction via the reality principle. Thus, we choose what appear to be circuitous routes in order better to ensure tension-reduction in the future in the face of obstacles to it's existing in the present. Freud supplemented the pleasure principle by the notion of the death instinct which also accounted for nonpleasureable behaviors, but this notion has been widely rejected as circular and unnecessary by most Freudians today, and it will be ignored here. In any case, the contradictions of much behavior to the tension-reduction principle are only *apparent* contradictions; they are explained as necessary detours rather than as suspensions of the principle.

CHALLENGES TO THE TENSION-REDUCTION PRINCIPLE

The chief advantage of tension-reduction as an explanatory principle is its elegance—its basic simplicity. Its disadvantages lie in the instances, alluded to above, where it fails to conform to our subjective experience, and with certain empirical evidence. With respect to contrary subjective experience, pleasure does not always seem to be merely the reduction of pain. Wanting to go to the movies or eat a meal, seem positive attractions, and only at times does this sort of desire seem subjectively to be based on the need to reduce a gnawing unpleasantness produced by tissue deficits. Of course, such a difficulty is not necessarily fatal, since many correct ideas have conflicted with common sense, as did the proposal, for example, that the earth revolved around the sun rather than the other way around.

As to empirical evidence which does not easily fit the tension-reduction principle, there are a great number of instances where people, and even infra-human animals, appear to seek stimulation rather than to reduce it. These instances are often difficult to explain away comfortably as being detours on the way to tension-reduction. For example, how does one explain thrill seekers (e.g., parachutists, auto racers, daredevils), or people who die rather than betray a trust, or those who risk their lives for a principle? Tension-reduction in such cases seems to be abrogated in favor of some other principle of motivation.

It has been shown, too, that animals who are not evidently driven by any of the usual primary drives still show curiosity, or exploratory and manipulative behavior. Harlow (1953) has demonstrated, for example, that when they are not hungry or thirsty, monkeys will work even harder to obtain the reward of being able to look out of a window at people and things going on about the cage than when they are caught up in primary drive tensions. Infants, too, appear to engage in more exploration and manipulation when evidently physically sated than when suffering from primary drive tensions.

Moreover, exclusive reference to tissue needs or deficits as the basis of drive-related behavior seems particularly deficient as an explanation in certain notable instances where such needs do not produce motivated behavior. McClelland et al. (1953, pp. 7–22) have very effectively marshalled evidence which dethrones tissue needs as the fundamental motivational source. Among other things, he cited experiments in which a non-nutritive substance, saccharine, served as an effective motivator merely by virtue of the sweet, pleasant taste it creates. He also referred to other instances where tissue deficits do not lead to motivated behavior when these lacks are not known to the person. A passage from McClelland et al. forcefully makes this point:

> ... Certain difficulties with this model [survival, tension-reduction] may be summarized briefly. In the first place, some survival needs produce a motive and some do not. For example, it is now known that vitamin B_{12} is necessary for the production of erythrocytes, and without B_{12} the organism will suffer from pernicious anemia and die. Yet a person suffering anemia or B_{12} deficiency behaves in no way like a motivated person, at least as determined by any of the usual measures of motivation. Another example would be the breathing of carbon monoxide which leads to sudden death and certainly to a tissue need, but which apparently produces no activity or behavior suggestive of a state of motivation. If anyone feels that these are merely isolated exceptions to the biological-need theory of motivation, a very brief perusal of the medical literature should convince him of the great number of pathological organic conditions that by definition constitute tissue needs, but which do not give rise to any kind of 'driving' stimulus or motive. Granted this fact, it follows that the presence of a biological need is not a reliable index of the existence of a motive (1953, p. 15).

Traditional tension-reduction explanations of the above anomolies appear forced, and other perhaps more satisfactory solutions have become increasingly popular in psychology. One of these recognizes that the tension-reduction principle is often valid, but insufficient, and attempts to supplement it with additional principles. The usual solution is to add to the original list of primary drives another category which is based not so much on what happens in the peripheral tissues, but on structures of the brain.

When this solution was originally proposed, it was assumed that such brain structures emerged with increasing encephalization, that is, with the evolutionary development of the brain. New drives such as curiosity, exploration, manipulation, etc., were invoked on the assumption that these were unique to higher organisms such as man. They do not operate because of tissue deficits (as in hunger) which are communicated by chemical action to the central nervous system, but entirely through neural processes which are not dependent on peripheral tissues. However, in recent years the evidence has grown that such drives operate in lower animals too, such as the rat and cat, as well as in the monkey and man. And increasingly psychologists and animal behaviorists have come to recognize such drives as characteristic of animal life (see for example, Dember, 1960). In any event, this solution of expanding the list of drives to include non-tissue-deficit types serves as a second type of motivational model, in addition to tension-reduction.

Approaches Supplementing the
Tension-reduction Model: Effectance

The most explicit and perhaps the most useful account of this newer line of reasoning as applied to personality may be found in the writings of Robert White (1960). His analysis begins as a sharp critique of Freud's psychosexual theory and skillfully points out that something more is needed to understand the behavior of the child. White wants to add the principle of "effectance" (wanting to have an effect on the environment), which he sees as encompassing better the important psychological events of childhood, and explaining better the exploration and manipulation which the person engages in over his lifetime. The person develops competence not merely to discharge instinctual drives better as Freud had argued, but because *effectance* motivation is an inherent property of the child at birth. It is, in short, as much of a primary drive as is hunger, thirst, or sex, and is ever so much more important than such drives in helping us understand the remarkable skills man manifests in dealing with his environment.

White thinks that drives such as hunger, thirst, and sex have been given too much importance in the analysis of the personality of civilized man. He concedes that the Freudian psychosexual theory explains much, particularly the sorts of pathology which can develop as a result of internal conflicts over the sexual and aggressive urges. But the aspects of behavior of interest to White, and which he feels are not encompassed by the Freudian approach, are powered by the effectance drive, rather than being derivatives of the sexual drives. White makes this point forcefully:

> The theory that we learn what helps us to reduce our viscerogenic drives will not stand up if we stop to consider the whole range of what a child must learn in order to deal effectively with his surroundings. He has much to learn about visual forms, about grasping and letting go, about the coordination of hand and eye. He must work out the difficult problem of the constancy of objects. . . . He must learn many facts about his world, building up a cognitive map that will afford guidance and structure for his behavior. It is not hard to see the biological advantage of an arrangement whereby these many learnings can get underway before they are needed as instruments for drive reduction or for safety. An animal that has thoroughly explored its environment stands a better chance of escaping from a sudden enemy or satisfying a gnawing hunger than one that merely dozes in the sun when its

homeostatic crises are past. Seen in this light, the many hours that infants and children spend in play are by no means wasted or merely recuperative in nature. Play may be fun, but it is also a serious business in childhood. During these hours the child steadily builds up his competence in dealing with the environment (1960, p. 102).

In subsequent statements, White proceeds to examine each of the psychosexual stages posited by Freud, matching the description of the child's erotic activity at each stage against observations of other things the child does as well. For example, in the oral stage in which the child is presumed by Freud to be preoccupied mainly with stimulation of the oral cavity—sucking, feeding, taking in things through the mouth, and maintaining comfort and security—White argues that the child does many other things, ignored by the psychosexual theory, things which involve manipulation of the environment thus producing competence. Such manipulation is an example, says White, of the operation of the effectance drive. His discussion of this is instructive:

> For one thing, there are clear signs that additional entertainment is desired during a meal. The utensils are investigated, the behavior of spilled food is explored, toys are played with throughout the feeding. Gesell suggests that at one year of age a toy in each hand is the only guarantee that a meal will be completed without housekeeping disaster. A similar situation prevails during the bath, when water toys are needed and when the germ of scientific interest may express itself by 'dabbling water onto the floor from the washcloth.' More important, however, is the infant's growing enthusiasm for the doctrine of 'do it yourself.' . . . Around one year there is likely to occur what Levy (1955) calls 'the battle of the spoon,' the moment 'when the baby grabs the spoon from the mother's hand and tries to feed itself.' From Gesell's painstaking description of the spoon's 'hazardous journey' from dish to mouth we can be sure the child is not motivated at this point by increased oral gratification. He gets more food by letting mother do it, but by doing it himself he gets more of another kind of satisfaction—a feeling of efficacy, and perhaps already a growth of the sense of competence (1960, p. 110).

White also draws a contrast between what he sees in the baby's behavior and what the classical psychoanalytic theory of psychosexuality appears to require: "The psychoanalytic hypothesis of oral libido requires us, first, to merge nutritional satisfaction with erotic satisfaction; second, to find the motivation of all the competence sequences in oral eroticism" (1960, p. 113). Such a merger could be produced by association of oral eroticism with feeding as Freud assumed; that is, during feeding, the mucus membranes of the mouth are stimulated. It might also occur through secondary reinforcement as argued by association-learning theory, that is, oral stimulation is connected with reduction of the hunger drive. And finally, it could occur through the process of symbolism, the one activity, oral stimulation, coming to be symbolic of the other, loss of hunger and security. About this White suggests:

Connections of this kind assuredly exist. I have no intention to dispute what Erikson, among others, has shown about symbolism in children's play and about the erotic and aggressive preoccupations that lead to play disruption. But we lose rather than gain, in my opinion, if we consider the child's undisrupted play, six hours a day, to be a continuous expression of libidinal energy, a continuous preoccupation with the family drama, as if there could be no intrinsic interest in the properties of the external world and the means of coming to terms with it. We lose rather than gain if we look only for an incorporative element in the infant's cognitive and motor behavior, remembering, for instance, that he puts the clothespin in his mouth but forgetting that he uses it to bang on the chair (1960, p. 113).

Similar analyses are made by White of each of the other two psychosexual periods, with the conclusion similar to the above that the decisive psychological struggles of the child do not occur solely in the feeding situation or in the bathroom with toilet training, but rather, in all settings in which the child is expressing his innate drive for effectance, that is, in the sandpile, on the tricycle, in learning to manipulate and comprehend the world. White does not deny that primary tissue needs from which hunger, thirst, sex, and other drives develop play a role in motivational development, but only that the really important human drives are to be active, to explore, to manipulate and control, to produce and accomplish, and these are encompassed under the general rubric of the effectance drive, that is, the wish to have an effect. It is biologically plausible that effectance, or whatever one wishes to call the drive, be expressed through the neural tissues which emerged with the phylogenetic development of higher species such as men, and is part of each man's inheritance from the past.

The position taken by White is important because it argues in contrast with the tension-reduction stance that much of our cognitive and social behavior should not be regarded as derived from so-called primary drives, such as hunger or sex, but rather, constitute the products of a primary or innate drive of their own. The person explores, manipulates, and thinks, not merely because such activity is instrumental to gratification of some primary drive, but because it is intrinsically gratifying to do so as a result of the way man is constructed. This supplements the tension-reduction formulation. In some respects, man is now said to be a *tension-producer,* as well as a tension-reducer, at times seeking the lowering of drive tensions, and at other times seeking to heighten such tensions. Many recent writers have argued that some optimal level of tension is the norm or baseline toward which man strives, that is, a level that is neither too high nor too low. Such a hypothetical level is difficult to specify exactly because there are no satisfactory operations to assess it, but ultimately such a concept might have more predictive power.

The above principle of which White's account is one of the clearest and most persuasive has not led to any new systems of personality theory.

However, it has taken many forms, penetrated widely into the literature, and has become a respected mode of thought in general psychology. One sees precursors of it in some of the neo-Freudian writers who have abandoned or qualified the tension-reduction principle, for example, in Jung, Rank, Adler, and Fromm. There are also many other current examples in personality theory in which the point of view is opposed to a tension-reduction view, including Murray (1938), McClelland (1951), Kelly (1955), and Maddi (1968). Although these differ in important respects, space prevents discussion of each variation. Rejection of total dependence on the theme of tension-reduction is also a cornerstone of a newer type of psychoanalytic thought, often referred to as "ego psychology" (e.g., Hartmann, 1964; Rapaport, 1967). Two features characterize this psychoanalytic ego-psychology movement: (1) The ego is presumed to develop partly as a result of the presence of inherent neurological structures, rather than entirely because of the failure of discharge of the life instincts. Thus, the ego has its own energy for growth and differentiation, so to speak, rather than depending for this upon the id, as Freud had postulated. As in White's analysis, adaptive thought is an instinctual or inherent property of the developing person. This aspect of the ego, that is, that which does not grow out of or stay embroiled in conflict and struggle over libidinal discharge, has been referred to as "the conflict-free ego sphere." (2) Psychoanalytic ego psychology turns its attention much more than did Freud to the adaptive functions of the ego, as contrasted with the Freudian focus on the ego's defensive role in intra-psychic struggles. A long standing gap between psychoanalysis and the more traditional concerns of general psychology is thus bridged somewhat by the abandonment of a strictly tension-reduction view of human motivation.

The Force-for-growth Model

"Force-for-growth" is an expression identifying a cluster of theoretical views about human motivation with one shared basic idea. It is that man contains within him the urge to grow, and when given the opportunity to express the highest qualities of thought, creativity, altruism, and humanitarianism of which he is capable, he will do so. Such a view is, perhaps, best represented by two writers, Carl Rogers (1951) and Abraham Maslow (1954), although elements of the idea of inherent potentiality for growth may be found in many of the neo-Freudians, such as Jung, Adler, Fromm, and especially in Rank. The central motive in man according to Carl Rogers is the need for "self-actualization." Rogers assumes that under appropriate conditions man will express higher values than those embodied in the primitive instincts of self-preservation, that is, avoidance of pain and the seeking of sensual pleasure. An example of this *force-for-growth* in operation is the adolescent who normally seeks independence and autonomy even though he is safer and more comfortable remaining dependent on his parents. Another is the willingness of a person to jeopardize his comfort and security in order to support an unpopular principle in which he believes. In spite of discomfort, then, an inherent growth process leads a person toward individuation and higher development.

The concept of *self-actualization,* as defined by Maslow, is that a person always strives toward realizing his inner potentialities. Maslow identified a hierarchy of needs and values, ranging from the most primitive which man shares with lower forms of life, to those characteristic of only the most advanced types of organism. The hierarchy of needs in man ranges from the lowest survival needs such as hunger and thirst, to higher needs including belongingness and love, esteem, and cognitive and aesthetic needs, such as a thirst for knowledge and a desire for beauty. According to Maslow, higher needs will not be gratified or permitted expression unless the more urgent primitive needs are satisfied.

The force-for-growth philosophy implies that, if man is given the opportunity, he will express his advanced nature. When he does not do so, it is because the social conditions of life continue to require a survival struggle to a degree that prevents the realization of his higher potential. Whereas for Freud cognitive and aesthetic needs are sublimated expressions of the primitive sexual and aggressive instincts and, in fact, come into being because these instincts are inhibited through social living, for Rogers and Maslow they are inborn qualities whose expression depends not on thwarting but on favorable life circumstances.

I said that the origins of the force-for-growth philosophy of man in personality theory can be found among the neo-Freudians, who increasingly emphasized the social basis of man's personality and who questioned the primacy of the life and death instincts as propounded by Freud. Thus, for example, Jung (1953) suggested that in middle life man becomes less dominated by libidinal urges and turns toward more philosophical, spiritual concerns about the meaning of life and his place in the universe. Alfred Adler (see Ansbacher and Ansbacher, 1956), too, maintained that man has the natural (inborn) tendency to concern himself with "social interest" and communion with other men. Otto Rank (1952) who comes the closest to being the direct forerunner of the force-for-growth school of thought, argued that the fundamental struggle in man is between the desire for social union and the need to become separate or individuated. The person who is most successful in synthesizing these two opposing tendencies was called by Rank "the artist," because he presumably engages in the creative act of simultaneously being at one with other men and remaining a separate, distinguishable individual. Psychoanalyst

Erich Fromm (1941, 1955) has gone even further, attempting to specify the kind of society that permits the individuation of man while sustaining his needs for security and belonging. Having re-examined history since feudal times, Fromm maintained that man has not yet evolved a society that permits the gratification of these conflicting but inherent needs.

We might note a kind of implicit evolutionary assumption in the force-for-growth point of view (and also in White), specifically, that as we move from primitive to higher animals, new structures of the brain evolve which introduce new needs and capacities. This assumption is most explicit in Maslow. Man is at the highest end of the phylogenetic scale. Thus, he carries with him many needs and capacities that are not found in lower animals. Self-actualization in man, therefore, requires the gratification of these later evolved needs. The force-for-growth concept has been criticized as mystical and value-laden, since it flirts so continuously with the evaluation of man in terms of normative judgments of high and low, advanced and primitive, good and bad.

Implications of the Three Motivational Models

Of the three viewpoints that have been reviewed above, White's is the least laden with implicit values about man, how he lives, and the quality of his society. The emphasis is on the drive for effectance, and its consequence is the development of competence for mastering the environment. The desirability of competence is the central value of the model, but precisely what competence consists of and what man might do with this competence is not the subject of immediate interest.

The drive for effectance could lead to diverse results. It could, for example, lead to an infantile, destructive lust for power, as in the cases of Hitler or Stalin, or it could express itself in self-actualization in the Maslow or Rogers sense, where the highest and most humanistic virtues are revered. It could result in artistic creativity, or in a banal, sterile output. It could even produce frustrated inaction, or bitterness toward those forces or persons who prevent one's getting things done. There could be innumerable forms of competence, depending on life circumstances. Effectance does not have any built-in direction, since it is merely the inherent desire to have an effect.

This relative *value neutrality* in the effectance model is in sharp contrast with the tension-reduction and force-for-growth viewpoints. The divergent values about man and society implied in these latter positions display themselves most clearly in two intellectual spheres. One concerns *conceptions of the nature of man* himself, that is, the inherent drive properties with which he comes into the world. The second has to do with *conceptions of man's society* and its role in shaping the human condition. Although one risks overstating things in making this contrast of values and stating its implications, the risk is worth it because the effort permits us to see a relationship between the assumptions of personality theory and some of the pressing social problems of our day. Let us begin with the fundamental conceptions of man which are held by the tension-reduction and force-for-growth viewpoints, respectively.

CONCEPTIONS OF MAN'S NATURE

One can perceive in the tension-reduction philosophy of man a competitive, conflict-laden, survival-oriented, perhaps somewhat pessimistic outlook. Man is seen as the latest state in a long line of evolutionary development based on the principle of *survival of the fittest*. By means of the process of natural selection through breeding, the species and biological properties best adapted to the environment evolved. Whenever man fails in his adaptation, it is because of changes in the environment in response to which selective breeding has not yet provided modifications suited to the new conditions of life. For example, man's natural aggressiveness might once have had value by facilitating his management of environmental dangers, but these same tendencies, and the emotionality accompanying them, are unsuited to the present industrialized social environment where aggression has few useful outlets. Now it results in internal disturbances whose consequences are psychosomatic disorders. In any case, the principle of natural selection is still in force, and man's biologically-given, primary drives still determine how he fares in the modern world. To the extent that these drives no longer facilitate biological or social survival, they have become unwanted residuals of an ancestral animal past, ultimately perhaps to be discarded.

In the above analysis, *self-interest* is the fundamental force that energizes and directs human behavior, although this force can be modified and redirected somewhat by the social system. Man struggles individually to survive and flourish by replenishing tissue deficits and discharging such drives as sex and aggression. However, this self-interest poses an interesting dilemma. In one sense it is the enemy of society which thrives on order and harmony. One man's success may mean another's failure. This means that if man is to live in relative harmony with his fellow man, the drives expressing self-interest must be controlled or transformed in such a way as to blunt their danger to other men and to the social system on which man today depends.

Freud saw the fundamental problem of mankind as the control and transformation of the animal instincts into "healthy," socially constructive, and acceptable modes of discharge. These instincts, in one sense, are bad, because they can destroy man and his society. In both the Freudian and association-learning versions of tension-reduction, the highly valued human patterns of moral concern, altruistic love, and esthetic appreciation are not biologically inherited, but are outgrowths of the thwarting of the instinctual drives. The motivating tensions thus produced create the subli- mations of these drives into socially desirable motives (Freud), or yield new social motives when the latter forms of behavior get associated with the reduction of such tensions (Dollard and Miller). Thus, the positive traits of mankind are learned or secondary, while the selfish traits of mankind are products of biological inheritance.

Nowhere is the idea of the necessary opposition between society and the animal part of man's nature more strongly emphasized than in Freudian theory, with its emphasis on primitive sex and aggression. A clinical example is the dramatic form of psychopathology known as multi- ple personality, a case of which, Miss Sally Beauchamp, was first fully described by Morton Prince (1920); later another case was reported by Thigpen and Kleckley (1957) which was made into a movie, "The Three Faces of Eve." Aspects of Sally Beauchamp's personality became "dis- sociated" from each other, as if the various conflicting impulses within her could no longer be integrated into a harmonious whole. During the course of the illness, three distinct personalities emerged, two of them particu- larly contrasting. One of the personalities was a sexually promiscuous, outspoken, and ribald woman who ridiculed the side of herself which was inhibited, moralistic, and prudish. The patient seemed to alternate being in one phase or the other, with little warning given as to when one or the other would dominate. The inhibited personality appeared to be totally unaware of the activities of the other uninhibited one. Most instances of multiple personality seem to manifest at least two personality extremes, one inhibited and overcontrolled (in a sense, oversocialized), the other uninhibited and undercontrolled (in a sense, animal-like). What could be more in keeping with the Freudian image of man as a mixture of primitive animal instincts and learned, internalized social constraints!

There is also a fine literary example of this dual image of man in Robert Louis Stevenson's famous novel, *The Strange Case of Dr. Jekyll and Mr. Hyde.* First published in 1886, its theme shows continuing popularity, as evidenced by the several movie versions of it which have been made in the U. S. (see Figure 9). Mr. Hyde is the "evil," animal part of man, consisting mainly of a mixture of sexual and aggressive (sadistic) impulses. Dr. Jekyll, a physician, is the "good" part which is tragically over- whelmed when he has the temerity to experiment with a chemical potion unleashing the animal part. Dr. Jekyll expresses to the other physicians of his time the shocking idea that these good and bad qualities exist together in all men.

One can see clearly in the Freudian viewpoint a presumed phylogenetic

FIGURE 9. Dr. Jekyll and Mr. Hyde as portrayed in the film by actor Frederick March. (Culver Pictures, Inc.)

continuity between man and lower animals. It is one of the ideas which shocked the Victorian world of Freud, as it shocked the physicians addressed by Dr. Jekyll in the Stevenson fiction. These men lived in a time when it was fashionable to believe that man was distinct from and above infra-human animals. In religious circles, only man was believed to have a pure soul. Church dogma attributed evil to the Devil, and to Original Sin which made man fall out of grace. To suggest a continuity with the animal world as Darwin did was to challenge man's uniqueness and to make him little better morally than the lower forms of life. Freud said, too, that man has all the base instincts found in other, lower animals. This deeply threatened and offended the Church and the public, and led to persistent and widespread condemnation of Darwin's and Freud's concepts. Although the positions are really not irreconcilable, they seemed so, and produced a long standing fundamentalist ideational struggle which has not ended to this day (see Beach, 1955, for further discussion of this).

It is important to recognize that Freud's views of animal behavior and instincts were quite inaccurate and overly simple, a fact that has become very evident through careful observations by modern ethologists and animal ecologists of animal *patterns of aggression.* There are many forms of aggression, and these may be based on quite different physiological mechanisms (Moyer, 1967; Rothballer, 1967). There are, for example, "intraspecies" and "interspecies" aggression, the stimuli, response topography, and functions of which are probably quite different from each other. *Interspecies aggression* involves attacks on animals of other species, as in the seeking of food by carnivores, or the maternal protection of young against predators. *Intraspecies aggression* consists of attacks on members of the same species, as when two males are in competition over territory or mating. If indeed these forms of aggression have different biological roots, and if one argues that aggression in man is carried down phylogenetically from his animal ancestors, then the question arises as to which of these forms, if any, provides the evolutionary origin of man's aggression.

Man is evidently the first primate to be a carnivorous predator (interspecies aggression), the great apes being mainly vegetarians. It is thought by some that this change represents the beginnings of man's aggression. Such interspecies aggressive tendencies may have been useful to early man, since they might have aided in his survival against other predators. Anthropologist Leakey (1967), however, has proposed that it was man's offensive smell and taste which preserved him more than anything else. In any case, most aggression in man seems to be of the intraspecies type, since his savagery toward other men is most striking and at the root of a large number of his social problems. Such aggression could be linked to the territorial aggressions found widely in the lower animals, that is, the tendency to fight other memebers of the same species over a section of ground, or over a mate.

There are some striking differences between man and infra-human animals in this, however. For example, when lower animals fight within their species, they rarely kill. They engage in what has been called, "ritual aggression" (see, for example, Matthews, 1964, and Hall, 1964). That is, when a male challenges another male for territory or a mate, there is much sound and fury but seldom a fatality, because the loser usually defers to the victor before he is seriously injured, and if he appears smaller and weaker, he may never make the challenge at all. Upon discovering his own vulnerability, he simply turns tail, exhibits a passive posture, and withdraws. The victor is quite content to let him go; he has proved his point and taken over the territory. Only when both animals are confined in a small space so that escape is not possible will one kill another as man does. It has been suggested, too, that man kills because his weapons make withdrawal before fatal damage is done difficult and that his long memory and strongly developed ego are fatal additions to the usual animal intraspecies aggressive tendencies.

The biological bases of aggression are far from clear, and there are those who find the argument that aggression has such an origin unsupported by evidence. They emphasize the social factors in aggression rather than the biological, arguing that learned responses to frustration provide the main basis of aggression in man. Whatever the ultimate answers turn out to be, questions about the origins of aggression are of great interest to biological and social scientists alike because of the great dangers to man of self-annihilation through modern warfare and weaponry.

Although this brief discussion of aggression may have seemed to be a digression, it was designed to prevent the usual kind of oversimplified analysis that stems from limited understanding of the complex problems of the biological origins of human drives. Freud's thinking on the subject of aggression was consistent with the knowledge of his era, and this knowledge has become outdated. Nevertheless, his general argument that man was suffused with drives which had to be controlled is a very forceful and widely respected position, and its implications for the solution of man's social problems are strikingly different from the image of man projected by the force-for-growth theorist.

Force-for-growth theorists acknowledge that man has the self-centered, survival-oriented drives emphasized by tension-reduction theories. Granting these, however, they argue that there are still other inherent and more important biologically-given properties in man. If they are nurtured, they can become predominant in man's behavior. The variants of these arguments are many, each attempting to specify in greater or lesser detail the fundamental drive attributes or needs that reach their highest flower in man. Overall, they emphasize man's relations with other men, that is, they postulate needs which express the social rather than tissue-centered nature of man. The fundamental needs of man are not seen as derived from more primitive tissue needs. Rather, they tend to be defined in social or interpersonal terms, although these too are regarded as biologically inherited dispositions motivating the person throughout his life.

Consider for a moment Abraham Maslow's (1954) approach. Motives are conceptualized as falling within a hierarchy, ranging from the survival needs, such as hunger and thirst, up the evolutionary scale toward higher needs, such as safety, then belonging and love, esteem, self-actualization, cognitive needs such as a thirst for knowledge, and esthetic needs such as a desire for beauty, in that order. The "higher" needs will not be gratified or permitted expression unless the prepotent and more primitive needs are first satisfied. In other words, the tissue needs and those related to safety and security, are urgent and tyrannical when threatened, but the "higher" needs involving self-actualization remain latent under conditions unfavorable to their emergence. The latter will be expressed only when a person is freed from the tyranny of lower-order needs.

Another example is the analysis by Erich Fromm (1947, 1955). His list of fundamental human needs includes *relatedness* or belonging, that is, to feel a part of the group; *transcendence,* to become a creative person rising above one's animal nature; *identity,* to be a unique individual; and having a stable *frame of reference,* that is, having a consistent way in which to perceive and comprehend the world.

Aside from making lists of fundamental human needs, there is not so much to say about motivational dynamics from the perspective of the force-for-growth theories, for these theories have been somewhat more vague about how motives work and the conditions under which they will emerge compared with tension-reduction theories. In recent years force-for-growth theorists have had much to say about the defects in man's society, sharing a common view that the failure of man to develop in a healthy way and to express his highest potentialities is the result of the damaging effects of the social conditions under which he lives. Concern has thus tended to be directed toward questions of how the social order should be arranged in order to maximize man's potentiality for growth, given the set of socially oriented needs that comprise his motivational system.

CONCEPTIONS OF MAN'S SOCIETY

It has already been pointed out that the tension-reduction model sees the social system as providing necessary restraints on the animal instincts. Such restraints are necessary for two reasons: first, so that means will be developed for overcoming inevitable obstacles to survival and comfort; and second, to make possible a secure, orderly, and stable mode of life for mankind. Again, Freud has been most explicit about how society developed and in what ways it transforms the primitive instincts.

Freud (1957) argued that the instincts of sex and aggression must be restrained by social rules and that man's culture is the outgrowth of these instincts and the organized ways of controlling them. With appropriate social rules, a strong ego develops which is capable of seeking safe and successful avenues for instinctual discharge. Without adequate limits and discipline permitting the development of a strong ego, man's personality would be warped by neurotic solutions, by character disorders in which there are insufficient moral development and inept life styles, or by psychoses in which there has been regression to infantile, pregenital forms of libidinal expression that are not suitable for adult life. Freud saw an analogy between the psychological development of the individual man and the evolutionary transition of man from the unrestrained expression of the sexual and aggressive instincts through the acceptance and internalization of social rules. This analogy may be illustrated by considering the mating behavior of the herd animal.

In the case of the migratory seal, for example, the mature bulls begin to arrive at the mating site in the spring ahead of the females. On arrival, the bull stakes out a plot of land, its size and desirability depending on his capacity to seize and hold it against all other competitors. When the females arrive, he creates a harem, and continues to resist challenges by other bulls. The largest and strongest "beachmasters" are most successful, mating with many females. Throughout the mating period there is continual competition over the territory and over the females. Each year, new competition emerges in the form of young males who are maturing and becoming powerful enough to challenge the old bull for his territory and harem. Old bulls who are no longer capable of driving off the challengers retire to the outskirts of the mating beaches, removed from the females and unable to mate; young bulls too puny to succeed also remain in the periphery. This mating struggle can be viewed as a phylogenetically primitive version of the Oedipus situation.

There is no incest taboo among the herd animal to cool down this perpetual struggle. However, man collectively has made a "social contract" which includes a universal taboo against incest. Thus, the son (except as an immature child) is prevented from accepting his mother as an erotic love object when he is adult. The Oedipus complex in infancy and childhood is a repetition ontogenetically of the phylogenetically primitive mating process of the herd animal, and it derives its motive power from essentially the same drive sources. Thus we see in Freudian theory that *the role of society is clearly to inhibit the unrestrained and destructive primitive urges of man so that a stable family system can develop, and to permit the emergence of the higher mental processes.* Man is then free to love unselfishly, to accept restraint on his impulses, and yet to discharge the libidinal energy in adequate, substitutive forms which can benefit the rest of mankind.

What has been said above about Freudian theory and the tension-reduction model suggests that such a view would have implications for our attitudes and behavior toward transgressions against the social order, for example, toward marginal social groups such as the slum dweller, vagrant, hippie drop out, welfare recipient, or alcoholic. Tension-reduction views should also tell us something about child-rearing. It turns out, however, that one's response to problem-groups and problem children depends on which of the features of tension-reduction one emphasizes. Freud actually argued that during the crucial early years of pregenital (oral and anal) psychosexual development, extremes of restraint or permissiveness were traumatizing, inhibiting the normal progression from one stage to the next. For example, too much oral supply (feeding, nurturance) would lead the developing child to expect it in perpetuity and make it unwilling to move toward the next stage (anality). Likewise, too little would lead to distrust of the environment and the continuing search thereafter to make up for the deficiency.

Some of the central assumptions of the tension-reduction point of view imply that man survives by virtue of developing competence to master the environment or adapt to it, and since the qualities relevant to such competence are, in part, passed down genetically through the process of natural selection, deviant groups may then be seen as human failures. In some instances, such failures are attributed to biological deficiencies; in others, they can be viewed as the product of a stunted or warped ego resulting from traumatic conditions of life. Undoubtedly, both biological and social processes are involved. In any case, where the emphasis has been placed on competition and the struggle for mastery, as it is above, the solution must lie in appropriate discipline and environmental limits, and where these have been lacking, in retraining. Such a stance has a Darwinian flavor which underlies the tension-reduction position; the assumption is made that the primary biological forces in man are those of self-interest and survival, altruism and other human ideals being seen merely as derivatives of such self-interest.

However, it would be oversimple to regard the tension-reduction model as lending itself exclusively to a discipline-centered orientation. Its protagonists would surely not argue that *any* social system is adequate merely because it restrains man's animal instincts. Although a strong ego (or in association-learning terms, an adequate habit system) is essential to healthy functioning, and such an ego cannot come into being without firm limits imposed by the social order, a repressive society is as defective as an overly permissive one. The former produces neurosis as in Freud's day; the latter, disorders of character or socialization, as perhaps today. Without adequate substitute forms of discharge, tension-reduction must fail. And excessive restraint makes it difficult or impossible to find creative solutions to life problems.

It must be remembered that Freud formulated his personality theory while attempting to treat neurotic patients who were, presumably, victims of a too repressive, Victorian society, and it would be out of character for Freud to argue that such repressiveness is desirable. On the other hand, when Freud's daughter, Anna, lectured in the United States after World War II, she is said to have made the interesting observation that the major maladjustments seen in clinics had changed from predominantly neurotics to character disorders, that is, to persons with inadequate socialization and competence for getting along in society. She attributed this to the shift from the excessive Victorian discipline of her father's day to excessive permissiveness in post World War II childrearing, with the impairment of self-discipline. In this connection it is ironic that Freud has long been presumed guilty of arguing in favor of unlimited permissiveness, and he was blamed for the breakdown of child-rearing discipline, merely because he was critical of the damaging effects of the repressiveness of his own times. Nevertheless, although one should not overstate the matter, the tension-reduction principle does somehow require affirmation of the importance of a firm restraining hand and a stable social order as the means by which primitive man is forged into civilized man. By restraining the animal in man, society makes possible the development of valued motivational social derivatives of the primary drives, since these latter are not inherent in man without the proper social experiences. Both too little discipline and limits that are too yielding are bad for the development of psychological health, each leading, however, to somewhat different forms of deviance. The precise limits of this generalization have never really been spelled out, and thus, without considerable research and evidence, the general principle does not lend itself very well to a program of child-rearing in which concrete recommendations are set forth.

How is the same issue dealt with by the force-for-growth model? Here, too, there is great danger of oversimplification. However, the force-for-growth protagonist seems to have been somewhat more inclined to take a militant position than the tension-reductionist, at least by emphasizing that society is the main culprit in man's psychological failures rather than a necessary asset in restraining the drives of self-interest. The force-for-growth theorists say that society has tended to resemble a jungle, so to speak, where survival is always threatened. Therefore, existing and past social systems have continued to keep man insecure, frightened, and helpless. This promotes the expression mainly of the prepotent survival needs, but inhibits the expression of the more fragile, but just as basic, higher social needs unique to man as a species. To force-for-growth theorists, the task of society is not the restraint of man's primitive drives, but rather the nurturance of those drives which contribute to his self-actualization. Only in a secure, supportive setting can the latter be expected to appear. Man's inner nature is fundamentally good, but society thwarts its expression.

If we consider from this point of view the marginal or deviant segments of the society, the onus clearly is placed on the society for not providing such individuals or groups with sufficient security to nurture the growth tendency which is present in everyone. The existence of such social failures only proves the inadequacy of the social system, rather than necessarily implying adaptive insufficiency.

Thus, force-for-growth theorists seem to be espousing a permissive ideal for the social system, and presumably for parental behavior, although the one-sidedness of this stance is probably the result of the wish to emphasize the evils of the existing forms of society, and the fact that such writers were attacking a more established view. In all likelihood, this sanguine view of man's capacity to express his highest nature without environmental restraints would probably be qualified by force-for-growth writers, were they pressed to detail concretely the ideal conditions of child-development. Most reasonable people recognize that discipline of some sort is an essential element in healthy development, and the argument tends to be over what kind of discipline, and about what are its healthy forms in contradiction to the unhealthy and confining ones. The difference between points of view turns mostly on emphasis. They are characteristically oversimplified by the public, and by those who for their own personal or ideological reasons want to argue for one or the other extreme position. The problem is a very emotional one. The more general and abstract the discussion is, that is, the less it refers to a specific context or to particular persons and behaviors, the more fruitless is the debate, and the more refractory it is to resolution by scientifically acceptable evidence. As it now stands, without the necessary specification and research, the issue can be dealt with only by speculative analysis which in the long run must give way to dependable knowledge.

Maslow has gone further than most force-for-growth theorists (except perhaps Fromm) in trying to conceptualize the essential quality of the society which might promote self-actualization. Recently (1964) he has found the general answer in the concept of "synergy," first introduced by cultural anthropologist, Ruth Benedict. Self-actualization requires that the person express his own personal identity without being alienated thereby from his society. To a greater or lesser extent, most cultures make this difficult or impossible, because gratification of oneself usually harms, or at least rarely benefits the group. *Synergy* expresses the extent to which the institutions of a culture make possible individual productivity while providing mutual advantage for the individual and the group. Maslow puts it as follows:

> ... the conclusion that emerges is that societies where non-aggression is conspicuous have social orders in which the individual by the same act and at the same time serves his own advantage and that of the group. . . . Non-aggression occurs (in these societies) not because people are unselfish and put social obligations above personal desires, but when social arrangements make these two identical. . . (1964, p. 155).

From the force-for-growth point of view, the solution of deviance and marginality is not further discipline, or the attempt to shape the person in socially desired directions by reward and punishment, but in making the person feel so secure and free from threat that he can afford to be what he is capable of becoming: a humane, socially conscious, artistic, creative, and altruistic individual. Punishment, especially when it is excessive, creates warped people instead of creating self-actualized ones. Any adaptive adequacy which may emerge from the survival struggle is apt to be devoted to selfish ends, rather than to the welfare of one's fellow man.

It is probably no accident that the force-for-growth philosophy has had a strong appeal among the intellectual youth of today who have rebelled against the defects of modern, industrial, competitive society. It is interesting, too, that a common answer to the criticisms of such youth is a tension-reduction answer, that without stress or struggle for survival, the affluent societies would not have achieved their spectacular wealth and mastery over the environment. It is also worth noting that a large segment of today's rebellious youth is accused of having it too easy, economically, compared with their insecure, depression era parents.

Although the above implications may have been somewhat overdrawn, it is particularly important to recognize that political and social ideology can be linked to the issues of personality theory. The divergent theoretical assumptions about the nature of human motivation are, in a sense, ideologies, dogmas, or philosophies, rather than scientifically tested propositions. At this time, so little is actually known about the conditions under which competence, altruism, love, aggression, etc., are to be found, that one must be very wary about accepting any of these philosophies as scientifically respectable. However, these philosophies do serve as alternative working assumptions whose acceptance and rejection tend to be made on the basis of plausibility and esthetic value. In the proposals for social change made by social scientists and political ideologists, these philosophies often remain as unstated assumptions. Someday perhaps, we will have a broader and more adequate empirical basis for choosing between them or for adopting different ones.

Other Issues of Personality Dynamics

In this chapter, theories of dynamics have been compared on one class of issues only, that is, the motivational principles under which man operates. Nothing has been said, for example, about the types of devices which people employ in coping with threat, or in dealing with conflicts between motives. Nor has attention been given to the emotional processes and the relations between emotion and thought. Most personality systems tend to assume that emotions, such as anxiety, are central motivating forces in the production of defenses and in the emergence of psychopathological behavior patterns, although the precise manner in which this occurs varies among these systems. For example, the motives underlying the conflicts which create anxiety, and the ways the individual learns to deal with them, are viewed quite differently among different personality theories. A full treatment of personality dynamics would require giving attention to such matters, as well as those which have been emphasized here. The reader should bear in mind that we have chosen certain issues on which to compare theories, but that this treatment is not exhaustive. We move next to the matter of personality determinants in Chapters 5 and 6.

Personality Determinants—Biological Factors

chapter five

Psychology is both a social science and a biological science, and in this chapter we are concerned with the latter. Man is a living creature made up of diverse biochemical substances, of cells and of cellular systems consisting of nerves, bone, muscles, glands, digestive organs, a circulatory system, and skin; therefore, he is subject to the same biological rules as other living things. There are also structural features which make him different from all other animals. In any case, the personality of man and of individual men could not be adequately understood without a grasp of the relevant biological details. These details include three main issues which make up the substance of the chapter, the biological and cultural evolution of man, the genetic influences on him, and the manner in which the physiological construction of man influences his behavior and personality.

Biological and Cultural Evolution

To understand personality from a biological standpoint requires first that man be placed in a phylogenetic context, since his anatomy and physiology are products of evolution from earlier and simpler organisms. About the evolution of man, Lerner has recently written that:

> ... all biologists agree that organic evolution is a reality, and that the currently dominant species on this planet (man) and all other existing kinds of life were not always the way they are now, but descended with modification from preexisting forms. The concept of evolution stresses the idea that the world itself was not always as it is, but has a historical past and evolved from simpler origins. And one of the features of the process of evolution is that it embraces a historical continuum in which there are no sharp borders. Thus, it is possible to distinguish nonliving material from living organisms in a general way although the exact point at which one turned into another is a matter of somewhat arbitrary opinion. Similarly, the precise point in history at which creatures that can be described as human beings first appeared on earth is a matter of definition (1968, p. 2).

Darwin's (1859) contribution to the ancient idea of *biological evolution* was to propose a workable mechanism for it, and to demonstrate by painstaking observations of animal and plant morphology that there was, indeed, structural continuity among the diverse species. The mechanism Darwin proposed was that man's biological characteristics evolved because of their adaptiveness to the environment through the process of "natural selection." By means of this process, characteristics which were antithetical to the survival of the species were dropped or suppressed, while those promoting species survival were retained and passed on to subsequent generations through genetic mechanisms. As a result of continuing natural selection and by means of feedback from the environment which determined whether a trait was adaptive or maladaptive, man eventually arrived on the scene. He had some properties which he shared with lower forms of life and others which were unique. Early man evidently appeared in the Pleistocene geological epoch about 500,000 years ago, and ultimately evolved into modern man perhaps about 10,000 years ago. As to the psychological qualities of modern man that distinguish him from other forms of mammalian life, Lerner (1968) suggests five: the capacity for a high degree of educability, the ability to communicate with contemporaries and with his descendants, an extended time sense, a consciousness of self, and the capacity to plan and direct his own evolution.

The physiological continuity which man shows with lower forms of life has been effectively documented by Darwin. His evidence included the finding that structually similar organisms could be found widely distributed over the earth, and hence they must have the same ancestors. A second type of evidence came from comparative anatomy and embryology, in which it was demonstrated that widely different species showed striking anatomical resemblance, both in their skeletal arrangement and in embryological development. An illustration of anatomical-skeletal continuity may be seen in Figure 10, and the striking similarity between the embryo stages of various vertebrate forms is diagrammed in Figure 11.

Biological evolution is a continuing process and is, presumably, still taking place today. Such continuing evolution depends on two factors: first, that there be genetic variation among the different organisms within the species, so that some traits may be selected and passed on to subsequent generations and others suppressed; and second, that these genetic traits be relevant to the fitness of the species for adapting to changes in the available environments. Geneticist Dobzhansky (1967) suggests that both conditions are probably met today, making the inference that evolution must be continuing a reasonable one. Many genetically influenced human traits, for example, intellectual capacity, vary from person to person, and it is likely that they affect the chances of survival and therefore the chance to reproduce before premature death. The basic elements of evolution are thus present today as they were in the past.

There is one other requirement for biological evolutionary change to take place. The environments of man must also be changing so that new adaptive demands are made on him. Only if the environment changes will there be natural selection as a result of adaptive success and failure under these conditions, thus permitting new traits systematically to emerge that are better suited to the new conditions, and old traits no longer viable in such an environment to be dropped out.

It is very evident that biological evolution is a very slow process, and it is difficult to document any important biological changes since modern man evolved approximately 10,000 years ago. However, man's *cultural evolution* has been extremely dramatic, and the rate of change in patterns of society during the past 5,000 years has surely been accelerated. Consider, for example, the changes in the past 200 years or so. There is no doubt that the present environment of man is markedly different from that hundreds of years ago, or perhaps even 50, particularly in the case of the industrialized societies of the world. Not only are there striking social changes, but there are physical changes too, many of which pose serious adaptive problems, for example, the increase in population, air pollution, the presence of harmful chemical agents in our water and food, etc. As to population, Petersen and Matza (1963, p.14) have observed that the world's human population was about 500 million in 1650. In three centuries, it expanded to five times that amount, reaching 2.5 billion in 1950. It is expected to be between 6 and 7 billion by the end of the century.

The implications of this rapid cultural change have been expressed by Aldous Huxley in the following provocative passage:

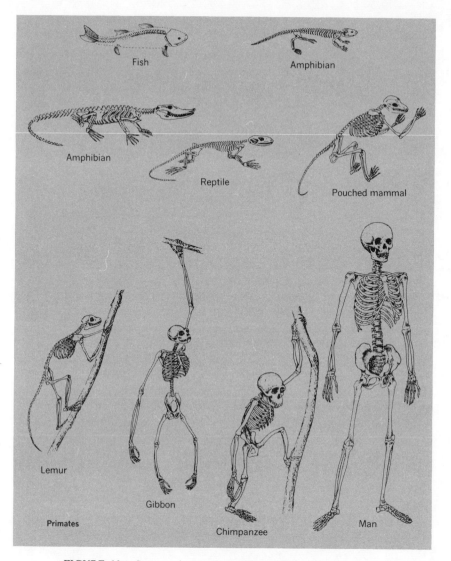

FIGURE 10.   Comparative Features of Skeletons on different rungs of the evolutionary ladder. Both fossil and living forms are represented. (From *Heredity, evolution, and society* by I. Michael Lerner. W.H. Freeman and Company, copyright © 1968.)

Anatomically and physiologically, man has changed very little during the last twenty or thirty thousand years. The nature of genetic capacities of today's bright child are essentially the same as those of a child born into a family of Upper Palaeolithic cave-dwellers. But whereas the contemporary bright baby may grow up to become almost anything—a Presbyterian engineer, for example, a piano-playing Marxist, a professor of biochemistry who is a mystical agnostic and likes to paint in water-colours—the palaeolithic

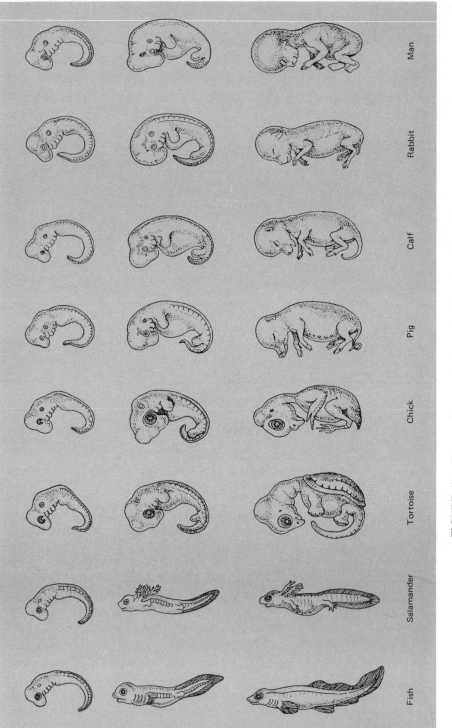

FIGURE 11. Comparative stages in the embryology of vertebrate forms.
(From *Biology: it's human implications* by Garret Hardin. W. H. Freeman and Company, copyright © 1949.)

baby could not possibly have grown into anything except a hunter or food-gatherer, using the crudest of stone tools and thinking about his narrow world of trees and swamps in terms of some hazy system of magic. Ancient and modern, the two babies are indistinguishable. Each of them contains all the potentialities of the particular breed of human being to which he or she happens to belong. But the adults into whom the babies will grow are profoundly dissimilar; and they are dissimilar because in one of them very few, and in the other a good many, of the baby's inborn potentialities have been actualized (1965, p. 32).

Genetic Influences

Charles Darwin believed that mental as well as physical characteristics were inherited and evolved from the struggle for survival. Without a hereditary mechanism whereby biological traits could be passed on to the next generation, there could be no evolution. One of the foremost early behavior geneticists was Francis Galton, Darwin's half cousin. Galton made many contributions to psychology, including the innovation of statistical methods and the development of mental testing. One of his most important contributions was the study of the inheritance of intelligence (1869). He showed that there is a much greater number of extremely able persons than might be expected by chance among the relatives of intellectually bright people, and he tried to refute the criticism that this might be the result of economic, social, and educational advantages by showing that the correlation was higher when the family relationship was genetically closer. The use of twins and other forms of consanguinity in assessing hereditary influences was thus introduced by Galton.

Darwin's work in evolution had created a climate clearly favorable to a hereditary point of view, and Galton's writings were further influential in advancing the cause of behavior genetics. However, a workable theory about the actual mechanisms of heredity was sorely needed. Johann Gregor Mendel helped supply such a theory with his research on the garden pea, although it took the world of science 34 years after it was published in 1865 to discover it. There were other major contributors around this period, for example, a Dutch biologist, Hugo deVries, a German botanist, Carl Correns, and an Austrian, Erich Tschermak, each of whom performed independent experiments that led to the recognition that Mendel had indeed discovered the formal basis of genetic transmission. Shortly after, several other researchers demonstrated that animals as well as plants follow Mendel's laws of genetics, and a British biologist, William Bateson, actually coined the term "genetics" to refer to this emerging area of biological science. By shortly after the turn of the century, many key hereditary notions, such as the gene, dominance and recessiveness, hybrid, genotype, and phenotype were already well known. And over the next several decades, advances were made in knowledge about the anatomy of genes and chromosomes, the process of mutation, and the interplay of genetic structures.

Most of the early knowledge of genetic mechanisms concerned molar units of analysis (dealing with the larger structures such as genes). In more recent years, progress in the understanding of the genetic mechanism has tended to be at the molecular level, that is, having to do with the biochemical molecules of which the genes are constructed, and the manner in which they influence the cytoplasm of the cell and its metabolic activity. The biochemical substances which have gained the most attention in recent years, and which have even become known to the lay person through the popular media, are the *nucleic acids.* One of these, ribonucleic acid (RNA), has been of particular interest to psychologists because of hypotheses about its role in the chemical transmission of memory. However, it is deoxyribonucleic acid (DNA) which seems to be of critical importance for genetics, because it contains the genetic information passed on to the developing cells of the embryo, and it directs the embryo's development into the full-blown baby by means of its chemical action. Whatever aspects of the person's physiological structure are inherited are evidently carried by the DNA molecule, of which the gene is a portion or segment.

The DNA molecule resides in every cell nucleus, and it serves as the template for the construction of RNA, which evidently migrates out of nucleus into the cytoplasm of the cell where it plays a key role in the synthesis of the cellular proteins. These proteins, some of which are enzymes serving as catalysts for biochemical activities, determine the functions of the cells. In effect, the DNA "tells" the cells of the body how to make the proteins which comprise the cell substance, which in turn controls how the cells should act. It contains the "genetic code" for protein synthesis, which it communicates to each cell of the body by means of its messenger, the RNA molecule.

The answer to the question of how nucleic acids influence cell development thus appears to be in the process of protein synthesis. Proteins are large biochemical substances made up of smaller substances called "amino acids." There may be several hundred amino acids (of 20 different types) linked together in a chain, and this chain comprises the structure of the protein. The links of the chain are arranged in some given order, and it is the order or pattern that defines the particular protein. Many combinations and permutations are thus possible in the protein molecule, and these combinations determine how the cells and the tissues (muscle, gland, bone, nerve) grow and function. As was said, the DNA influences this growth and function by instructing the cells how to make the proteins, that is, how to order the chain of linkages among the 20 types of amino acids comprising the cellular proteins. In this way, DNA carries the genetic information about the sort of creature that is to be produced and by means of RNA, gets that information to every cell in the body of the developing organism.

VARIABILITY AND HERITABILITY

To understand the role of heredity in the production of any trait requires a grasp of two key concepts, "variability" and "heritability." Confusion, particularly over the latter, has contributed greatly to misunderstandings on the part of laymen and scientists alike about the application of genetics to social problems and to the relations between heredity and environment in human development.

Interest in the issue of genetics itself arises because within a species such as man there is much *variation* in physical and psychological traits. Since many of the traits of offspring seem similar to those manifested in parents and grandparents, it is reasonable to assume that such traits must be passed on from generation to generation. One reason for the variation in traits among people is that the varying properties found in different people are transmitted to their own offspring, but are not possessed by all.

It is also evident that each of us lives different lives and is exposed to different environmental experiences, and this too could play an important role in producing the variability among us. But every trait is the result of the *interplay of both factors,* genetic and environmental. The question is thus raised as to how much of the given variation which is found in a particular trait, say physical height or intelligence, is the result of hereditary influences, and how much is the result of environment.

The concept of *heritability* is the quantitative estimate of the amount of such variability that is attributable to genetic factors. It is a precise and technical concept, which requires first that the degree of variation in a trait be assessed in some given species and in a given environmental context. Heritability is a ratio or proportion, technically the square of the amount of variation that is due to genetic factors divided by the square of the amount of total variation observed for the trait in question. In other words, it is essentially the proportion of total variance of the trait that can be shown to be attributable to inheritance.

The concept of heritability can be understood more clearly if we imagine some extreme hypothetical situations which, of course, never occur in reality. Suppose, for example, we had a large group of individuals with identical genes, the sort of thing that occurs on a small scale when we have identical twins. And suppose this population with identical hereditary properties is placed in highly diversified environments, each individual going into a different environmental setting to live. In this case, any variations we found among the traits manifested by the respective individuals would be entirely the result of environmental factors. Heritability would be zero—none of the variation could be attributed to genetic factors, these being the same in every case. On the other hand, suppose we had another large group of individuals who were heterogeneous in genetic background, as would be the case for unrelated individuals, or for that matter, for any two individuals who were not identical twins. Now we place this group in a homogeneous environment, recognizing in our hypothetical example, of course, that this would be technically impossible, since in reality there would probably never be two environments exactly alike. In this instance, any variations among traits that might be observed could not be the result of environmental variation since there was none, and thus, heritability would be unity—genetic factors would account for all of the variation. Between these two extremes, of course, lies the bulk of instances in which heritability varies in the degree of trait variance it can account for, lying somewhere between zero and one.

Hereditary and environmental contributions to trait variation depend on a number of specific factors, for example, the trait in question, the specific environmental context of that trait, the species involved, and the context of other hereditary traits. Each of the above factors determines heritability. For example, given a comparable environment, some traits are more influenced by genetic factors than others—the role of heredity is greater in purely physical traits such as stature than it is in psychological traits. Some traits are influenced by a single gene inherited directly from the parent, as in the case of hair and eye color, while others, such as height, are produced by many genetic factors which combine to produce the effect. There is no single gene for the shape of the nose, although that shape is undoubtedly influenced by many genes. This is important because any given genetic factor may have different (sometimes opposite) end effects depending on the other genetic components with which it interacts. As was said, the environmental context in which heritability is evaluated is important too. For example, in a culture where everyone has an adequate diet, the heritability of weight will be high because the total variation would not be influenced very much by nutritional variations. On the other hand, where diet varies markedly, the index of heritability will be correspondingly lower, since dietary variations will have much to do with the weight variations found in that population.

What this means is that heritability can never be judged in the abstract, but only in a particular context, that is, in some given environment, in a particular species, in respect to a particular trait, and in a given genetic matrix. The index of heritability will change as any of these factors is changed. Thus, it is totally misleading to speak in general of the role of inheritance in intelligence, since technically such a role will vary greatly wherever and whenever the assessment is made, depending on all of the above considerations. This point is stubbornly missed and confused by laymen and scientists alike, who, often with perfectly honorable intent, use genetic principles to explain social problems and display intense emotional hangups on the heredity-environment issue.

A good example of the hazards of speaking about heridienary determinants in the abstract is the controversy stirred up among social scientists by Arthur Jensen (1969) who suggested that there may be hereditary bases for the observed intellectual differences among Negroes and whites. In this paper, Jensen also provides an extensive summary of the heritability of intelligence. It is totally impossible to resolve such a controversy in the abstract, without specification of the population being referred to, the exact trait being considered, and knowledge of the environmental context under which it is functioning. More will be said about this problem of race differences a little later. A fuller account of the emotional hangups connected with this problem may be found in Lazarus (1969). Only if the concepts of heritability and variability are clearly understood can the reader avoid the same pitfalls into which the uninformed, and often even the learned, seem to fall.

THE STUDY OF HEREDITARY INFLUENCES—
METHODS, FINDINGS, AND ISSUES

Although it is important to guard against the careless and overgeneral attempt to identify the hereditary component in psychological traits, this component can and has been studied systematically by a variety of methods. Rarely has the quantitative variable of heritability been evaluated in such studies, but some insight is usually provided into the role of genetics in many human traits. The most commonly studied psychological trait is intelligence, possibly because of its great importance in human adaptation, and the fact that it can be measured with reasonable reliability.

The earliest work which attempted to show that certain characteristics run in families and are therefore, by inference, inherited, made use of the *family biography*, or the pedigree method. Galton's own research, which surveyed a number of different families for evidence of a hereditary basis for genius, belonged to this type. There were a number of others (e.g. Dugdale, 1877; Goddard, 1912) also which received considerable attention. But the problem with the family biography approach is that it cannot separate hereditary and environmental influences. The approach fails because genetically undesirable parents bring up their children under unsatisfactory conditions. Therefore, even if their genetic legacy is tainted, the situation in which the descendants are reared is also likely to be grossly inadequate. It is simply impossible to identify the respective roles heredity and environment have played by means of this approach by itself.

However, the family biography can be successfully supplemented by more sophisticated statistical analysis and controls, as in the highly respected research on a biochemical defect known as phenylketonuria (PKU), sometimes called "Folling's disease" after its discoverer. Folling had shown in 1934 that some instances of mental retardation were associated with the abnormal excretion of large amounts of phenylpyruvic acid in the urine. Later, Jervis (1937) demonstrated clearly that the defect was inherited. By studying the family biographical patterns of the victims, Jervis came to the conclusion that the disease followed the classical Mendelian pattern of recessive genes, and that it was probably caused by a single gene pair. Because of this careful detective work revealing the fact that the disease followed Mendelian ratios, and partly as a result of the straightforward diagnosis of the disease through urinalysis, most of the deficiencies of the family biography method were avoided in this case, as they had not been in Dugdale's and Goddard's works. All doubt about the hereditary nature of PKU was dispelled when the mental defect was later traced to reduced ability of the body to convert phenylalanine, an essential amino acid, into tyrosine (Jervis, 1947, 1953). The resulting mental retardation is now thought to be caused by the toxic neural effects of the accumulated phenylalanine. If the child is given a diet free of this substance early in life the disorder can be materially improved.

The case of PKU has been given great attention in psychological circles in spite of the fact that it accounts for a very tiny proportion of the cases of mental retardation, because it shows the manner in which some defects can be directly inherited. It is sometimes considered to be a prototypic example of the genetic-constitutional determination of inadequate mental functioning. The argument goes something like this: As with other forms of mental retardation, PKU was once unknown, as was its cause. Hence it is possible that these other forms of mental retardation whose cause is now unknown will also be shown ultimately to result from inherited defects. This argument has, however, been challenged. One might point out, for example, that severe mental retardation is very rare, while most cases of retardation are of the mild variety. Thus, severe forms of retardation are probably in a class by themselves and are not representative of the more usual, mild instances. Moreover, as Zigler (1967) has noted, most cases of mental retardation should not be thought of in terms of the inheritance of a single gene carrying the defect (as in the case of PKU), but rather as the product of the combination of many genes. Varying levels of intellectual ability are normally distributed among the population so that some individuals, unluckily, fall at the lower end of the distribution. Zigler's argument makes the distribution of intellectual ability analogous to a game of chance, such as poker, in which four of a kind or a straight flush is unusual statistically; however, such hands will appear from time to time, just as exceptionally poor hands do. Many cases will occur in which intellectual level is weak, but not really because a disorder has been inherited. PKU is clearly a specific *defect,* while low intelligence, although it is undesirable, need not be so at all.

Researchers attempting to isolate heredity from environment have also turned to studies of *twins,* in particular to the theoretically ideal "co-twin control" method invented by Galton. This technique requires studying identical twins who have been reared apart under different environmental conditions. Ideally, the *co-twin control* method properly administered holds genetic factors constant (identical twins have identical heredity) and permits the isolation of the effects of environmental variation. One difficulty, of course, is that instances of identical twins reared apart are few in number. A second difficulty is that it is harder to determine whether twins are really identical than most people realize. Third and most important of all, most such twins are separated very late in childhood or placed in environments which are fairly similar. The converse of this approach, holding environmental factors constant and varying heredity, is technically impossible to bring about.

Despite the relative rarity of opportunity, a number of researchers have undertaken studies of identical twins—investigating behavioral characteristics such as intelligence as well as physical factors such as height, weight, and incidence of disease—after the twins have been separated and placed in foster homes by public welfare agencies. They all have tended to unearth great similarities among the separated identical twins in the incidence and pattern of diseases and often even in the results of intelligence tests. For children who have been tested on intelligence before adoption and then studied after some time in a foster home, intellectual functioning remained similar between twins in spite of the environmental variation. Yet there were also changes, especially when environmental variations were extreme. These changes were least evident in physical characteristics and most evident in behavioral characteristics such as intelligence-test performance.

In extreme instances of environmental variation, the higher-scoring twin had invariably received considerable educational and cultural advantages as a result of the foster placement. One study reports on a woman who had an IQ of 116 and was a college graduate, although her identical twin had an IQ of 92 and had no schooling beyond the second grade. Here is a case where, in spite of identical inheritance, twins differed strikingly in intellect, presumably as a result of altered and markedly unequal environmental circumstances.

Another example of the use of twins to assess the hereditary component of psychological traits is research by Irving Gottesman (1966). If it can be shown that identical twins who have identical heredity are more similar with respect to a trait than fraternal twins who do not, a strong case can be made for a hereditary contribution to that trait. Gottesman employed personality tests such as the California Psychological Inventory and others to compare the identical or monozygotic (single egg) male and female twins with fraternal or dizygotic (two egg) twins. The sample of subjects consisted of 79 pairs of identical twins and 68 pairs of fraternal twins. The variances for both types of male twins on three of the CPI scales are shown in Table 3 (the lower the variances, the more similar are the twin pairs), along with the heritability indexes which Gottesman calculated. The higher the heritability index, the higher is the proportion of the total variance contributed by heredity. Considerably greater similarity was found between identical twins than between fraternal twins.

One variation on the twin approach has been employed extensively by Franz Kallman (1953) in his research on the hereditary contribution to schizophrenia and other psychoses. Kallman's variation is called the "method of concordance" because it deals with the likelihood that one member of a sibling pair will have a specified condition (for instance, schizophrenia) when it is known that the other member has it. Comparing the index of *concordance* among identical twins, fraternal twins, full siblings, and half siblings, it is possible roughly to gauge the hereditary contribution. Although the index of concordance is not as precise a measure of this as the index of heritability, the reasoning is quite the same.

Essentially, Kallman's method is this: He digs through hospital records of patients with schizophrenia, manic-depressive psychosis, or involutional melancholia to identify those who have an identical twin, fraternal twin, full sibling, or half sibling. He then seeks to determine the adjustive status of that twin or sibling. The index of concordance is simply the percentage of times that the second member of the pair has the same pathology as the hospitalized first member of the pair. Kallman reported that the index of concordance for identical twins is dramatically higher than that for fraternal twins, which in turn is higher than for half sibs and unrelated pairs of individuals. Figure 12 presents Kallman's indexes of concordance for three types of psychosis and for the several types of genetic relationship.

Table 3

Some of Gottesman's Data on Personality Test Variances for Identical and Fraternal Twins

CPI TEST SCALE	IDENTICAL	FRATERNAL	HERITABILITY INDEX
Dominance	41.342	80.706	0.49
Sociability	46.082	90.838	0.49
Achievement via conformance	76.297	66.625	0.00
Self-acceptance	53.848	99.787	0.46

From Gottesman (1966, p. 203)

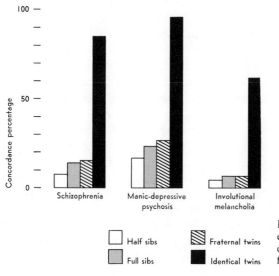

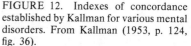

FIGURE 12. Indexes of concordance established by Kallman for various mental disorders. From Kallman (1953, p. 124, fig. 36).

Kallman does not hold that the various disorders studied are directly inherited but rather that genetic factors dispose a person to become sick. In support of his position, he cites the reasoning in the case of tuberculosis. A person cannot become tubercular unless he comes in contact with the disease-producing bacteria. Thus, the disease cannot be directly inherited, only the disposition or lack of resistance to the illness. The same argument is offered for schizophrenia and other psychoses. If a person has a strong genetic disposition to respond to life stress with schizophrenia and he is exposed to the appropriate environmental conditions, the illness will occur. Kallman does not suggest the nature of this disposition physiologically, which of course would ultimately have to be known to establish fully the logical case, but he thinks his data offer good evidence that we should look for the genetic and physiological determinants of psychosis.

Kallman's research remains highly controversial, and it is difficult to assess the degree of genetic component of the various psychopathologies from it because of methodological problems. Indeed, it has been severely criticized by psychologists interested in the etiology of mental illness. Some object—and the probability that this may have happened is strong —that Kallman severely exaggerated the concordance rates for identical twins, although to what extent cannot be known at present. The same person who obtained the records of mental illness, Kallman, also determined whether the second member of the pair showed evidence of the illness. This would pose a sticky problem when the second person was not actually hospitalized and judgment had to be exercised about the extent or nature of his psychopathology. Since Kallman knew the original genetic classification and had strong convictions about the role of genetics, he may have unwittingly exaggerated the incidence of concordance. The method of concordance also has some fundamental weaknesses. For example, the living environments of identical twins are probably more similar than those of fraternal twins, since parents are acutely conscious of identicalness, and since twins too tend to regard themselves as alike and therefore dress alike and react alike. Thus, the high incidence of concordance for identical twins could be due in large part to this uniform environment, as much as to genetic uniformities. Moreover, the twins studied by Kallman had lived together most of their lives, hence the crucial environmental influences which might have contributed to illness in one were probably present also in the case of the other.

A number of other investigators have repeated Kallman's research with essentially comparable results (see Thompson, 1965). However, the studies suffer from methodological difficulties and thus are no more definitive than Kallman's. The imperfect data are much more likely to be accepted as proving a hereditary determination of severe mental illnesses such as schizophrenia by those psychologists who tend to favor a biological approach, and to be rejected by those with a social psychological viewpoint. The issue of the role of heredity in mental illness remains a controversial one.

Another method for studying the effects of heredity on behavioral traits is experimental and makes use of *selective breeding* for the trait in question. An example is the research of behavior geneticist, Theodosius Dobzhansky (1967) with Drosophila, a species of fruitfly. Behavioral tendencies of these flies to move upwards or downwards when released from a tube, or to be attracted or repelled by light, have been selectively bred over many generations to produce distinctively different types of Drosophila. Even earlier research by Robert Tryon (1940) is another example. Tryon bred generations of rats for brightness and dullness in performing a laboratory maze. Starting with 142 unselected white rats, he assessed their effectiveness in learning the maze, then bred the bright rats with other bright rats, and the dull ones with other dull rats. He did this for 21 generations. After only eight generations, even the dullest of the bright rats did better on the maze than the brightest of the dull. Such data clearly demonstrate a hereditary component in rat intelligence. It is of course not without hazard to generalize from rat or fruitfly to man, or from the process of learning mazes to other intellectual functions. Still, such findings provide impressive evidence of the genetic component in adaptive intelligence. One must be impressed by the exciting possibilities inherent in genetic research into adaptively useful behavioral traits which are part of personality variation.

THE RACE ISSUE

During World War I it was discovered that white army inductees obtained higher scores on tests of intellectual functioning than Negro inductees. However, the data also showed that blacks growing up in certain Northern states, such as Pennsylvania, Ohio, New York, and Illinois, were superior even to white recruits from the South. The most impressive subsequent study was done by a social psychologist, Otto Klineberg (1935) who showed that Southern Negro children improved in intelligence test scores after having moved to New York City, and that the improvement was related to the length of time they had been there. Thus the differences could not be due to selective migration, but clearly showed that environment had a marked effect on intelligence test scores. There are few researchers in this field today who are not aware of the validity of this point.

Most behavior geneticists doubt that there are any important differences among the races in broad adaptive traits such as intelligence. For one thing, the concept of race itself is vague and ill-defined, and as is pointed out in the UNESCO statement on race, there is no evidence for the existence of so-called pure races. Lerner writes that, "On the basis of known gene frequencies, and the assumptions that (1) fitness is independent of color and (2) random mating will take place among Negroes without further gene flow from the European pool, it is predictable that in another generation hardly any Negro will not be the bearer of some white genes" (1968, p. 234). Gottesman, a psychologist clearly oriented toward the search for genetic factors, also adds his comments to the crescendo of sophisticated negative opinion that has been expressed about the validity and usefulness of the concept of a genetic basis for "race" differences in adaptive functioning, writing for example, "My evaluation of the literature on race differences has led me to conclude that the differences observed between the mean IQs of Negro Americans and other Americans can be accounted for almost wholly by environmental disadvantages which start in the prenatal period and continue throughout a lifetime" (1968, p. 63). All this does not mean that there are no genetically determined differences in constitution among human groups; there obviously are, or else race would be an entirely meaningless concept, which it is not. Rather, it means that such differences are relative (there are no pure races) and are not of major importance in the adaptive functioning of human racial groups.

In his handling of this matter, Lerner quotes from the famous anthropologist S. L. Washburn in a presidential address to the American Anthropological Association, in which he goes even further, saying, "I am sometimes surprised to hear it stated that if Negroes were given an equal opportunity, their IQ would be the same as the whites. If one looks at the degree of social discrimination against Negroes and their lack of education, and also takes into account the tremendous amount of overlapping between the observed IQ's of both, one can make an equally good case that, given a comparable chance to that of the whites, their IQ's would test out ahead. Of course, it would be absolutely unimportant in a democratic society if this were to be true, because the vast majority of individuals of both groups would be of comparable intelligence, whatever the mean of these intelligence tests would show" (1968, pp. 235–36).

The final sentence of the above quotation illustrates the defects of a form of thought which has been discarded by knowledgeable behavior geneticists in recent years, one that has been referred to as *typological thinking*. There is a strong tendency to pigeonhole individual people into categories or types. It is a useful way of simplifying things, but in behavior genetics typological thinking is a very misleading habit of thought. It encourages, for example, the image of a single gene, responsible, say, for intelligence, or for any other complex psychological trait in which one might be interested. If the person has the gene, then he ought to have the trait. Such an image conforms to the Mendelian laws of heredity which are so useful in analyzing certain simple traits such as those Mendel studied in the pea plant. It also occasionally works well with rare disorders, such as PKU. But in most instances of human psychological traits, such a form of thinking is inadequate, and no longer provides an accurate picture of genetic processes, or the way geneticists think about the problem. Combinations of genes are necessary to produce particular physiological and behavior effects, each trait usually being the product of interaction among large numbers of genes. This is known as *population* or *statistical thinking* in contrast to typological thinking.

Geneticists today speak of the *gene pool* to refer to the hypothetical total number of genetic influences which may be found within a species, or in a group of individuals. And even when selective breeding has occurred, this original gene pool is evidently not lost. Thus, for example, the many genes related to "brightness" and "dullness" in the rats which Tryon had bred over many generations were not lost over these generations, but remained latent within both populations even after they had been bred into two distinct behavioral types. When they were no longer being selectively bred for brightness or dullness, the original distribution of maze learning ability rapidly returned to each group. As pointed out by Dobzhansky (1967), this is a very useful property for organisms, since even though there has been selective breeding in the past, when new changes occur in the environment, the process can still reverse itself; that is, the basis of natural selection can be readily changed without the species becoming terribly vulnerable and unable to draw upon its full range of adaptive mechanisms. The gene pool remains slow to change irreversibly, and it is not known how much time might be needed for this to happen. The bridges are not burned by selective mating, and retreat to earlier types of traits is possible.

Such a situation implies that races or types in which the gene pools are distinctively different are not likely to develop easily. It also means that the types or categories into which people are placed in classification by traits are less important than are the individual differences, which cannot be readily explained by membership in a type. Dobzhansky effectively states the case against typological thought:

> Man in the street is a spontaneous typologist. To him, all things which have the same nature are therefore alike. All men have the human nature, and an alleged wisdom has it that the human nature does not change. All Negroes are alike because of their negritude, and all Jews are alike because of their jewishness. Populationists affirm that there is no single human nature but as many human natures as there are individuals. Human nature does change. Race differences are compounded of the same ingredients as differences among individuals which compose a race. In fact, races differ in relative frequencies of genes more often than they differ qualitatively....
>
> To say that we do not know to what extent group differences in psychological traits are genetic is not the same as saying that the genetic component does not exist. It is a challenge to find out. If individuals within populations vary in some character, be that blood grouping, or stature, or intelligence, it is quite unlikely that the population means (averages) will be exactly the same. What matters is how great is the intrapopulational variance compared to the interpopulational variance. Skin pigmentation is individually variable in probably all races, but the interracial variance is evidently larger. Although precise data are not available, it is at least as probable that the relation is reversed for psychological traits. In simplest terms, the brightest individuals in every class, caste, and race are undoubtedly brighter than the average in any class, caste, or race. And vice-versa the dullest individuals in any of these groups are duller than the average of any group. There are sound biological reasons why this should be so. Very briefly, in the evolution of mankind the natural selection has worked, nearly always and everywhere, to increase and maintain the behavioral plasticity and diversity, which are essential in all human cultures, primitive as well as advanced (1967, pp. 47–48).

ENVIRONMENTAL INFLUENCES

By no means all of the research on the determinants of adaptive intelligence or other personality traits has been designed to extract the influence of genetic factors—much of it has been oriented toward the influence of environmental variations. Some of it needs to be discussed here to balance the discussion of hereditary influences. Since this turns our attention away from biological influences and toward the subject of the next chapter, it seems best to touch on such work only very lightly. We shall limit ourselves to a brief discussion of a striking piece of research by Skeels (1940, 1942, 1966) on the impact of an impoverished versus enriched environment on intellectual development. One reason that the research of Skeels is unusual is that it involves a follow-up of the same children 21 years after the original observations were made.

Two groups of children were first observed, 13 in the experimental group, 12 in a contrast or control group. All were mentally retarded and had been placed in an orphanage. The experimental group had been moved out of the orphanage to an institution with much stimulation and warm relationships with mother substitutes. The contrast group stayed behind in the unstimulating, impoverished environment. Marked differences were later observed in the intellectual level and functioning of the two groups, although they had started at about the same level, with the experimental group having actually been slightly inferior. In two years, the experimental group had gained 25.8 IQ points, while the controls had lost 26.2 IQ points. Eleven of the former children were adopted later and continued to show improvement in intellectual level, while the two not adopted had declined somewhat.

Twenty-one years later all the cases were located and again the comparison between groups was made. None of the 13 children who had been moved to the superior environment had become a ward of any institution, public or private. Their median education was completion of the twelfth grade; four had one year or more of college; of these one had graduated college; and another was taking some graduate work. All were self-supporting. In the contrast group, one had died in adolescence in a state institution for the mentally retarded; four were still wards of institutions, one in a mental hospital, the other three in institutions for the mentally retarded. Their median education was less than third grade. The enriched and deprived environments had made themselves felt very substantially in the overall level of functioning of the two groups.

GENERAL CONCLUSION CONCERNING GENETIC INFLUENCES

What can be concluded from the above review of some of the research and research methods on genetic factors in the development of psychological traits? The fundamental conclusion is in a sense banal, that psychological characteristics are influenced *both* by hereditary and environmental factors. The conclusion is banal largely because it is so general, and so self-evident.

There can be little doubt that hereditary influences do, indeed, exist. What is mainly lacking in our knowledge at the moment are the details of the relationship, that is, those facts necessary to specify in more technical fashion the heritability of a given trait under particular conditions, and some knowledge of the physiological structures that mediate the genetically influenced trait. For example, if one assumed with Kallman that schizophrenia has a hereditary basis, at least in part, evidence is still lacking about the physiological differences between the schizophrenic and nonschizophrenic in order to account for the susceptibility to the disorder. Let us recognize that what is inherited, after all, is an anatomy of some sort, a physiological structure which functions in certain ways, and grows out of the hereditary influence on cell differentiation. Variations in this structure must underlie, in part, many of the psychological differences that we observe. How anatomical and physiological differences might lead to variations in personality must be considered next.

Physiological Influences

The general argument that an animal's physiology contributes to its behavior is grossly supported by taking a phylogenetic perspective, that is, by comparing the physiological structures of animals at different phylogenetic levels and observing that their characteristic patterns of behavior vary. When, for example, neurological structures are relatively similar, as they are within phyla or species, characteristic behavior is also similar; however, when the neurological makeup differs markedly, as it does particularly across phyla, striking behavioral differences also appear. But the statement of such a relationship and nothing more is too general and obvious. What is needed is that the details of this influence be clarified and documented. The problem of relating physiology to psychological functioning gets more difficult, complex, and subtle within a species, such as man. There are two reasons for this: first, because when we are working within a species the variations in physiological structure are not so obvious, although they clearly do exist; and second, man is the most complex of animals, physiologically and psychologically, and his behavior is governed by many more variables which can easily escape our notice or understanding.

The subject of personality tends to emphasize man rather than infra-human animals, but much of the evidence for the relationship between physiology and stable patterns of behavior (from which personality is inferred) comes from studies of animals. This is partly because of the greater complexity of man and the greater difficulty of studying him, and partly because of restrictions on the kinds of research that can be performed on him. Nevertheless, there are also marked individual differences among infra-human animals within the same species, and it is quite reasonable to conceive of such animals as possessing personalities too, although the jump to man is always suspect. Our objective in this section is to illustrate physiological influences on adaptive behavior and to analyze the ways in which these relationships can be applied to personality.

The influence of physiological factors on behavior can be studied in two ways. One is by experimental methods to create temporary physiological states and observe their behavioral effects; the other is to examine stable, naturally occurring differences among animals in glandular, neurological, or other organ structures as possible correlates of variations in behavior. The use of drugs that produce certain effects on the nervous system and hence on behavior is an example of the first approach. While the socially oriented psychologist is attempting to understand psychological functioning and malfunctioning in terms of disturbances in social relations, the physiological psychologist is concerned with explaining these disorders at the level of physiological structure and function.

Physiological factors can affect behavior either directly or indirectly. In *direct influence,* normal behavior is altered by damage to tissues or by structural or functional conditions in the nervous system. For example, metabolic disturbances that result from inadequate functioning of the endocrine gland system may produce behavioral effects, such as hyperactivity, sluggishness, and reported anxiety. Damage to the brain from physical injuries or diseases such as syphilis can produce impairment in adaptive behavior and marked changes in a person's relationship with other people. There is no doubt that these disturbances are definitely produced by damage to the brain tissue, although the mechanism whereby the damage is reflected in behavior is not entirely clear and will not be fully understood until the precise relationship between the brain and psychological functioning is known.

Indirect influences occur when physiological states have social consequences which in turn affect the individual's behavior. Physical handicaps often present striking examples of indirect influence because they may produce negative or disturbed reactions in other people that make the handicapped person to feel inadequate, to attempt to compensate for the defect, perhaps to withdraw from social contacts, or to resort to one of a variety of other forms of adjustment. A girl who is physically unattractive may develop an insecure or compensating personality, strongly influenced by this physical fact. Similarly, a child endowed with considerable physical strength and large stature will probably discover in playing with other children that he is stronger than they, and thus develop a personality different from that of a lad who is sickly and puny.

The above point suggests that the effects of physiological factors on personality are also likely to be dependent on social factors, and it will be the interaction of both that determines the end product we call personality. Yet research into the physiological and social origins of the development of personality has actually given relatively little attention to these interactions. The physiological psychologist inclines toward the isolated study of physiological variables, and the socially oriented psychologist conversely addresses himself primarily to the analysis of social influences. This isolation occurs in spite of the fact that personality theorists of either persuasion usually assume such interaction as the normal state of affairs.

The potential range of examples of physiological influences on adaptive behavior is large, and one must be highly selective in a brief treatment. Two examples will be given here. The first concerns the relationship between body build and temperament. The second has to do with the effects of hormones on adaptive behavior. Although the illustrations are selective, essentially the same general points could be made about other physiological factors that have been omitted because of lack of space.

BODY BUILD AND TEMPERAMENT

An early prototype of the basic idea of the relationship of physiology and personality is the classical Greek theory of Hippocrates that temperament depends on the relative proportions of four main body humors— black bile, yellow bile, blood, and phlegm—each corresponding to four types of person, the melancholic, choleric, sanguine, and phlegmatic, respectively. The major modern representative of this theme is the "constitutional psychology" of William H. Sheldon (1940, 1942). Its immediate ancestor was the work of Kretschmer (1925), who had divided people into four physical types, (1) the frail, linear *asthenic,* (2) the vigorous, muscular *athletic,* (3) the plump *pyknic,* and (4) the inconsistent *dysplastic* for whom portions of the body could be asthenic and other portions simultaneously pyknic or athletic. Kretschmer maintained that temperament and even the type of mental disorder an individual might develop depended on the body type with which he was endowed. Thus, for example, schizophrenics were apt to be asthenic in body build, while manic-depressives were likely to be pyknics.

In addition to pursuing this line of research much further than Kretschmer, Sheldon developed a system of scale measurements for the varieties and dimensions of body build as well as for the varieties and dimensions of temperament. He also suggested an embryonically oriented theory of the relationship between body build (or "somatotype") and temperament, in which it was assumed that various portions of the body's tissues, say the digestive organs (endomorphy), the muscle and bone (mesomorphy), or the nervous system (ectomorphy), have each been differently emphasized in the development of the individual, resulting in different patterns of psychological response.

Sheldon assumed a direct influence of the dimensions of body build on temperament, although he also acknowledged that cultural attitudes toward and stereotypes about body builds may also influence the growing person as well. For example, there is a widespread tendency to assume that fat people (pyknic body build) are jolly, while thin people (asthenic body build) are anxious, serious, and intellectual. Shakespeare gives expression to this idea in Julius Caesar's remark, "Yond Cassius has a lean and hungry look; he thinks too much: such men are dangerous (*Julius Caesar,* i, 2, 192)." With such a cultural stereotype, it would not be surprising for fat people to grow up with a different personality than thin people, the expectations of others being an important influence on one's self-image.

Sheldon has reported extensive research demonstrating a moderate link between body type and temperament. Considerable doubt, however, exists about the mechanisms underlying this relationship, since correlational evidence cannot answer the question about whether the influence is direct or indirect, or even whether there is any cause-and-effect relationship involved at all. Few advances on the problem have been made since Sheldon's pioneering efforts. The basic ideas behind it remain highly controversial among psychologists interested in personality, and the problem has never entered the mainstream of personality psychology.

THE BIOCHEMICAL CONTROL OF BEHAVIOR

Nowhere is the impact of physiology on adaptive behavior more clearly expressed than in the influence of hormones. Everyone is aware of the existence of the *endocrine glands,* the network of hormone factories which secrete biochemical substances of great potency directly into the bloodstream, there to be carried to internal organs throughout the body. One usually speaks of the endocrine glands as a system, because one gland influences the other rather than working in isolation. Within this system, the *pituitary* appears to be the most important; it secretes many hormonal substances which regulate other glands in the system. Figure 13 lists the endocrine glands and portrays their approximate locations in the body.

The potency of endocrine hormones for influencing behavior and adaptive functioning becomes most evident when there is a disease or defect of one of the secreting glands. Striking examples include the effects of too little or too much *thyroid* hormone. Behaviorally, too much results in agitation and sleeplessness among other things, while too little is apt to produce lethargy and fatigue. These effects are likely to be known by the lay person because so many people take pills to overcome thyroid deficiency. Another equally striking example involves the pancreas, sections of which (the islet cells) secrete a powerful hormone known as *insulin.* Insulin regulates the amount of sugar in the blood stream; its action is to withdraw sugar from the blood and to store it in the liver. This is important because the functioning of the muscles of the body and, indeed, of

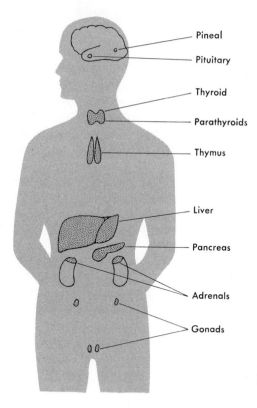

FIGURE 13. The endocrine glands and their approximate locations.

the cells of the brain depends on the oxidation of sugar. If there is too little sugar available, adaptive thought and action cannot take place; if there is too much, the person suffers from the disease of diabetes. Thus, the amount of insulin released from the pancreas must be enough to keep the blood sugar level from becoming excessive and yet provide enough to permit the brain and muscles to function successfully.

Occasionally an individual suffers from an insulin disorder, and the symptoms communicate dramatically the vital role of hormones in psychological functioning. One such disorder, for example, is an insulin-secreting tumor of the pancreas. Under these conditions, insulin continues to be secreted into the blood stream regardless of the blood sugar level. In such a case, excessive withdrawal of sugar from the blood and cells of the brain produces severe symptoms, such as physical weakness, mental confusion, double vision, and even coma or convulsions. An individual chronically beset by this disorder may not realize the nature of the difficulty, but feels unable to deal adequately with the ordinary requirements of living. In severe cases he may even display paranoid symptoms, or periodically experience psychotic-like attacks. All of these profound mental effects are produced by a hormone-secreting tumor that may be no larger than a small match head.

In recent years the *adrenal glands* have received much attention from psychologists because they are so important in stress and emotion. There are two main portions of the adrenals, both producing specialized hormones which have different functions. The outer portion of the gland is known as the "cortex," and produces several hormones called "corticosteroids." These regulate metabolic activities, such as protein, fat, and carbohydrate breakdown, and in this way are very important in sustaining adaptive activities over long periods of time during which the animal is exposed to stressful circumstances. The functions of these adrenal cortical hormones have been particularly emphasized by physiologist Hans Selyé (1956) whose writings and research on the body's adrenal-based physiological defenses against stress have been very influential. In consequence of this work, stress reactions are often studied by measuring the secretion of adrenal hormones in the blood or urine.

The other main portion of the adrenal gland is the inner part, called the "medulla." Here there are secreted at least two (and probably more) hormonal substances, "adrenaline" and "nor-adrenaline." There is some evidence that *adrenaline* is emphasized in emotional reactions such as fear, while *nor-adrenaline* is the major hormonal component in reactions such as anger, although this generalization is probably overly simple, and the empirical case made for it is rather weak. Two lines of evidence are involved. First is the observation that herbivorous animals seem to have higher secretion ratios of adrenaline to nor-adrenaline than carnivorous animals. This would make sense if anger and attack were associated mainly with nor-adrenaline, fear and withdrawal with adrenaline. The evidence thus suggests that glandular makeup is consistent with the characteristic life adjustment of the species.

A second line of evidence is that adrenaline and nor-adrenaline produce measurably different, though overlapping, end-organ effects when injected into the person. There are also common-sense observations which seem to be consistent with the idea that the biochemical correlates of anger and fear are different. For example, anger is thought to produce a reddening or flushing of the face, and we use the expression, "red-faced" anger. On the other hand, fear seems to be associated with blanching or paling of the face and a drying up of the mucus membranes. Who has not found his mouth almost too dry to speak clearly on facing an audience for the first time? Some classic studies by Wolff (1950) have also confirmed the above common-sense impressions. A patient was observed with a disorder which required keeping his stomach open for a time. A window was installed in the opening so that the gastric activity could be observed. When the patient seemed to be angry, the stomach lining was engorged with blood, appeared red, and became moist; when he seemed afraid the lining was pale and dry. It is quite likely that such effects are produced both by activity of the autonomic nervous system, and of the endocrine glands, in particular the adrenal medulla.

Let us consider one more illustration of the role of biochemical substances in adaptive behavior before we attempt to examine the manner in which personality itself may be shaped by physiology. The illustration concerns hormonal influences on *aggressiveness*. Animal species vary greatly in aggressiveness. For example, the Norway wild rat must be handled with great care to avoid its fierce attacks. However, after many years of breeding this animal for purposes of experimentation, researchers have produced a very tame animal which can be handled easily and roughly without the risk of attack. The wild Norway rat has adrenal glands that are far larger than those of the domesticated version.

It has been assumed for a long time that aggressiveness is also related to sex hormones, since male animals very typically are more aggressive than females. One of the striking pieces of evidence about this comes from a study by Clark and Birch (1945, 1946) who experimented with chimpanzees. Most animal species, including chimpanzees, maintain social dominance hierarchies (sometimes referred to as "pecking orders"). Some animals behave consistently in a dominant fashion over all the others; others are dominant over some but submissive with others, still others falling at the very bottom of the dominance scale. Dominance usually means considerable control over the food supply, with the dominant animal usually satisfying himself first. Clark and Birch observed that when two chimpanzees were allowed to fight over a peanut which was presented a number of times in a cup between them, one of the two ultimately tended to emerge as the dominant animal—he always took the peanut first each time until no longer hungry. However, when the experimenters injected the subordinate chimp with a dose of male sex hormone, he overturned the dominance relationship that had been established earlier, and tended to establish dominance over the other chimp.

This is a very clear and interesting example of the influence of the male sex hormone on adaptive behavior. However, since human behavior seems to be far less controlled by such hormones than the behavior of infrahuman animals, it is not altogether clear to what extent the findings of Clark and Birch have applicability to the human context, although it is not implausible that some such mechanisms could also be at work in human individual differences in aggressiveness.

HOW HORMONES AND OTHER PHYSIOLOGICAL
FACTORS MIGHT INFLUENCE PERSONALITY

In the above account, illustrations have been provided of the biochemical control of adaptive behavior. They show that immediately circulating hormones momentarily affect the actions and reactions of animals, particularly infra-human animal species. Remember, however, that the subject of personality depends on two themes, first the existence of more or less stable or enduring patterns of psychological functioning, and second, manifest individual differences in these patterns. Thus, to get from the above examples of how hormones influence behavior to the manner in which they might affect personality, we have to make three logical, inferential leaps.

The first is to make the assumption that stable individual differences in some behavioral traits could be a result of different amounts of hormone coursing through the system. For example, we might expect different degrees of aggressiveness in people to be associated with different secreted amounts of, say, male sex hormone. This does not, of course, necessarily imply a one-to-one or exclusive relationship. The person's social experience probably plays an important role, too, in increasing or toning down the biologically shaped aggressiveness. The resulting behavior pattern is undoubtedly a product of the interaction of both hormonal and social factors, and it is unlikely that any complex personality or temperamental quality could be the result of only a single physiological influence. Thus, the male sex hormone might provide some of the impetus for aggressiveness. However, there are probably a host of other biochemical and neurological elements which operate together in some complex and unknown geometry to determine the behavioral outcome, not to speak of the unquestioned role of social experience or of the immediate situation as well.

The influence of hormones on personality is not a new idea. About 30 or 40 years ago when medical research and practice first began to recognize the powerful impact of hormones on behavior, overly simple assumptions about individual differences in personality and glandular makeup began to burgeon and to reach the lay public. It was assumed, for example, that what had been learned about thyroid deficiency and its treatment could also be applied to the individual who functioned within normal limits, for example, to increase his energy or help him to relax. In time it was discovered that successful treatment for cases of endocrine defect would not work in normal cases; moreover, the endocrine glands functioned as part of an organized system, so that injections with a hormone usually had repercussions, often serious ones, throughout the entire system. With the discovery of the complexity of the problem, initial enthusiasm about hormones cooled. Today, although the potential implications of the hormonal control of personality still have the same force, we recognize how far we are from the degree of understanding of the problem that would be necessary for the practical control of adaptive behavior.

The second inferential leap is somewhat more complicated, and even more fascinating to consider than the first. It is that hormones have a marked effect on the development of the person from conception on, and thus could influence personality by influencing the formation of the physiological structure and function which gets established early in life. Furthermore, the very hormones which determine how the physiological structure will develop are in turn influenced by early life experiences (in infancy and perhaps even *in utero*). In sum, individual differences in hormonal activity (produced both through genetic influences and early life experience) could create physiological structures quite variable from person to person, or animal to animal, thus resulting in varying patterns of behavior throughout the remainder of life.

Evidence concerning the above principle comes from the work of Seymour Levine (1966; also Levine and Mullins, 1966) in which the effects of male and female sex hormones at critical periods of development of the rat were studied. There appear to be distinct differences between the male and female brain that determine sexual activity. Levine argues that in mammals the brain is essentially female at birth, until a certain stage of development when the male's brain undergoes sex-related changes. In the rat this stage occurs a very short time after birth. If testosterone is absent at this stage, the brain will remain female; if it is present, then the brain will develop male characteristics. Females injected with testosterone at this early period fail to develop normal female sex behavior in adulthood. They also fail to acquire normal female physiological patterns—their ovaries are dwarfed, and their ovulation cycle is absent. Similarly, males who are castrated during the first few days after birth, and hence deprived of testosterone at this critical period, show signs of female physiology and female behavioral receptivity in adulthood. Similar findings have been reported in the guinea pig. Moreover, if a newborn rat is administered thyroid hormone, its thyroid functioning is permanently suppressed for the rest of its life. This suggests to Levine that there is a portion of the brain which might be called the thyroid "thermostat" or regulator, and that it has in effect been permanently adjusted too low by the early administration of thyroid hormone. Thus, there is evidence to support the inferential leap of the second type, that hormonal levels early in life produce changes in the central nervous system, such that regulatory activity of circulating hormones later in life is permanently altered too. Although the nature of these changes in the brain is not known, Levine argues that they must have occurred if we are to understand the permanence of the hormonal effects over the animal's lifetime as a result of the experimental treatments in infancy.

There are, of course, two ways in nature that hormonal influences on the developing physiological structure could be produced. First, there is the possibility that genetic influences will create varying levels of glandular production of a given hormone. In this event, some animals will start out with more of the hormone than others. A second possibility is that the experiences to which animals are exposed will produce different circulating amounts of a given hormone at critical early periods in life. It is known that the handling of animals by humans, interactions with other animals, stressful situations, etc., all influence the circulating levels of hormones such as hydrocortisone, adrenalin, and testosterone. For example, when an animal ecological system becomes too heavily populated for the given food resources of the environment, a survival struggle that generates severe stress is created. Under such stress conditions, the adrenal glands secrete far more hydrocortisone than usual. As a result, the animals become less resistant to disease and less capable of mating and reproducing. Christian and Davis (1964) have suggested this as one of the biological mechanisms by means of which animal population levels are kept relatively constant. When the population grows too large, survival and breeding are impaired, and population size is reduced; when it falls below a given point, survival and breeding again improve, with a subsequent increase in the population size. The overall level of population in the long run fluctuates around some normal, constant level (except in modern man, which appears to be a special case). In any event, early life experiences affect hormone levels, which in turn permanently influence the nervous system on which later regulation of adaptive behavior by circulating hormones and environmental forces depends.

We have saved the largest inferential leap of all for last, that is, the possible connections between principles derived from infra-human animal forms, even such low ones as the rat, and those appropriate to man. Does the work of Levine have anything to do with the relationship of physiology to personality in man? To suggest it does requires that we overlook provisionally the differences among the physiological structures (for example, the brain) of man and the infra-human animal world, although as we go from the macrostructure of tissue systems to the microstructure of individual cells and subcellular structures, the differences in structure and function become less impressive. Thus, a human gene will act biochemically in essentially the same way as a gene of a rodent. The same hormones are found in rats and men. Yet human behavior is infinitely more complex than that of lower forms of animal life, just as man's overall physiology is also more complex. Man's behavior is also far more flexible and more sensitively keyed to environmental forces and learning than is that of lower animals.

Therefore, it is hazardous and probably unwarranted to argue that Levine's findings, and others like them, have direct and specific applicability to man, although they might well have a general relevance. One of the things which make this work on lower animals potentially fascinating is precisely the possibility that the principles derived from it will have some relevance to man. Few of us really have much interest in rats as such, but we do have a great deal of interest in those things that we as humans share with them. The inferential leap, however, must be highly disciplined, and we must be continuously on guard against overgeneralization in the absence of comparative data in each species.

Although the socially oriented personality researcher has little direct interest in documenting the inferential leaps considered above, he should take seriously the search for rules about how physiological structure affects adaptive behavior and personality. Although his own attention is likely to be directed elsewhere, he knows full well that man is a living creature like other animals, and as such, understanding him will require biological as well as social rules. The social determinants of personality are examined next in Chapter 6.

Personality Determinants—
Social Factors

chapter six

Two statements serve as basic themes for this chapter: (1) For man every behaving situation is really a social one, whether the person is alone or in the company of others. When one is with another person, the presence of this other is a powerful influence on how one acts and reacts; but even when one is alone, the reactions of others to what he does or thinks can be imagined or remembered, and this too has considerable influence on him. (2) Over the course of development from the very earliest moments of post-natal life, every person has a host of experiences with other people, and these influence the developing personality structure which, in turn, governs his social behavior. Thus, there are two levels at which social influence can be examined, the contemporaneous social situation (sometimes referred to as interactive) and the developmental history of social influence on which the personality is, in large part, based. In short, *contemporaneous* or interactive determinants refer to the effects of the immediate social situation on reactions, while *developmental* determinants refer to effects of events in the past which contribute to reactions in the present. These levels will be discussed in detail in this chapter under the headings, "contemporaneous social influence" and "developmental social influence."

Contemporaneous Social Influence

In any situation of social interaction, the actions of one person, A, are perceived by the other person, B. Person A, therefore, has served as a stimulus for person B; and vice-versa, person B has been a stimulus for A. Feedback about his effects on B has also been provided A (B to A), and feedback has also gone from A to B, influencing the subsequent behavior of each party to the interaction. Moreover, the original action of A which started the process was undoubtedly performed with certain expectations based on past experience about how B would probably react (developmental social influence). Even the most simple social exchange is thus exceedingly complex, as was emphasized some time ago by sociologist George Herbert Mead (1934).

The properties of other persons as psychological beings and the reasons for their actions are not known to us directly, but can be grasped only through inference from what is observed. Thus, another element of major importance in social interchange is that the actions of one person must be perceived and interpreted by the other to be meaningful. A social interchange involves all of the basic psychological processes which the field of psychology attempts to study and understand, including perception, learning, memory, thought, motivation, and emotion. Social psychologist, Solomon E. Asch has captured this point very well in the following passage:

> To naive thought nothing is less problematic than that we grasp the actions of others, but it is precisely the task of psychology to remove the veil of self-evidence from these momentous processes. For example, it is customary to dispose of the problem by referring to our dependency on others and to the fact that the acts of others have consequences for us. But dependence presupposes knowledge of human facts. We reach firm psychological ground only when we realize that our dependence is mediated by a psychological process of following and making sense of the actions of others. There is an almost infinite variety of qualities that we note and understand in persons. We see their actions in relation to objects, as when we say that they come and go, push and pull. Similarly, we note activities in them that are more "mental", as when we say that a person searches and finds, that he is surprised, that he concentrates, guesses, studies. In the same way, we note the actions of persons directed to other persons—that they help, fight, advise, buy, sell, criticize, bribe, scoff, teach, retaliate. Finally, we grasp certain characteristic qualities of persons— their spontaneity, intelligence, alertness, indolence, or pride. It is our task to clarify how we come to understand such acts and properties of persons (1952, pp. 139–40).

Social situations can influence virtually every human psychological function that we can study. They can affect what and how we learn, how we perceive and judge the environment and the events in it, the language with which we describe and conceptualize events, our motives, the manner in which we cope with life demands, the feelings we have for others, and the manner in which we experience and express emotional reactions. In this brief discussion of contemporaneous social influence, very few of the social influences, or the kinds of psychological functions which they determine, can be reviewed. We shall examine a few concrete research examples of contemporaneous social influences, primarily ones dealing with the way we perceive things. The studies cited below have played an important role in the development of modern social psychology. Then in a second section we shall explore some of the mechanisms by which such influence is presumed to occur.

EXAMPLES OF CONTEMPORANEOUS
SOCIAL INFLUENCE

Representative instances of contemporaneous social influence have been revealed and analyzed by social psychologists in many ways and settings. A favorite approach has been to place subjects in contrasting social settings and make observations about how they act. This approach has its modern origins in experimental work by Sherif (1935), and Sherif and Cantril (1947), and by Asch (1952, 1956), in which the acts observed were *perceptual* in nature.

In a very well-known study, Sherif (1935) gave subjects the task of judging the apparent movements of a stationary pinpoint of light. When such a pinpoint of light is viewed in a completely dark room without any reference points it seems to move, a phenomenon called by Sherif, "the autokinetic effect." The extent and pattern of this movement vary from person to person and are determined by purely internal psychological factors. When subjects work alone over a number of trials, each develops a stable, characteristic *autokinetic effect.* One subject may report relatively little movement (a few inches, for example) in a particular direction, while another subject may report a large movement in a different direction. This becomes his own individual norm or standard which is repeated consistently from trial to trial.

However, when subjects work in groups of two or three, each announcing his own judgment aloud, a marked influence of one subject on the other is then found. Gradually group rather than indivudual norms are established. The group norm tends to represent a compromise among individual norms, with extreme cases pulled in by the group in both the degree and patterning of the estimated movement. Sherif's subjects who had had previous experience with the autokinetic phenomenon, and who had established their own individual norms, gradually gave up their individual norms in response to the behavior of the group. Moreover, these group norms persisted even after the subjects were allowed subsequently to work alone. Subjects who had had no such experience rapidly achieved group norms in their judgments, and these group norms persisted into the period when these subjects later worked alone. In other words, individual norms always gave way to the social interaction, with the group norm ultimately being adopted by the individual and persisting in the individual situation. Sherif's experiments dramatically illustrated the powerful effects of being in a group situation.

Asch's research (1952, 1956) with socially based influences on *perception* provides a somewhat different illustration of the same principle. His experiments have come to represent a classic paradigm for experimental research in which the structure of groups is manipulated by the experimenter so that the effects on an individual can be examined. In the best-known study, subjects had the task of comparing a series of standard lines with several alternatives, and of announcing to the experimenter in each case the alternative line that was the same length as the standard. When the subject did it by himself, there were virtually no errors, suggesting that this perceptual task was not particularly difficult. The same task was also done, however, in a group with a number of other persons, each of whom had been secretly instructed by the experimenter on exactly how to respond. In one of the group situations consisting of seven confederates and one "real" subject, Asch had all the confederates give the same incorrect answer before it was the "real" subject's turn. He found that about one-third of the time, the "real" subject made "errors" in the direction of the group norm or standard. Table 4 shows what happened when the frequency of subject errors in the solitary situation was compared with that in the group situation. As can be seen, the number of errors increased dramatically, all of them being the result of "yielding" to the pressure of the social group.

MECHANISMS OF CONTEMPORANEOUS SOCIAL INFLUENCE

In both Sherif's and Asch's research there is striking evidence of contemporaneous social influence. The problem remains, however, of understanding what made the subjects vulnerable to that influence. A considerable proportion of the research on social influence has been aimed, not merely at demonstrating such effects, but at comprehending their mechanisms, that is, at answering the theoretical question of why.

In the discussion that follows, three kinds of mechanisms are proposed and studied, although these do not exhaust the possibilities. (1) The first concerns the possibility of disapproval or rejection by the group, which maintains power over the individual by virtue of his needs for affiliation, and because of the group's control over valuable resources. (2) The second has to do with the need for confirmation of one's judgment by other persons. (3) The third focuses on personality dispositions to erect and use

Table 4

Distribution of Errors in Experimental and Control Groups of Asch Study on Group Pressures

NUMBER OF CRITICAL ERRORS	FREQUENCY OF ERRORS IN EXPERIMENTAL GROUP* ($n = 50$)	FREQUENCY OF ERRORS IN CONTROL GROUP ($n = 37$)
0	13	35
1	4	1
2	5	1
3	6	
4	3	
5	4	
6	1	
7	2	
8	5	
9	3	
10	3	
11	1	
12	0	
Mean	3.84	0.08

*All errors in the experimental group were in the direction of majority estimates.
From Asch (1952, p. 5)

defenses in threatening contexts where there is conflict between the person and the group. These mechanisms are not mutually exclusive. The illustrations below come from Asch's interviews of subjects in his conformity experiments, from an attempt by Breger to study defenses against expressing hostility, and from Schachter's demonstration of the way in which a group actually uses its power against deviant individuals. Finally, we shall see an example (a study by Lipsitt and Strodtbeck) of the impact of social situations in which the nature of the effect was clearly dependent on relevant personality characteristics, in effect, an example of the interactive effects of contemporaneous social influences and developmental social influences.

There have been two main methodological approaches to the study of the mechanisms of contemporaneous social influence. One was initiated by Asch himself, and consists of attempting to obtain from the subjects through interviews a picture of the psychological processes occurring during the social pressure situation. The other consists of experimental attempts to evaluate the hypothetical conditions under which such pressure will or will not change behavior.

Asch interviewed each subject after the basic experiment described above, confronting him with the instances of his yielding to the group and seeking an explanation from him. When confronted with their mistaken judgments, some subjects admitted that they had realized the seven other "subjects" had been wrong; however, the unanimity of the "other subjects" made them experience severe distress about being deviant and led to yielding to the sensed pressure. Other subjects reported experiencing equal distress, but with such an array of evidence against them, decided that they somehow must have misunderstood the task. Finally, a small proportion of subjects expressed utter surprise at discovering their errors and reported not remembering any conflict or even being influenced by the other subjects. These interview responses suggest that there may be three quite different processes involved in this situation of social influence: (1) the threat of disapproval or rejection for being deviant, which a subject can attempt to cope with either by adamantly "sticking to his guns" in spite of the distress, or by volitionally knuckling under to the group; (2) the threat posed by doubts that one has correctly appraised the requirements of the task, leading to a search for confirmation or disconfirmation of one's judgment, and to yielding or nonyielding depending on the conclusion of the search; and (3) the resolution of threat by a kind of denial or repression in which the person accommodates perhaps without even being aware that he has done so.

Many experiments have been performed with one or the other of the above mechanisms in mind. One by Breger (1963), for example, has emphasized the *defensive personality characteristics* of yielders as implied in the third alternative above. He reasoned that yielding or conforming individuals should also have difficulty expressing hostility, because yielding to social pressure and inability to express hostility both represent ways of coping with the threat of social rejection. Breger's subjects were female college students who were placed in a situation not unlike that presented by Asch. However, unlike the Asch procedure, and to increase the numbers of subjects that could be tested, the confederates were never actually seen. They were presumably seated behind partitions, and the subject thought he was overhearing their judgments through an error. In addition to yielding scores, the hostility expression of each subject was also assessed in two ways. One measure of hostility was based on fantasy. The subject told a series of stories in response to a set of pictures (a test called the Thematic Apperception Test that will be described in Chapter 7). The contents of the stories were scored for overt and covert hostility. Overt hostility was inferred from stories that contained references to arguments, anger, fighting, revenge, murder, etc.; covert (or covered-up hostility) was inferred from story references to sickness, deaths, and accidents (where harm is not so obviously intended as it is in themes of overt hostility).

The other measure of hostility was based on behavioral reactions to a two-person situation involving instructions to perform a boring task under unfair criticism. The subject could overtly express his hostility to this mistreatment without prodding by complaining or directing angry remarks to the experimenter; or, if he did not do so, a confederate urged him by saying in an angry voice, "Boy, he makes me mad; having us do that stupid thing, and then telling us we're wrong. Doesn't that get you?"

Subjects' reactions or comments could then be evaluated as to hostility. Overt hostility might be conveyed by such statements as, "I'd like to slug him," "I don't need this," or "I could drop it," etc. Covert hostility can be conveyed by such statements as, "I feel like I'm mentally retarded or something," or, "I'm very nervous; my hands are shaking," etc.

Breger found that those who yielded to the social pressure expressed less overt hostility, and showed more covert hostility, than subjects who remained independent of such pressure. This was evident both in the story-telling projective test, and in the behavioral response to the experimenter's abuse. The findings as reflected in the story-telling task for those who yielded, those who were independent, and those who were in-between are illustrated in Table 5.

Breger's conforming or yielding subjects do seem to have personalities disposing them more than nonyielders to avoid expression of hostility and to favor repressive-avoidant forms of coping with conflict situations. It is not clear, however, whether the process of coping by yielding takes place without awareness on the part of such a person. It could be seen, for example, as a deliberate and conscious attempt to ingratiate oneself with others in the group, although this is not the interpretation favored by Breger. Moreover, although defensive activity may constitute one of the mechanisms involved in yielding to social pressure, research has also implicated the other two mechanisms noted earlier. Our choice of Breger's study as an illustration was based on the concern with personality-oriented research as the subject matter of the present volume. A text emphasizing social factors might well have chosen studies focusing on other conditions such as the use of secret or open reporting, the numbers of "real" subjects and confederates, and other social aspects of the conformity situation that have been researched. The determinants of yielding are complex, some of them residing within the person and others in the social context.

The belief that deviating from social standards is apt to be punished has a realistic basis, as was demonstrated in a classic experiment by Stanley Schachter (1951) showing how groups exercise their *power* over individuals. An ingenious experimental situation was created to test what might

Table 5

Conformity and Hostile Expression

CONFORMITY GROUPS	NUMBER OF CASES	EXPRESSED HOSTILITY	COVERT HOSTILITY
Independents	22	5.18	2.68
Middle	35	4.46	3.31
Conformers	22	4.00	4.55

Adapted from Breger (1963, p. 253)

happen to the deviating individual. By advertising, Schachter created a number of "natural" groups made up of college students who wished to engage in discussions about current social issues. At their first meeting he asked each group to discuss and give judgments about a court case involving a delinquent who was shortly to be sentenced for a criminal act of which he had been found guilty. The group had to decide whether to recommend clemency or strong discipline to the presiding judge. The case was so presented that a position in favor of clemency would be the predominant reaction.

Into this setting, and following in the tradition of Asch's use of confederates to create different social structures, Schachter introduced three types of accomplices, each trained to behave in a particular fashion. One always adopted the dominant position of the group and stuck to it throughout the discussion. A second always began by taking a deviant position from the group, but later was won over by the group's arguments. A third took a deviant position and maintained it regardless of the social pressure to do otherwise. Many such groups were created in this research study.

In the early stages of the discussions, Schachter found that the group usually directed intensive conversation toward the deviant, presumably in an effort to convert him; but as time passed without change in his stance, the members of the group ceased to communicate with him, thus tending to isolate him from social contact. When asked to evaluate the members to determine who would continue to participate in later discussions, the group also rated the deviant as less acceptable than the other types of confederates. Perhaps most revealing of all, the consistently deviant individual was less often elected to important committees, and when he was elected or nominated for an administrative function, it was more often to an unimportant committee where labor without power or influence was involved. These latter findings are schematized in Figure 14 which shows the frequency above or below chance expectancy with which the deviant was nominated either for the unimportant correspondence committee, or the important executive committee. Schacter's research highlights one of the important ways in which the social group influences the individual, that is, by controlling rewards and punishments and acceptance or rejection.

A final experimental illustration of research into the mechanisms of contemporaneous social influence is a study by Lipsitt and Strodtbeck (1967) which moves the problem one step beyond the separate manipulation of either situational social forces or personality traits by combining both in the same study. Essentially, the experiment involved the assessment of subjects' personality characteristics and exposing them to one of four versions of the court transcript of a jury trial. Employed were 380 male naval enlisted personnel between the ages of 18 and 29. Sex-role

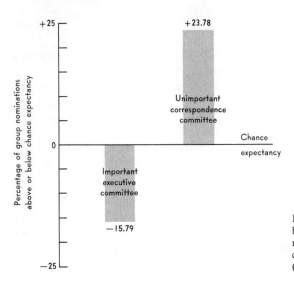

+25 ⌐

Unimportant
correspondence
committee

+23.78

Percentage of group nominations
above or below chance expectancy

0

Chance
expectancy

Important
executive
committee

−15.79

−25 ⌐

FIGURE 14. Percentages above and
below chance of assignments of "deviate"
members to important and unimportant
committees. Adapted from Schachter
(1951, pp. 190–207).

ıdentities of these men were assessed first for "unconscious" sexuality by
means of a projective test. The test required the subject to complete each
of a series of incomplete drawings consisting of a few simple lines by
drawing them into any kind of picture they chose. The projective drawing
test was scored by experienced judges on the basis of a variety of criteria
for male and female symbolic expressions. For example, expanded drawings were scored male, while drawings left open were judged female.
Active objects, such as motorboats or steamboats, were scored male, while
passive objects like sailboats and containers were scored female. The criteria were clear enough to make it possible for the judges to achieve a high
degree of agreement in judging. The overall score for this test was conceived by the authors as a measure of covert or *unconscious* masculinity
or feminity, the assumption being that subjects would not be aware of the
trends in themselves communicated in their drawings.

A second method of assessment was also used, consisting of a questionnaire to which the subjects responded with true or false answers, and
which presumably revealed the subjects' *conscious* sex-role identification,
since the implications of a large proportion of the questions could be seen
through. Some examples include: "I want to be an important person in the
community"; "I prefer a shower to a bath"; and "I would like to work as
a dress designer." On the basis of both test results, subjects could fall into
one of four types, unconscious feminine-conscious masculine, unconscious
masculine-conscious feminine, conscious masculine-conscious feminine,
and unconscious masculine-unconscious feminine.

The experimental task consisted of listening to the transcript of the
trial in order to make a decision about whether the accused was innocent
or guilty. The accused was a former American soldier being tried for
treason as a result of alleged activities while he was a Japanese prisoner
of war after the fall of Corregidor in 1942. During the actual trial the

130

judge had allowed the introduction of testimony about the defendant's alleged homosexuality on the grounds that it related to the character of the defendant. (On appeal, it was held that this testimony was irrelevant and prejudicial.) The judge had also made a controversial "charge" to the jury containing the assertion that it was appropriate for the jury to consider the defendant's character in arriving at a verdict of guilty or not guilty. This original transcript was edited by the experimenters so as to create four experimental conditions. These conditions involved variations around two basic themes based on the emotionally arousing testimony about homosexuality, and the judge's controversial charge to the jury.

The four experimental conditions were as follows: The (ah) transcript serving as the basic case contained *neither* of the two types of touchy material. The (AH) transcript contained *both* the testimony about homosexuality (H) and the judge's charge to the jury (A). The (aH) transcript contained the basic case plus *only* the testimony about *homosexuality.* And the (Ah) transcript contained the basic case plus *only* the judge's *charge to the jury.* The stage is thus set to determine the extent to which the decision about innocence or guilt is influenced by the two types of emotionally loaded material acting on the various personality types. This was done by exposing subjects from each personality subgroup to each of the various experimental treatments.

Lipsitt and Strodtbeck report three particularly interesting findings. First, the (Ah) transcript, which contains only the judge's charge to the jury to the effect that the defendant's character is relevant to the judgment of guilt or innocence, produced an increase in the tendency of all personality types to find the defendant guilty. Evidently the judge's point about moral character being relevant to the verdict resulted in a more punitive stance in general.

Second, in the (aH) treatment where homosexuality alone was introduced, the personality group evaluated as *unconsciously feminine and consciously masculine* gave a greater number of guilty verdicts than would be expected by chance. Of that group, 87 per cent voted guilty, compared with a little over 50 per cent in the other groups. In effect, for this group, the introduction of homosexuality into the trial produced a distortion of the basic judicial issue. The authors suggested that this type of person with suppressed feminine impulses has learned to inhibit and feel punitively toward his own feminine tendencies, and hence does not hesitate to be punitive toward the defendant for his overtly expressed homosexuality.

Third, in the (AH) treatment condition, in which both the judge's charge and the homosexual testimony were included, the personality group identified as both *consciously and unconsciously feminine* showed a marked tendency to give not-guilty verdicts (15 out of 23 cases), compared with the other groups which tended to vote guilty (e.g., 11 out of 19 guilty votes in one group, 10 out of 12 in another, and 10 out of 13 in the third). The authors suggested that in these subjects their own conscious as well as unconscious homosexual inclinations led them to be especially sensitive to the accusation of homosexuality brought against another and used as evidence against his character; they overreacted to a sense of injustice which they felt was reflected in the impugnment of the defendant's character by an irrelevant consideration.

We must be cautious in accepting the assumption of the authors that the projective test scores measured unconscious sexual identification, while the questionnaire measured its conscious counterpart. The evidence for this assumption is weak, although it is one of the possible explanations for the finding of individuals who show a discrepancy between two different measures of the same trait, in this case, of sex-role identification. But even if this assumption is rejected, the study by Lipsitt and Strodtbeck provides strong evidence of the powerful influence on the decision process (judging guilt or innocence) of the manner in which the contents of the immediate social situation communicate with relevant personality dispositions. In other words, the effect of the stimulus (e.g., the homosexual evidence) clearly depends on the kind of person who responds to it, that is, the significance of that input for him. Although such a conclusion should be rather obvious, the principle underlying it is all too commonly overlooked in research on contemporaneous social influence.

The reader should also bear in mind that we have earlier spoken of two main types of social determinants, contemporaneous social influence and developmental social influence. The study by Lipsitt and Strodtbeck illustrates both at the same time, effectively making the point that the influence of the former clearly depends on the latter, and vice-versa. It is only for convenience and clarity that we separate them, since in life both are always operating simultaneously, one affecting the impact of the other. Let us turn then to developmental social influence which is the part of the problem more immediately relevant to the subject matter of personality.

Developmental Social Influence

How is the personality itself fashioned over a lifetime by the social system into which the child is born? To answer this, some variables of social structure need to be identified, since it is these variables which variously impinge on us as we develop, and along with the biological givens with which we are born, help shape our individual personalities. The task of analyzing the social structure of any society—that is, the ways in which people and their daily and life roles are organized—belongs mainly to sociology and cultural anthropology, and as one might expect, there have been many divergent proposals about how this is best accomplished. We cannot enter here into the debates about the best way of analyzing the social structure. In the discussion that follows, two broad types of social variables will be used to illustrate how society influences personality: the variable of culture and the variable of social class. As in our discussion of contemporaneous social influence, our first task will be to give some examples of the influence of cultural and social class variations on personality. Following this, we turn to theoretical analyses of how such influence is accomplished, that is, to the mechanisms by which personality is fashioned by variables of social structure.

CULTURAL INFLUENCES ON PERSONALITY

The interplay of personality and culture is potentially a vast topic, and interest in it among social scientists has grown greatly in recent years. This is attested to by the increasing number of books and journals that have been published reviewing the findings and methodological problems of cross-cultural research on personality.

Among the most interesting specific instances of this relationship are studies which have examined the patterns of psychopathology in different cultures and subcultures. Cultures vary greatly, for example, in their expressed attitudes toward alcohol and drugs; in the manner in which illness, death, and bereavement are viewed; in orientation toward emotional expression; in the role patterns of various members of the family, and so on. Such variations, in turn, influence greatly such disturbances as alcoholism and drug addiction, and physical and mental illness.

Let us begin with *alcohol* and *alcoholism*. Considerable differences in rates of alcoholism exist among various national and ethnic groups. As has been noted by Opler (1959), certain groups such as the Chinese in New York and the Italian and Jewish populations have an unusually low incidence of problem drinking. The Irish, in contrast, have a great deal of difficulty with drinking, and in this group personality disorder is very likely to be accompanied by alcoholism as well.

Heavy drinking is also very common among the Japanese, but the national attitudes toward drinking seem to permit drinking patterns that rarely lead to serious occupational and social problems, or to the personality deterioration associated in our society with alcoholism of the "skid row" type. William Caudill, an anthropologist with long experience in the Japanese culture, has written provocatively about this:

> It is striking that there is much drinking by men in Japan, and a great deal of male dependency and passivity, but there is little alcoholism as this would be defined in the United States. Some aspects of this question may be illustrated by a simple thing like a whisky advertisement in *Bungeishunju* (a popular monthly magazine) which says a great deal about attitudes in Japanese culture when it shows a pleasant old gentleman smilingly anticipating the pleasure of drinking the six bottles of whisky he has saved up, while

his gray-haired elderly wife kneels on the floor and counts her money. The caption reads, "To each his own happiness." Further understanding is provided by the fact that the wife in the Japanese family manages the money and, circumstances permitting, gives her husband an allowance on which to go out and do his drinking. It is not likely that such an ad, nor the cultural circumstances represented in it, would occur in the United States, and from this example it is possible to gain some appreciation of the influence of the cultural context on the patterning of instinctual gratification.

One might say reasonably enough of the above example that it is merely an ad in a popular magazine, although the ad gains a certain validity from the fact that it would not be likely to appear unless it were acceptable in the culture and useful in selling whisky. That such an ad, however, had its counterpart in behavior was brought home to me in the experience of several of my friends in Japan. I had one friend with whom I spent many evenings drinking and talking. He had a habit on one night each week of taking the allowance provided for the purpose by his wife in the family budget and going out to drink with his cronies. When he arrived home late in the evening his wife would meet him at the door, help him off with his shoes, prepare a snack for him in the kitchen, and then assist him to bed. Equally, I had another friend whose job entailed great responsibility and power. He liked to drink American whisky, and I would occasionally bring him a bottle as a gift. He saved these bottles and others, until his store amounted to several dozen. His plan was to wait until a suitable vacation period permitted him the leisure to drink them up. This vacation became a reality in the interim between one important job and another, and he was able to put his plan into effect.

These examples would seem to indicate that the Japanese man does not anticipate rejection from others because of his drinking and is less likely, at least through stimulation from this outside source, to feel guilty about his drinking (1959, pp. 215–16).

It is notable that in Japan the drinking pattern is evidently a highly disciplined one, in which drunkenness occurs during periods of leisure, rather than as a companion to the ordinary responsibilities of life. The Japanese man demands of himself a high degree of tension-producing discipline and responsibility, and he releases these tensions by explosive episodes of drinking at times and under circumstances that do not impair his functioning. In order to understand the varying patterns of drinking and alcoholism among different peoples, it is evidently necessary also to understand the diverse cultural values associated with them.

Reaction to *pain* and *illness* also varies greatly among different cultural groups. For example, interviews with Jewish-American and Italian-American mothers by Zborowsky (1958) have shown that mothers of both ethnic groups who had recently immigrated were overprotective and overconcerned about their children's health, compared with mothers from families who had lived in the United States for many generations and had become fully assimilated. The more recently immigrated also tended to exaggerate pain and respond to it emotionally, while the "Old Americans" were more stoical about pain and adopted an "objective" stance in reacting to it. Also consistent with the above are findings of Mechanic (1963) who noted that American Jews visited doctors and took medication much more often than either American Protestants or Catholics, even when their educational and economic levels were held constant. And in a study comparing Irish- and Italian-Americans, Zola (1966) observed marked differences between the two groups in their presenting medical complaints, even when the actual diagnosed disorders were the same. The chief complaint of the Irish-American group was more commonly centered around the eye, ear, nose, and throat, compared with other parts of the body in the case of Italian-Americans. Zola suggested that the symptoms of illness reflect the particular preoccupations and values of that culture. In support of this point, he noted that when the Irish and Italians in his sample were asked to identify the most important part of their body, more Irish than Italians emphasized the eye, ear, nose, and throat, thus making understandable their penchant for medical complaints centering around these bodily areas. Of course, the relationship could theoretically also go the other way round, with values about the body being determined by the nature of medical complaints, but this is not the way Zola has interpreted the direction of causality here. In any case, there seems to a strong relationship between a culture's values and its characteristic ways of dealing with matters of health and illness.

One of the most interesting examples of the link between culture and illness patterns may be found in studies by Singer and Opler (1956; also described in Opler, 1959) of the personality characteristics and symptomatology observed in Irish-American and Italian-American schizophrenic patients. Schizophrenia is the most serious and widespread of the psychotic disturbances, and Singer and Opler carefully examined through observation, case history data, and personality tests, 60 male schizophrenic patients in a mental hospital in New York City, ranging in age from 18 to 45. Half of the patients were Irish-American, half Italian-American, all of them varying from first to third generation Americans. Both groups were Catholic, comparable in education and socioconomic status, and had been hospitalized at about the same time. Thus, the only important way in which they differed was in their Irish or Italian ethnic background.

The choice of Irish and Italian ethnic groups to compare was based on clear knowledge about certain differences between them in family structure and personal values, differences which might be reflected in the specific manner in which the symptoms of serious mental illness might express themselves. For example, in the Irish family the mother plays a dominant and controlling role, whereas in the Italian family the father dominates and the mother defers to him. Moreover, in the Irish context, sexual activity is subordinated to procreation; sexual courtship is mild and extended in time, with marriage being long delayed and celibacy encouraged; sexual feelings are typically regarded as sinful and are a source of guilt. In contrast, in the Italian setting, sexuality is an accepted part of life and tends to be cultivated as part of the assertion of healthy maleness. In short, inhibition and delay of gratification and a maternally-dominated family are clearly emphasized in Irish culture, while in the Italian there is an expressive acting out of feelings along with a male-dominated family. On the basis of these cultural differences, Singer and Opler anticipated marked differences in the manifest emotional pattern expressed by Irish and Italian schizophrenic patients.

Marked differences in symptomatology conforming to the cultural differences were indeed found. The Irish patient was more inhibited and beset by fear and guilt, while the Italian patient was more emotionally expressive. Moreover, the Irish schizophrenics felt hostility keenly toward female family figures but largely controlled it, while the Italian patient tended to be more overtly hostile, aiming this hostility mainly at male parental figures. Alcoholism was a frequently observed symptom among the Irish and extremely rare in the Italians.

In these above examples and many more that space prevents citing, personality (as evidenced by patterns of psychopathology) is closely intertwined with the cultural context in which the person is reared.

SOCIAL CLASS INFLUENCES ON PERSONALITY

Societies of man, as those of many infra-human animals, tend to be organized into strata or hierarchical layers. Social classes form one of the most common of stratification principles. Since the research of sociologist W. Lloyd Warner (e.g. Warner and Lunt, 1941), it has been evident to social scientists that Americans arrange themselves in such social classes and usually recognize their position in this hierarchy when asked. Although the details of this early research need not concern us here, its most important message was twofold: (1) The manner of life and the values on which life was predicated vary as functions of social class. (2) Social class variations create rather strong barriers to social interaction among the members of each class. Such social barriers are of great sociological and psychological interest and suggest a tremendous disparity between the American ideal of social equality and the American reality of social stratification. Not only does social class influence who interacts socially with whom, but it also has a strong impact on such personality-relevant characteristics as motives, values, life styles, the ways in which people view themselves, via the life experience it produces and the manner in which parents rear their children. Social psychologist Roger Brown puts the matter pleasantly in the following passage:

The life style differences arborealize into the flimsiest trivia. Upper-class Americans like martinis before dinner, wine with dinner, and brandy after dinner; beer is a working-class beverage. The upper class likes a leafy green salad with oil and vinegar, while the lower class likes a chopped salad or head of lettuce with bottled dressing. If you are middle-class you say *tuxedo,* where the upper-class says *dinner jacket;* in England you say *mirror* where the aristocracy says *looking-glass.* If you, like me, give your trousers a little hitch when you sit down so that they will not bag at the knee, then you are quite irredeemably middle class (1965, pp. 132–33).

Naturally, the importance of social class differences lies not in the trivia of a few preferences, expressive styles, or the manner in which one handles his trousers when sitting, but in the major life values and patterns of behavior the person adopts. Each social class tends to live in given residential areas which are inhabited by people who share common socio-economic, educational, and occupational characteristics, and common attitudinal and value patterns, even to the extent of their voting behavior. For example, Robert Tryon (1955a, 1955b, 1959, cited in Krech, Crutchfield, and Ballachey, 1962) was able to predict with considerable accuracy (a correlation of $+.90$) the voting behavior of people of varying social class memberships in San Francisco in the election of 1954 which concerned a number of local and state political propositions. Through his surveys he found that given community areas were quite stable as places where people of given social strata would live. Some living areas were of "high quality" or exclusive, others comprised mainly less well-educated, skilled, and semi-skilled workers, and still others were made up of ethnic and racial minorities living in crowded and segregated neighborhoods. De-facto segregation of ethnic and racial groups in living areas and in school communities is all too well-known today to dispute. People who grow up in different sections will probably be exposed to, and develop personalities built out of different values and attitudes toward education, psychiatry, premarital and extramarital sex, masturbation, religion, and liberal versus conservative political thought, and have different degrees of access to medical and psychiatric attention and hence different life expectancies, to name some of the personality-relevant differences that have been found between the social classes.

What about barriers to social interaction produced by social stratification? Studies have clearly shown that voluntary social relationships such as friendship and marriage have tended to follow social class lines. For example, the social activities of 199 men in Cambridge, Massachusetts were studied by Kahl and Davis (1955). Each participant was asked to name his three best friends, and the social class (based on occupational levels) of all those named was then examined and compared with that of each informant. Those who were named as friends were generally in the same social class as the person naming them. In another similar research, Hollingshead (1949) studied high school students who were linked together in social cliques and found that they were usually of the same social class. For example, among the students who dated, 61 per cent belonged to the same social class and 35 per cent to immediately adjacent classes. Only 4 per cent were two classes apart. Hollingshead also showed that in New Haven, Connecticut where his surveys were conducted, marriages generally occurred within the same or adjacent classes. Although these studies are fairly old, there is no reason to assume that the relationship between social class and social interaction is different today.

Of all the life-style variations associated with social class membership, perhaps the most interesting and important concerns the manner in which children are reared, since to be preserved class variations must be passed on to subsequent generations by *childrearing* patterns. Striking class-based differences in childrearing have been found. These first came to the forefront following publication of a study by Davis and Havighurst (1946) which was based on data obtained in 1940. They found that middle-class parents were considerably stricter with their children than lower-class parents. The specific childrearing practices surveyed by these researchers reflected great interest in toilet training and weaning as a result of the impact of the Freudian theory of psychosexual development. Among other things, Davis and Havighurst observed that middle-class parents weaned their children and began toilet training earlier than lower-class parents.

The findings reported from Davis and Havighurst's research and those of others were believed for a time to reflect stable social class differences in childrearing. Then, over 15 years later, Sears, Maccoby, and Levin (1957) reported the opposite, that middle-class mothers in Boston were actually more permissive toward their children than lower-class mothers. What appeared to be a contradiction in findings was reconciled subsequently by Bronfenbrenner (1958) who suggested that the childrearing practices originally noted by Davis and Havighurst had actually changed over the ensuing years. He cited, for example, the content analysis by Wolfenstein (1953) of a bulletin on childrearing practices entitled *Infant Care,* published by the U. S. Children's Bureau over the years 1929 through 1938. In the 1930's, there had been great emphasis on regularity and the tendency to feed and arrange sleep times for the child by the clock. The dominant attitude was that one should never yield to the baby's resistance or demands, and that the parent must win out over the child in the struggle for domination. But in the next decade, the attitudes toward the child had totally changed. The child was now viewed as engaging in a valuable and harmless effort to explore his world, and was regarded as needing mainly benevolent attention and care. Parents were advised to give in to the child's demands in order to make him less demanding later on. The attitude had shifted from one of severeness and rigidity to one of permissiveness and flexibility.

Why had the social class differences originally observed by Davis and Havighurst also changed? The answer is not clear. The inference is made by Bronfenbrenner that the literate and educated middle-class mothers and fathers of the 1930's and early 1940's had been strongly influenced by the mass media and the books written by professionals in the mental health and child-care fields. It was largely the educated middle-class parents who read these publications, an example of which is the tremendously popular book by Benjamin Spock, *Baby and Child Care,* which epitomized the relaxed attitude toward raising children. This doesn't explain, however, why professional workers changed their view of childrearing or whether they were even responsible for the change among the laymen. Perhaps the middle-class professional members of society merely went along with the dominant and changing social view. In any event, there had been a shift in the middle-class value system, a shift which is today reflected in the fact that deviant youth groups, such as Hippies and political activists, seem to come mainly from the relatively affluent middle-class, rather than from lower-class society. The influence of the "Protestant Ethic" which emphasizes discipline, self-control, and the postponement of gratification had greatly weakened among the middle-class, post-depression, post-World War II children. As for the lower classes, it is possible that they have not yet caught up with the middle class. That is, the lower classes have absorbed the original middle-class standards of yesteryear (of the 1920's), and have not yet cast them off as the middle-class has done. And they are still trying to gain the economic and social advantages which have been taken for granted by the ensuing generations of the middle class.

In the modern era when communication of standards has tended to shift from magazines and books which require high literacy and education, to television which brings essentially similar messages about childrearing to middle-class and lower-class mothers alike, the social class differences once noted may tend to disappear altogether. It is also possible that the same leveling process could occur across cultures as they become less isolated from each other, thus reducing the bond between culture and personality, too.

It is tempting here to ask the question about the relative superiority of permissiveness or authoritative approaches to childrearing, but such a question requires an analysis of the qualities of personality that one values, as well as more information about the effects of these approaches on personality. There is no scarcity of opinion. Elsewhere we have noted the allegation that the types of mild psychopathology seen in clinics had shifted from mainly neuroses in Freud's day to mainly character disorders today, implying that the shift from strong authority to permissiveness in childrearing had been responsible. But such statements tend to be based on rather casual impressions rather than on hard data.

Nevertheless, the question is of great interest to the layman and to researchers in the field of child development. For example, Diana Baumrind and A. E. Black (1967) at the Institute of Human Development of the University of California have recently reported some results of an eight year study of three groups of nursery school children. She found that parents who were most warm and permissive produced children who were the least self-reliant, exploratory, and self-controlled. On the other hand, the children of authoritarian parents were discontented, withdrawn, and distrustful. The middle group, whose parents were controlling and demanding (Baumrind called this authoritative after Fromm), yet also warm, rational, and receptive to the child proved to be the most self-reliant, exploratory, self-controlled, and content with themselves and in their relationships with others. Thus it would appear that neither extreme of authoritarianism or permissiveness results in the actualization of many of our positively valued traits of personality. Studies along these lines offer some promise of establishing through empirical data the childrearing practices that promote those personality traits we most highly value, regardless of their association with some given social class. In any event, it begins to be clear that childrearing patterns within social class groups are not at all rigidly fixed.

Consideration of childrearing practices as a function of social class variables illustrates another point of great importance to the social scientist concerning the levels of analysis dealt with by different disciplines in their theory and research. Social class is essentially a sociological variable, that is, it deals with the manner in which societies of people are organized, rather than with individuals per se. The point becomes clearer if we consider for a moment how social class membership might affect personality development. Social class is an aspect of the social system, and it is only at the points where such membership confronts and affects the individual person that we can understand its impact psychologically. If the behaviors of mothers do not differ as a function of social class, or if the individual's experience does differ if he belongs to one or another social class, then social system variables such as social class have no psychological implications. Childrearing practices are an important dimension of developmental social influences because the social experiences of individual children are the social basis of personality formation. Social classes are of interest to psychologists because persons growing up within them are likely to be influenced in predictable ways, although not all mothers are affected in the same way by such variables, and it is the individual mother's behavior toward the child that in the final analysis is one of the critical social variables of developmental social influence. This problem of levels of analysis has been explicated most effectively by Smelser and Smelser (1963). The core of the problem of developmental social influences is to be able to identify past experiences of the individual person, whatever they may be, and however they may be related to the social structure, that help to produce a given personality which, in turn, reacts in the present to a social event.

The Mechanisms of Social Influence on Personality

The key idea, of course, is basically very simple—the person acquires through his social experience the norms or standards of the society in which he lives. Thus, for example, the child growing up in a middle-class family in the 1920's and 1930's is likely to have had very different experiences with discipline than a child growing up in the same era in a lower-class family. Or, a black child will have a very different set of experiences relevant to the development of a concept of himself than a white child. Not only does each of us grow up in a particular culture and subculture (including social classes, ethnic groups, regions, urban or rural settings, etc.), but each person has a particular set of parents; thus, every child's family will have its own distinctive characteristics as a social unit. But to complicate things even more, even the parental family unit is a combination of two distinct people, the father and the mother, each with a unique personality and value system. It is no wonder that each person becomes a distinctive individual, in certain ways like no other individual, even if we were to ignore the matter of individual differences in biological makeup. We need to know the rules by which such variations produce distinctive kinds of individuals, and the basic idea that we acquire the standards of the setting in which we live is too general to allow us to understand the process of social influence on personality development.

There are two main psychological mechanisms which have been proposed by theorists concerned with the socialization of the child. In both cases the child's parents are the primary agents since they are usually the main adults in contact with the child at the early critical stages of personality development; however, the mechanisms apply equally well to any social figures with whom the child has a close functional relationship. One mechanism emphasizes the learning principle of reinforcement; the second assumes some form of identification in which the person takes over the attitudes and behavior patterns of someone else. We shall discuss each separately.

SOCIALIZATION THROUGH REINFORCEMENT-LEARNING

This principle states that we learn whatever directly results in the reduction of tension or pain, or the production of satisfaction. The values and behavior patterns of parents and other, significant adult individuals are said to be acquired by the child because these adults systematically employ rewards and punishments to shape the behavior and attitudes of their children. Earlier, we saw a social analogy of this sort of reinforcing power relationship in the experiment by Schacthter (1951) on the manner in which a social group punishes an individual for being deviant.

The theoretical principle of reinforcement has been more important and probably has had more support among psychologists over the past half century or so than has any other alternative method of explaining learning and development. When an animal is rewarded for making certain responses, there is an increasing tendency for him to continue to make that response again in the same context. Likewise, when a person is rewarded for behavior by things he wants, such as money, praise, good grades, etc., his tendency to do whatever it was that led to the reward in the first place is increased. Conversely, punishment for undesired behavior, such as speeding in one's car, making too much noise in a library, stealing, fighting, and so on, tends to result in the inhibition of such behavior in the future. As a very general rule of thumb, our behavior is, indeed, controlled by whether or not we anticipate that it will be followed by a positive condition of tension-reduction or a negative condition of pain or harm. One of the clearest formulations of this principle was offered some years ago by Miller and Dollard (1941) in a book entitled *Social Learning and Imitation.* A modern version may be found in Aronfreed (1968). Reinforcement in the shaping of behavior is also strongly emphasized today by psychologists interested in behavior modification, a point of view which is exemplified by the recent text of abnormal behavior by Ullmann and Krasner (1969).

However, the effects of negative reinforcement or punishment in "stamping out" responses are far from simple or clear, even in simpler organisms such as the rat and the pigeon; and reinforcement adherents who have dealt with complex situations by no means adopt a single-minded conception of its role in the development of personality. Its effects are clearly dependent on the conditions under which reinforcement has taken place and the complex mix of variables to which the person is exposed in any new situation. Although reinforcement is of great importance in guiding human behavior and in the development of personality, it has become increasingly evident that, because it was the only major principle for so long, it has been considerably overextended as the basis of learning.

A particularly good example of the insufficiency of a simple reinforcement principle may be observed in efforts to train persons to control aggression. The outcomes of these efforts are sometimes contrary to expectation. For example, reinforcement-learning principles imply that the parent who severely and consistently punishes the child for aggressive acts will eventually stamp out the undesirable behavior—the child is continually reinforced negatively for his aggression, and positively for inhibiting it. Nevertheless, it has been observed that delinquents and criminals are likely to have physically cruel, rejecting parents, and to have been subjected to much punishment in their childhoods. Punishment alone has not stamped out their aggressiveness and deviancy—quite the contrary. Sheldon and Eleanor Glueck (1950) had earlier suggested that delinquents were unimpressed with punishment because they had had so much experience with it from their rejecting parents. And more recent detailed studies of the family backgrounds of delinquents by William and Joan McCord (1956, 1958) provide further evidence that the violently aggressive delinquent has typically been severely rejected by his parents and often brutally beaten. This retention of the pattern of aggressive disobedience in such boys despite frequent and severe punishment is embarrassing to a strict and exclusive application of the reinforcement-learning point of view, and suggests that other forms of learning (e.g., by imitation) must evidently be involved.

Brown makes this point in the following passage:

> Parents who beat their children for aggression intend to "stamp out" the aggression. The fact that the treatment does not work as intended suggests that the implicit learning theory is wrong. A beating may be rewarded as an instance of the behavior it is supposed to stamp out. If children are more disposed to learn by imitation or example than by "stamping out" they ought to learn from a beating to beat. This seems to be roughly what happens (1965, pp. 394–95).

The effects of punishment probably depend greatly on a host of other factors as well, such as its consistency, the joint use of reward when appropriate behavior occurs, the attitude (e.g., love or hate) with which it is given, the concept on the part of the child that he can or cannot control the occurrence of the rewards or punishments by his actions (i.e., nothing he can do seems to make any difference), the values of peers toward the infraction, whether the object of the punishment is a boy or girl, and so on. The complexity of the problem of childhood discipline and its effects is apt to be unrecognized by the lay person, but is strongly emphasized by many writers in the field of child development who have reviewed the research evidence (e.g., Becker, 1964).

SOCIALIZATION THROUGH IDENTIFICATION

The basic idea in this type of mechanism is that we take on behavior patterns and values on the basis of seeing them in others and imitating or modeling them. Various terms have been used to refer to this type of process, such as identification, internalization, introjection, modeling, and socialization.

It is important to recognize that when someone else's behavior or values are copied this can be done with varying degrees of attitudinal involvement. Social psychologist Herbert Kelman (1961) has suggested several degrees of such involvement with "compliance" representing the weakest and "internalization" representing the strongest. For example, we can act in *compliance* with the values of the other person without having actually taken on these values as one's own. This may be done only to obtain a favorable reaction from the other, as when the attitude being expressed is privately disagreed with or when we laugh at a joke without thinking it funny. In *internalization,* another's influence is accepted and made one's own because it is intrinsically rewarding to do so.

When Freud spoke about identification, he meant an unconscious acceptance of the parent's values, with these becoming a deeply ingrained part of the person's own system of values. The term identification or internalization usually implies more than a "skin deep" acquisition or show of behavior. Rather, it is an acceptance of it as one's own, sometimes without the recognition that it is being done.

There are four variations of the identification principle referring to different theoretical bases on which the process rests:

1. The identification is said to take place on the basis of the *similarity* of the person to the object of identification. Thus, in the Freudian system, the boy normally takes on the values of the father (and conversely the girl takes on those of her mother) partly because of the boy's perceived similarity to the father—he is marked by everyone as a boy who will ultimately take over the father's role—and he perceives his sexual similarity to the father as being masculine (e.g., having a penis) rather than feminine. Freud attempted in this way to explain not only the mechanism underlying the adoption of the moral values of the parents, but at the same time, to explain sex-typing, that is, the tendency of the boy to adopt a masculine role and the girl to adopt a feminine role.

2. Identification is considered to be based on *envy* over the possession of the good things of life. In effect, the child is more apt to identify with those adults whom he sees as possessing the important good things of life.

3. Identification is thought to be based on the *power to contr* the disposition of the good things of life.

4. Identification is based on the need to *neutralize threat* from some powerful person. This is the form of identification which was most emphasized in Freudian theory, and has been referred to by such psychoanalytically oriented writers as Bruno Bettelheim (1960) as "identification with the aggressor." You will remember that in Freud's psychosexual theory the boy represses his sexual (Oedipal) urges toward the mother and his hostility toward the competitor-father in order to avoid the danger of castration. In doing so, he internalizes the father's values, becoming like him. This process of *identification with the aggressor* in Freudian theory is the main basis for the formation of the superego or conscience. Bettelheim gives some striking examples of identification with the aggressor in the

behavior of concentration camp inmates during World War II, and Elkins (1961) suggests the same sort of mechanism for the American Negro slave. Such identification forms one of the meanings underlying the expression, "Uncle Tom." It implies the adoption (perhaps unconscious) of the white man's values by the black in an effort to curry favor or feel secure in the white man's world. Such identification stems from the powerlessness of the person (the child, the concentration or prison camp inmate exposed to "brainwashing," and the Negro slave) that makes him feel too threatened to express any indivuality. Crucial to this sort of mechanism is absolute control by the powerful parent figure over rewards and punishments.

In recent years a growing number of studies have been designed to compare some of the alternative mechanisms of socialization which have been touched upon above. One of the best recent experiments has been performed by Bandura, Ross, and Ross (1963), who created four kinds of models for identification to occur, each representing a slightly different basis of identification. One adult model controlled a wonderful collection of toys, another adult was the fortunate receipient of them, a third model consisted of a child who watched without getting anything, and a fourth model was a child who received the toys just as in the case of the second adult. Each of the models was made to engage in some actions which could be easily imitated, and the experimenters observed which model was copied by the child. It was found that the subjects (all children) imitated mainly the adult who controlled the toys, rather than the other models. Thus, it would seem that control over resources rather than possession or consumption of them served as the basis of imitation or modelling in this experiment. And although imitation and identification are not equivalent concepts, perhaps some of the same conditions underly both.

Other research has attempted to compare the relative potency of reward and punishment compared with identification in the control of behavior. However, the data are as yet too limited to permit very definite conclusions, and in all probability, both identification and reinforcement mechanisms are involved in most life situations. The complex character of the mechanisms underlying socialization is very well summarized in a recent statement by social psychologist Roger Brown:

> Parents can affect the behavior, the conduct of children in at least two ways: by direct reward or punishment and by providing a model for imitation. It now looks as if power were the prime factor making a model attractive for imitation though such facts as nurturance and vicarious rewards may also be important. With two parents to manifest power and administer direct reward and punishment there are many possible kinds of family patterns, many kinds of learning problems presented to children. For some kinds of behavior, for example speaking the local language, all forces work in the same direction. Both parents model English and both reward for it. For some kinds of behavior the pattern will be complex, for example assertive-

ness. Perhaps father manifests considerable assertiveness and has more power in the family than his non-assertive wife. Perhaps both parents reward assertiveness in their son and not in their daughter. Both children might be expected to try out being assertive on the model of their impressive father and the son's performance would be confirmed by approval but the daughter's would not be. Does the daughter perhaps retain a desire to behave assertively, a latent identification with her male parent, that leads her to try out assertiveness in new groups where the reinforcement program may be different? Learning by identification is certainly a complex geometry and it is likely that what we now know is not more than the rudiments (1965, p. 401).

SOCIALIZATION AS PASSIVE OSMOSIS VERSUS ACTIVE DIGESTION

In recognizing how much we acquire from the social environment in which we grow up, we must not forget too that only certain things are taken from any adult figure to be part of our personality, while other things are rejected or ignored. Remember that we do not emerge as identical or perhaps even very similar to either of our parents. As we mature we pick up some of the values of each parent, and reject others. When we say that a boy is like his father, we are correct but tending to ignore the many ways in which he is also different; and when we say a boy is different from his father, we are also correct but tending to ignore the many ways in which he is similar.

There is a very important implication of the above qualification, namely, that a person is an evaluating organism, sifting through and selecting those models with which to identify, and those attributes to adopt as his own. As Brown (1965) has observed, the best concept may be that of active digestion, not of passive osmosis. In osmosis, one tissue passively soaks up the substance on the other side of a semi-permeable membrane, as a sponge soaks up fluid. There is no judgment and little selectivity involved in the process, only an automatic absorption of that which can pass through the membrane filter when the pressure is greater on one side than the other. In digestion, some things are accepted and transformed or altered by the system through catabolic processes; other things are rejected, depending on whether they fit the requirements imposed by the biochemistry of the substance and are capable of the metabolic transformations produced by the enzyme action. In the socialization of the person, the parental or societal values are not automatically absorbed, but are selectively dealt with, and we know very little about how this actually works.

The latter model of socialization, implying evaluation and selection, is rather clearly implied in the work of Piaget (1948) and his followers (e.g.,

Kohlberg, 1963) on the acquisition of morality. In the young child, moral concepts are indeed at first rigidly and quite passively drawn from parents and other adult authorities. Such rigidity corresponds to the relatively primitive, sensori-motor stage in the development of adaptive intelligence. Piaget showed how preadolescent children follow strictly the "rules of the game" as laid down by adults even when it would make more sense to do otherwise. Wrongdoing is seen literally as the violation of rules, rather than in terms of intentions, abstract justice, or the ultimate objectives of the game.

However, beyond about eight or so years of age, the child's conception of morality becomes increasingly psychological rather than objective, relative rather than absolute, and capable of being modified on the basis of group decision. Such a change in the process of socialization corresponds to the growing emphasis on conceptual rather than concrete, stimulus-centered forms of thought. The person becomes increasingly a thinking, judging individual, active in his search for useful principles, rather than a passive receiver of what the culture imposes. He thus becomes increasingly capable of picking and choosing those things with which to identify and those things to reject.

One wonders to what extent the values a person has acquired more or less passively in the early stages of development remain with him as permanent unconscious "gut reactions," so to speak, and are merely overlaid with the more rational and flexible qualities that Freud called secondary process thinking and Piaget referred to as conceptual modes of thought. Psychologists commonly make the distinction between the primitive, or developmentally early layers of mental activity, and the more advanced and later ones. Whether basic identifications formed early in life are ever lost or ever cease to influence our adaptive life, is not very clear. The idea that they are not lost is one of the cornerstones of the psychoanalytic approach to psychopathology. The current vogue of seeking contact with the more primitive and inaccessible aspects of one's experience through drugs or dyonesian forms of therapy or group activity, such as in Esalon and Synanon, stems from this assumption of two levels of psychological functioning—the impulsive, primitive, and unconscious, and the controlled, rational, and surface mental life. It is argued that the search for understanding of oneself requires contact with this primitive portion of one's mental life. In any case, the process of identification may involve both of these levels of mental activity, each operating in accordance with somewhat different rules.

In this chapter we have seen how social influence works in two areas of psychological functioning, contemporaneously, and over the developmental life history of the person. These are not separate and independent problems, since the mechanisms of immediate social influence not only operate at each moment, but also help us account for the formative processes that shape the personality over the long run. Thus, for example, the processes of identification and of reinforcement are undoubtedly occurring to the person in each social situation. These same processes, taking place over the life span of the person, comprise a cumulative story of social experience that has produced his particular personality. Once the personality begins to be established, then along with contemporaneous social influences, it too affects the person's social action and reaction. Thus, the latter two sets of influence, that is, the social siutation and the personality structure are crucial determinants of the person's behavior from the very first moment that the personality begins to form. The study of one is incomplete without consideration of the other.

Biological Versus Social Determinants: The Principle of Interaction

All personality theories concede that man is a biological organism and that he has some inborn nature, although the exact nature and mode of operation of this inborn nature clearly present a controversial issue. A major difference among personality theories lies in the relative emphasis given to that nature. Some points of view give heavy weighting to the biological givens, and the role of these in shaping personality and adjustment, while others virtually ignore biological forces and stress the role of experience and the structure of the society. We shall see below a number of examples of this continuum of emphasis from the biological to the social in specifying the determinants of personality.

Freud, for example, was a neurologist who had already made some important contributions to that field. He took a position very close to the biological pole of the biology-culture continuum. He saw culture mainly as the unfolding of man's biological nature; the variations in culture were less significant in his eyes than the universal features of all cultures emerging as a result of these biological givens. The psychosexual stages were seen as clearly biologically determined universal patterns to be found regardless of the social system in which they developed. Social systems themselves were outgrowths of these biological forces. It was not the child's experience which motivated the psychosexual transition through the sequence of pregenital forms of libidinal expression—such shifts were the products of biological maturation, and the developmental sequences were presumably products of the hereditary genes of the species.

This strong biological emphasis was rejected or modified by other theorists of the neo-Freudian tradition. You will recall, for example, that although the neo-Freudians accepted the idea of biological givens, these were expressed in social terms; they spoke of the need for autonomy, belonging, identity, relatedness, etc. In most neo-Freudian works, in fact, the list of basic human needs tends to be expressed more in interpersonal terms than in tissue-centered terms. Thus, although they did not disregard biological givens, those givens were clearly oriented to man's social existence.

There is another way in which personality theories have turned their emphasis from the biological to the social spheres. It can be nicely illustrated with concepts of the Oedipus complex. Freud (e.g., 1957) saw the Oedipus complex as a product of biological forces which expressed themselves in certain libidinal drives and in the choice of love object. However, one of the neo-Freudians, Karen Horney (1937), has taken an opposite stand. She argued that the Oedipus complex was not universal, and furthermore, that when it appeared, its roots lay in the social structure of the family. Thus its causes were social, not biological.

According to Horney, the Viennese middle-class family was largely patriarchal, with the father controlling the power to dispense rewards and punishments. Horney saw the competition between father and son not as a product of libidinal urges toward the mother, but as stemming from the boy's envy over the father's social power. Though Freud was presumed correct in recognizing that the boy often wished to be in the father's place, except in rare instances such envy had nothing to do with sex—it had to do mainly with social roles and authority patterns in the family. In other words, in Horney's view the Oedipus complex is caused by certain types of social experience, rather than by biologically given, libidinal forces.

The same argument can be made with respect to each so-called *psychosexual stage*. They are all products of socialization. For example, the focus on anal activity is a product of bowel training taking place around the second year of life. Thus, the Freudian biologically-oriented argument is turned completely around by Horney who proposes that social experience rather than biological unfolding determines the observed patterns of development.

Cultural anthropologists have been greatly influenced by the Freudian developmental theory. However, Freud's biologically-centered view also presented some perplexing difficulties. Although the interest of the anthropologist lies in the diverse patterns of culture which may be found in different societies, Freud's biological emphasis seemd to imply that cultures were, at least in fundamental respects, more similar to each other than different. This made the differences among cultures seem trivial, since it left little room for anything more than superficial differences in the social structure. Nevertheless, some anthropologists adopted the Freudian position, and others accepted it with modifications. An example of the latter is Abram Kardiner (1939, 1949), who suggested that there were a number of basic variations among different social systems. He assumed that these came about through variations in the physical factors in the environment, such as geographic isolation, soil and water conditions, available food supply, climate, etc. Nevertheless, Kardiner supported the Freudian view by assuming severe limitations in the number of possible variations, constrained as they were by the biologically determined psychosexual forces.

According to Kardiner, to understand the interplay between the culture and the developing personality of an individual we must know the culture's child-rearing practices with respect to each psychosexual stage. If a culture demanded orderliness, conformity, and neatness, and enforced these principles rigidly, it would influence the outcome of the anal stage of child development so that widespread obsessive-compulsive personality tendencies would emerge in its members. A very different kind of personality would emerge from a culture whose approach to toilet training was easygoing and undemanding. Similar analyses could be made of the culture's approach to feeding and weaning and its resultant impact on the oral stage of development. In short, Kardiner viewed cultural variations as important determinants of personality because of the manner in which they facilitated or interfered with the normal psychosexual progression.

A much more socially oriented position is taken by Erich Fromm (1949), who rejected the psychosexual theory and, even more than Freud or Kardiner, regarded personality as a product of cultural forces. Fromm argued that cultural variations were not important because of their effect on the psychosexual stages, but rather because of their influence on the *atmosphere* of the parent-child relationship. For example, whether love and affection, or coldness and rejection are provided would have an important bearing on how the child handled its security and autonomy needs as it grew up. The pattern of parental authority was also important. A child's response to an autocratic parent is likely to be either excessive submissiveness to or complete rejection of authority.

The analyses of culture and personality offered by Kardiner and Fromm have, in recent years, been brought into question because of doubt cast on the concept of national or *cultural character*. The idea that most people of culture have a similar personality structure based on the cultural pattern seems far too much of an oversimplification. It is evident that great variations exist among the members of a given culture. Nevertheless, the basic ideas of Kardiner and Fromm, particularly as applied to individuals rather than the whole of a complex society, are still quite relevant to the general problem of how the social structure influences personality. The issues of theory and methodology of studying personality cross-culturally have been thoroughly examined by Singer (1961), who has also reviewed much of the specific modern research on personality and culture.

Even greater emphasis on the social origins of personality is found among those sociologists and social psychologists who emphasize the concept of *social role,* and exhibit little interest in the native biological conditions stressed so much by Freud and the neo-Freudians. In the case of the former, the fundamental units of analysis are the interactions of people and the effects of these interactions on the development of the person. Such interactions are largely governed by the organized social roles of the culture. Social institutions prescribe how a person must behave *(role patterns)* and how he should regard himself.

The writers who conceive of personality in terms of role theory and the interaction of self and role appear indeed to exhibit little interest in man's biological nature. They occupy a position closest to the culture pole on the biology-culture continuum. Yet, while their analysis is made at the level of social interaction rather than biological disposition, they must leave room for the universally recognized *interaction* of biology and culture in the development of personality (although they do not trouble themselves about it), just as the more biologically-oriented writers must accord some place (however small and underemphasized) for the effects of learned social experience.

One last point may be made about the general issue of the role of biological and social factors in the shaping of personality. In the light of modern knowledge it is altogether untenable to cast the issue in either-or terms. Even in the lower animals, instinctual behaviors that were once thought of as invariant and fully determined by neurological and hormonal mechanisms turn out to be quite dependent on both environmental controls and biological processes. An excellent illustration of this may be found in the research of ornithologist Daniel S. Lehrman (1964) on the reproductive behavior cycle of the ring dove. When male and female ring doves are placed together in a cage with a glass bowl and some nesting materials, an extremely predictable reproductive cycle is observed to take place. First comes courtship, with the male strutting about, bowing and cooing at the female. After some hours, the bowl will be selected as the nesting site. The male gathers nesting materials and brings them to the female who stands in the bowl and constructs the nest. After a week or so, during which time copulation has taken place, the female appears to become highly attached to the nest and is very difficult to dislodge from it. About seven to eleven days after the courtship began, the female produces the first egg, typically late in the afternoon, and then another one in the morning. The male takes a turn sitting, and both birds alternate. In about 14 days, the eggs hatch and the young are fed by the parents from a pouch in their gullets that secretes a liquid food. At 10 or 12 days of age, the young leave the nest but continue to beg for food until they are about two weeks old, when the parents begin to refuse to feed them and the young squabs learn to peck for grain for themselves. This refusal tends to terminate the cycle, but it will begin again almost exactly as before when the young are about 15 to 25 days old.

Lehrman has conclusively shown by his experiments that each stage in the reproductive cycle is dependent upon the proper stimulation from other parts of the cycle as well as from environmental stimulation. For example, a lone female lays no eggs; a lone male has no interest in nesting materials, eggs, or young. If a male and female are kept in isolation and then brought together in a cage with nesting materials and with eggs already laid, they do not sit on them but act almost as if the eggs were not there. However, they do proceed through their own reproductive behavior cycle, beginning to court, to build their own nest, to lay eggs, etc. Only then will the eggs be sat on. The steps in the sequence are all important, each one having to take place before the next one follows. Although the instinctual behavior is, indeed, partly controlled by neurological and hormonal processes within the animals, these processes in turn are set off by specific environmental stimuli, such as the effects of the presence and behavior of one mate on the endocrine system of the other. These stimuli must be present at the right moment for the instinctual behavior cycle to unfold.

In more general terms, even in the rather automatized, so-called instinctual behavior of the simpler animals, there is a constant *interaction* between biological and environmental forces. One does not act independently of the other; both interact, or mutually influence each other. At the human level, the newborn child arrives in the social world with a considerable assortment of tempermental characteristics or dispostions which influence how the social environment will react to him; and in turn, the social environment affects the manner in which the biological maturation will take place. An excitable, irritable infant may be an exhilarating experience for an energetic parent, but a source of intense annoyance and stress for the lethargic parent. Conversely, the lethargic child might bore the former parent, but not the latter; or such a child might need the kind of stimulation which the energetic parent could give. And the irritable child might profit better from parental handling which screens and protects him from overstimulation. In all probability, such parental reactions brought into being by the child's inherent characteristics, will in turn act on the child, too, in molding his development.

Such *interactions* between biological and social forces suggest the limited scope of an analysis of personality which is based on an either-or point of view concerning biological and cultural determinants. In the discussion of biological factors one must bear in mind that half of the story of the determination of personality is being neglected; and in the discussion of social factors, one must remember too that such determinants always operate in the context of a particular biological system. The only valid reason for separating them is for convenience and simplicity of presentation.

The Assessment of Personality

chapter seven

Research in personality depends on two types of activities: 1. the evolution of fruitful theoretical concepts about personality and 2. the measurement of the qualities of personality postulated in such theory so that empirical observation and experimentation on the constructs can be pursued and theories evaluated. Without a science of assessment, there could be no science of personality, any more than geology, for example, could exist without an empirically based system for differentiating rocks, or biochemistry without methods of distinguishing between biochemical substances.

The task of assessment can be conceived in two ways, first, the measurement of individual attributes or traits which comprise the personality structure, and second, the assessment of the "whole" person with emphasis on the integration of the individual parts. After all, an adequate psychological description of a man is arrived at not just by mentioning one or two characteristics, but by drawing a broad, complex picture of that person, i.e., covering a wide and representative range of his functioning, and tapping the depths of his resources for managing the unusual as well as the routine demands of living. The latter task depends on our ability to accomplish the former.

From a somewhat skeptical point of view, the assessment of the "whole" person might be described as a rather vague goal. One might ask, for example, when or whether we ever adequately describe a man physiologically. At what point does a medical chart succeed in capturing the essence of one's health? Description of multiple dimensions of personality is at least a quantitative increase from the description of a single dimension. But those who argue for the assessment of the "whole" person seem to be saying that this is not merely the addition of dimensions, but a qualitatively different step in which an organized system is somehow better captured. Anyway, assuming that it can be done in a fashion distinguishable from merely adding dimensions of description, attempting to capture the "whole" person is certainly far more ambitious than measuring a single quality. Furthermore, it would be an approach particularly compatible with psychologists of an idiographic bent, while assessment of individual traits would seem to be favored by nomothetically oriented psychologists. Moreover, in spite of this sort of distinction, most personality descriptions are relative, that is, to be meaningful they must be stated in a way that permits comparison with other individuals. Both kinds of approaches are also subject to common, basic principles, the outlining of which is the major task of this chapter. We shall use the term assessment to refer to both the measurement of single traits and the description of the "whole" person, but the reader should keep in mind the presumed distinction.

Assessment or measurement of personality traits depends on getting samples of a person's behavior, either in a natural life setting or in a contrived laboratory situation. We have seen many examples of this in the research on personality illustrated throughout the earlier chapters of this book. Quite obviously we are not just interested in the particular situation in which the observations are made, but rather in generalizing from that situation to others to which the person is likely to be exposed, and which we are not likely to be able to observe directly. Not only must our observations of the behavior as it occurs in the assessment situation be accurate, but it is of vital importance that generalizations to other contexts also be possible. The field of assessment utilizes some special principles which concern the above goals of accuracy and generalizability.

Principles of Assessment

There are three basic concepts on which the technology of assessment is based, "standardization," "reliability," and "validity." These should be reviewed before specific techniques of assessment are considered.

STANDARDIZATION

When observations are made of how a person behaves, such as in a test of how much information he has or of the extent to which his blood pressure rises when he is insulted, these observations must be evaluated. If one wishes to compare one individual with others, data are required about how others act in similar situations. This makes it possible to say whether, for example, the individual in question is more informed or easily aroused than others, less so, or somewhere in between. Data of this kind are called "norms"; they are standards which permit interpretation of the behavioral attribute measured in any given individual.

The normative data may come from the general population, or some particular portion of the population against which one wishes to compare the individual under study, say men, women, people in a given age bracket, those who have a given level of education, people living in cities or suburbs, and so on, depending on what the relevant comparison is that one wishes to make. For example, if we wanted to know whether a man's blood pressure is normal, we would need data on the blood pressure of other men. However, if the man in question is 50 years of age, and the group from which the norms are obtained averages 20 years of age, we are almost certain to judge the man's blood pressure as deviant because we know that blood pressure increases with age even in perfectly healthy persons. Therefore, a more appropriate normative sample for such an evaluation might be other men of the same age. A great deal depends on the kind of question we are asking, and from which the evaluation is to be made. There may be many normative samples rather than only one, each used for quite different purposes. An individual's behavior can be understood and interpreted only if there are appropriate norms or standards about other persons for comparison (inter-individual standards), or norms for that individual on other occasions (intra-individual standards). Interpretive statements about how fearful, dependent, effective, happy, or whatever, the person is, depend on such standardization data.

RELIABILITY

There are two basic kinds of reliability concerned with (1) the representativeness, stability and generality of the behavior sampled, and (2) the degree of agreement between observers.

Representativeness, stability, and generality of the behavior sampled. Total observation of the person in every situation to which he is exposed would provide the assessment psychologist with the most complete raw data from which to form a conception of his personality. Obviously, however, this would be an impossibility even for a close relative to accomplish. It took one pair of psychologists 435 pages of a book to record in some detail the activities of a seven-year-old boy during *one day* of his life, and not even completely at that (cf. Barker and Wright, 1951). Considering the multitude of events, imagine the task of documenting through observation the whole life span of an individual, or even important experiences over so limited a time period as one year! The Library of Congress could not store the data, and no individual could hope to absorb even a small portion of it. For this reason, assessment must be based on a very limited sample of a person's behavior, often as limited as one particular test situation, or perhaps a few such situations lasting only a few hours.

Since inferences about personality are made from a limited sample of observations, three aspects of reliability become especially significant in assessment. One concerns the *representativeness* of the sample. One may ask, for example, whether the reactions observed on a particular day are typical of that person, or vulnerable to fatigue, changes in mood, etc. If they are vulnerable to such factors, then it will be hazardous to make inferences based on one or two observational samplings. Second, the behavior in question may not be at all *stable* even in the same type of situation, in which case the measurements will change from one occasion of testing to another. A behavior could be essentially stable, yet show marked variation as a function of mood or fatigue, in which case reliability will be low except when such mood or fatigue variables are controlled. Finally, reliability also involves the *generalizability* of a behavior from one type of situation to another. An observed behavior could be representative and stable in one particular type of situation, but disappear or change in a different situational context. If the testing is done over several such contexts, it will appear most unreliable.

An attempt to evaluate a person's intelligence by means of testing provides an excellent illustration of these three components of reliability. If the test is repeated several times, the score on the test would undoubtedly vary on each occasion, perhaps a great deal (low reliability), perhaps only slightly (high reliability). This variation could be the result of any or all of the several components, lack of representativeness of the score, lack of stability of intellectual functioning, and poor generalizability across different situations. An example of the first would be variations in attentiveness during the testing; second, intelligence might vary with age, and if there were a fundamental lack of stability in intellectual performance, then keeping fatigue or attention constant would still fail to produce a stable score in a child at different times of life. Finally, intelligence measured by verbal tests might be quite different when measured by performance tests; and a person who does very well when tested individually (and given support and encouragement) may do poorly in group testing situations. Of course, low reliability could also result from inadequacies of the measuring instrument, errors in scoring, etc., which represent still a different level of explanation of low reliability.

When reliability is low, each testing will produce its own score, and it must be determined which of these scores is the "true" one, that is, the one which most nearly represents that individual's hypothetical ability. The more variable such scores are (that is, the more unreliable the performance on different occasions) the less is the confidence that can be placed in the accuracy of our assessment of the individual's intelligence. We often assume that intelligence is intelligence no matter what the circumstances. This is only so in a very relative sense, and for many personality traits it would be a marked exaggeration. In fact, it is appropriate to say that *any* personality trait is manifested only in a specific range of stimulus situations, or in particular contexts. Some may occur over a wider range than others, but no trait would be expected to operate all the time.

Agreement among observers. Reliability with respect to observers is concerned with the accuracy of their observations, description, and interpretation of a behavior sample, rather than its representativeness, and it is evaluated by the degree of agreement among the observers. If the behavior of the subject under study is variously described or interpreted, then one has no way of knowing which, if any, of the descriptions or interpretations is correct. Such inaccuracy could derive from many causes. Observers may selectively observe or emphasize different aspects of the complex behavioral event, remember it differently, or see it in a different light. Thus, for example, in judging hostility from a person's response to some remark, one observer may view an angry statement as an instance of defensiveness in a vulnerable individual who is easily threatened, while another may see the same statement as evidence of unwarranted hostility.

The use of permanent and objective records of the behavioral event, such as a tape recording, motion picture film, or videotape, tends to reduce errors of memory and to eliminate some of the distortions that stem from the inability to review the same event a second time to confirm an original impression or to check on it in the context of later events. Even a half-hour recording of a complex social event, however, is filled with too much material to keep clearly and objectively in mind. Inevitably the whole record must be compressed into a limited number of abstractions and interpretive judgments which add to the likelihood of variations in the characterization of the events by different observers.

Two solutions are possible: 1. The types of behavior which serve as the focus of attention may be intentionally limited so that little or no observer judgment is required. A prime example of this is the "objective" test of personality, where the subject need only answer each item with a simple "yes" or "no" response. Since the response alternatives are very few, there is little or no problem of observer reliability. 2. Effort can be made to train observers so that the criteria used in their observations and interpretations are clear and agreed upon, and then to demonstrate the degree of agreement among their judgments. In this event, the judges are the measuring instruments, and if they cannot agree about the behavior episode in question, then little of scientific value can be done with their observations. Such disagreement is similar to a defective bathroom scale which at one time shows a man's weight as 150 pounds and at another time records the same man's weight as 200 pounds. Clearly this variation is beyond the limits of usefulness. Since inferences about personality often depend on elaborate patterns of social behavior in complex situations, adequate observer reliability is one of the most fundamental requirements of personality assessment.

VALIDITY

Whatever observation or measurement technique is employed in assessment, it must be shown to be valid to justify its use, that is, there must be evidence that it measures what it purports to measure. This is surely self-evident. Therefore, to move from the banal to the significant we must first recognize that there are several kinds of validity, depending on the purposes of the assessment and the kinds of evidence on which the validity is to be judged. Two main varieties can be distinguished, "criterion-related validity" and "construct validity." Criterion-related concerns whether one sample of behavior, say that obtained on a test, is correlated as claimed with another sample of behavior obtained at the same time (concurrent validity), or obtained later (predictive validity). Construct validity deals with a trait that cannot be directly observed, but is a theoretical construct that can only be conceived or identified through inference from some behavior. Often it is merely a creative hypothesis about a possible process which connects a series of otherwise unrelated events. Thus, in construct validity, interest centers on a theoretical (hypothetical) quality of the person (the construct), and validity refers to evidence that this quality can justifiably be inferred from some behavior sample or test. The distinction between the two types of validity can be illustrated concretely by examining briefly an example of research on each.

Criterion-related validity. One of the best illustrations of a successful empirical effort by psychologists to predict one form of behavior from another (i.e., *criterion-related validity* of the predictive type) comes from the work of Alfred Binet and Th. Simon in France at the turn of the last century. As there was a practical need to identify students who could not profit from schooling, Binet accepted the task of attempting to find ways of predicting school performance in Parisian children. He joined forces with Simon who had already been working on the problem, and in collaboration they selected a variety of tests requiring imagery, memory, comprehension, judgment, and reasoning, and gave these to school children. Binet and Simon's experiments, reported in 1905, demonstrated, first, that performance on these tests improved with age, and second, that it was substantially correlated with independent estimates by teachers of the child's brightness, and with his school grades. Later, a modified and standardized version of the Binet-Simon scale was developed by Lewis M. Terman (1916) at Stanford University, and it became the Stanford-Binet, probably the most highly regarded test ever made for the measurement of intelligence.

Remember that we have been speaking of criterion-related validity which refers, strictly speaking, to the empirical question of whether one form of behavior can be predicted, or concurrently goes along with, another. However, the background of Binet and Simon's work also points up the fact that rarely is our interest in such validity *strictly* empirical or practical. More commonly, it starts from a theoretical question, or the theoretical question arises after it has been shown that two important behavioral variables are indeed related and we wonder about the mechanism of this relationship. In the case of the above research, a practical need generated the effort which, in consequence, could be readily separated from the more abstruse theoretical issues underlying the empirical relationship itself. Nevertheless, once we begin to use the word "intelligence" to identify the process or trait underlying the surface findings, we enter the area of interpretation or theory. By saying, in effect, that the behavior in question (in this case, performance on certain tests) is indicative of some inner psychological processes which we call intelligence, a theoretical construct (see Chapter 1) is introduced.

As it turns out, there had been interest in the concept of intelligence even before Binet and Simon did their practical empirical research. For example, a distinguished psychologist in the United States, James McKeen Cattell, had conceived of intelligence (mental ability) as being made up of basic neurological properties (e.g., the speed of nerve conduction) that determined how rapidly a person could make a response to a signal (reaction time). Cattell was one of the first to systematically approach the problem of individual differences. It seemed plausible to Cattell that the better adapted the animal the faster it should be able to respond to the environment. So he created a number of sensori-motor tasks based on this principle to test the "adequacy" of the nervous systems of different individuals. However, the principle was evidently wrong. A student of Cattell's, Clark Wissler (1901), correlated school grades (as one criterion of intelligence) with performance on Cattell's sensori-motor tasks and found they were not related. This left the field entirely to Binet and Simon who had correctly chosen complex mental tasks as their measure of intellectual functioning. Nevertheless, even today the definition and theory of intelligence are by no means settled, and there remains considerable controversy about its nature.

Although the distinction between criterion-related and construct validity is blurred in the case of Binet and Simon's work, as it is in most actual validity research, there are times when the most important thing is to determine the empirical question of whether one behavior is predictable from another, regardless of whether the process underlying the relationship is understood or even of great interest. When the focus of the research is on predicting some observable behavior, such as school grades, learning to be a pilot, becoming emotional, smiling, being a successful executive, voting for a given political candidate, purchasing an advertised product, or what have you, we speak of criterion-related validity; if the emphasis is on measuring some theoretically postulated quality of the personality such as intelligence, impulse control, strength of conscience, etc., then we speak of "construct validity."

Construct validity. As our main illustration of *construct validity,* we turn to some research aimed at evaluating a measure of the degree of "socialization" of the person. A questionnaire scale developed by Gough (1957) and called the California Psychological Inventory contains one section or subscale dealing with *socialization.* The questions cover a number of common social attitudes and ways of responding. Examples include, "Before I do something I try to consider how my friends will react to it"; "I often think about how I look and what impression I am making upon others"; "I find it easy to 'drop' or 'break with' a friend"; "I have often gone against my parents' wishes"; and, "If the pay was right I would like to travel with a circus or carnival." Gough interpreted these items as tapping in part the ability of a person to sense and interpret social nuances and subtle interpersonal cues. Therefore, a scale made up of these items could measure the extent to which a person would behave in accordance with social expectations, in effect, the extent to which the person has internalized the values of his society and was socialized. Construct validity requires evidence that the scale does, indeed, measure the theoretically inferred process implied by the construct. The emphasis here is not on prediction or empirical correlation, but on the theoretical analysis of personality, although of course, empirical correlations must be used as evidence about construct validity.

Certain strategies of research by means of which the construct validity of the test can be evaluated follow rather clearly. For example, theoretically speaking, differences among individuals in socialization score should be associated with the extent to which such individuals transgress social norms and behave in an antisocial fashion. The reasoning is as follows: if degree of socialization refers to the extent of internalization of social values, then the more socialized the person the less will he show evidence of antisocial behavior. Such a finding would support the interpretation of the test scale as socialization, while failure to obtain such data would throw the construct validity of the scale into doubt. A comparison was made by Gough (1960) of the socialization scale test scores of groups whose members had on the one hand been nominated as "best citizens," and on the other hand were disciplinary problems, county-jail inmates, imprisoned delinquents, and felons. There was a very strong relationship between score on the test and the chances that the individual belonged to a group either behaving deviantly or showing highly visible acceptance of the social norms.

Another research strategy to evaluate construct validity is to attempt to relate the test scores to personality traits which logically ought to be present on the basis of the theoretical interpretation. In one such study, for example, Reed and Cuadra (1957) showed that, as would be anticipated, persons with low socialization scores were less skillful in sensing and interpreting cues of social approval or disapproval. These researchers had student nurses describe themselves by means of a series of adjectives, and also to guess how other nurses with whom they frequently interacted would describe them. Subjects with high socialization scores were more successful at gauging the reactions of others than were those with low socialization scores. This type of construct validity research makes it possible to interpret with some confidence the trait which is being measured by a personality test in accordance with some theoretical orientation. Such efforts are fundamental to the development of tools for measuring individual traits of personality, and ultimately to the furtherance of the technology underlying assessment of the "whole" personality.

Although I have been speaking of the construct validity of a test, such as the socialization scale of Gough, strictly speaking, such an evaluation also relates intimately to the theory on which the construct is based. Construct validity is entirely theory dependent, that is, the interpretation of the test score hangs on whether the theoretical meaning of the construct is well conceived. Thus, if a test of socialization is constructed, for example, certain predicted relationships follow from how socialization is interpreted. That is, the anticipated antecedents or sources of socialization and, likewise, the expected consequences of socialization depend on how the concept itself is understood. Such theory provides the logical basis for the empirical deductions which can then be tested in empirical studies.

The above point means that if Gough's conception of socialization were different than it is, he would have expected that the trait would have different origins and effects than was actually assumed in his own research (e.g., Gough, 1960), and in that of Reed and Cuadra (1957) cited above. For example, if one conceived of socialization as a process by which an insecure and dependent person sought social approval by conforming to social norms, he might have predicted that imprisoned delinquents would act as they did when the norms were those of people they didn't care about, but under threat of disapproval by their peers or other persons with whom they identified, they would be expected to show a high degree of conformity to the latter's social norms. In short, their observed lack of socialization might be based on a set of social norms created by an alien society, rather than a set based on social groups whose approval they counted on. Thus, socialization would be a relative, rather than an absolute, thing.

The point is that the construct validity of a test is inextricably bound up with the validity (or at least serviceability) of the theory on which it is based. In effect, when the findings of construct validity research are supportive, they also support the theory on which it is based. When the findings are negative, they suggest either one or both of the following: (1) that the test does not measure the presupposed quality, or (2) that the theory is wrong, since it leads to inaccurate empirical predictions. Failure to obtain positive results often suggests that the theory itself be abandoned or modified. Thus, it is not entirely accurate to refer to construct validity research as though it had to do only with the validity of a test; it also involves the whole fabric of the theory as well. For the beginning student, this is a difficult idea to grasp fully. The interested reader is referred to one of the best and most complete discussions of the problem by Cronbach and Meehl (1955).

SITUATIONAL FACTORS AND ASSESSMENT

The natural bias of the personality psychologist has been to search for enduring personality structures or dispositions leading the person to act in certain ways regardless of the situation. The focus is thus on tendencies within the person which push him to behave as he does, rather than the external circumstances which pull him in one way or another. It is evident, however, that both forces are involved in any behavioral event, and to focus exclusively on the internal structure is to ignore the important other half of the story deriving from the impact of situations. It may be that personality assessment is moving somewhat away from the extreme trait orientation (cf. Mischel, 1968). Anyway, here is the key point: To the extent that situations do have substantial influence on behavior, then the attempt to forecast behavior on the basis of assessment procedures is bound always to face severe restrictions, since the situations to which the person will be exposed in the future can never be accurately known in advance, and these will to a large degree determine how he acts.

On what basis then can a prediction be made about future behavior from observed behavior in an assessment situation? One possibility on which assessment psychologists rely is that if enough is known about the person over a variety of situations, then inferences can be made at least about how he *usually* responds, assuming he shows some more or less typical pattern. Moreover, a concept can be formed about the classes of situations under which the person will act in such and such a fashion. For example, it may be observed that one individual tends to act defensively and apologetically in situations where he is criticized; another individual responds to the same criticism with anger and verbal attack. The prediction can then be made that in other situations of criticism, similar forms of reaction might be expected from the two persons. The accuracy of such predictions depends on the degree of generality of the disposition to react, that is, the range of situations over which such behavior may be expected, and this can only be determined empirically. Thus, a behavior forecast based on assessment should not be a wildly overgeneralized statement that the person will behave in some fashion in each and every situation, but rather a prediction limited to a given class of situations. Such a class should include situations that are "functionally equivalent" for that individual in generating either anger or apologetic behavior, as the case may be. The more evidence on which such an inferential concept is based, and the more clear and well-established its theoretical basis, the more accurately can the limits of the predictive generalization from personality assessment be established.

The keys to prediction are thus twofold: First, the inferences derived from an assessment should be based on well-established empirical evidence about how the person acts in a variety of situations in the past or present; second, such inferences should also be based on well-established theoretical principles about the situations which are functionally equivalent to those comprising the sample situations employed in the assessment sessions. In effect, we need to know for any given type of person what constitutes a threatening criticism, a loss, a sign of a safe social interaction, a rewarding experience, a source of joy, etc. Only then can we be in a position to expect that a particular situation in the future will call forth a specified reaction. This is no simple problem, and a great deal of research is required to provide the knowledge from which the keys can be fashioned. The general point being made above should be fairly obvious on reflection, but it is frequently overlooked not only by laymen who tend to think of assessment either in magical terms or as phony crystal-ball gazing, but also by psychologists who should know better.

More recently, some excellent research has been performed by Endler and Hunt (1968) in an effort to emphasize situational factors in assessment, and to pinpoint the proportions of variation in behavior which are the result of situational, as opposed to personality, dispositions. The sources of variation due to a number of factors on any test can be separated out and studied. Endler and Hunt's efforts have centered around two questionnaires designed to measure anxiety and hostility. The tests were designed so that subjects could indicate one of several forms of response defining both anxiety and hostility. In the case of anxiety, for example, these might include physiological reactions such as sweating or

trembling, subjective reactions such as feeling uneasy or inability to con-
centrate, and behavioral reactions such as sleeplessness or irritability. In
addition, these responses could be related to a number of eliciting situations, such as being criticized, meeting strangers, having to speak in public, etc. Similar categories of response and of eliciting situations were also
constructed for the hostility scale. Thus, there were three main sources of
variation in the subjects' answers to the questionnaires, the type of response, the eliciting situation, and a third which is always present in
assessment and is usually the main focus of interest, persons, that is, the
varying individuals making up the sample of subjects tested.

Some actual examples of the varied *situations* sampled in the *hostility
questionnaire* of Endler and Hunt were: "You are talking to someone and
he (she) does not answer you"; "You accidentally bang your shins against
a park bench"; "Your instructor unfairly accuses you of cheating on an
examination"; "You are very tired and have just gone to sleep, when you
are awakened by the arrival of some friends." One can see that the eliciting situations for hostility are quite different from each other. Variations
in the mode of *hostile responses* may be illustrated by the following examples: "Heart beats faster"; "Want to strike something or someone"; "Lose
patience"; "Feel irritated"; "Curse"; "Become tense."

Subjects were given the questionnaire materials to answer, analysis of
which involved separating statistically the extent to which the variations
in response were produced by persons, situations, and response modalities. In the hostility questionnaire, individual differences (personality) accounted for 15-20 per cent of the total variation in responses to the
hostility relevant questions, modes of response accounted for 14-15 per
cent, and situations accounted for 4-8 per cent (there was a sex difference
which need not concern us here). In contrast, in the analysis of the
anxiety questionnaire, the respective proportions of variation in response
were 4-5 per cent for persons, 25 per cent for modes of response, and 4-8
per cent for situations. Thus, the proportion of variation due to the mode
of the response and the personality of the respondents was not the same
for the trait of hostility as it was for the trait of anxiety—personality was
far less important in determining anxiety than it was in determining hostility.

Endler and Hunt's research begins systematically to recognize that the
assessment of any behavioral reaction depends not only on dispositions of
persons to react in some way, but also on the modality of the response
(e.g., verbal attack versus physical attack), and the situation in which the
behavior occurs. Until the rules concerning these and other respective
determinants of behavior are well understood, the assessment of such
traits as hostility and anxiety will inevitably be less accurate than required
for the effective forecasting of behavior. As we shall see later in the
discussion of structured tests, this point of view has led to new proposals

about the design of such tests in order better to identify the various stimulus sources of reaction.

Techniques of Assessment

In the earlier sections of this chapter attention was directed to basic principles of assessment. Now we turn to the specific sources of information which assessment psychologists employ, that is, the techniques through which sample behavior is obtained for observation and interpretation. We shall review four basic techniques including the life history, the interview, the psychological test, and a variety of procedures for obtaining and coding direct observations of behavior.

THE LIFE HISTORY

A life history is a chronological story about the main facts of a person's life and development. Its use is based on the assumption that the present personality is the product of a continuous process of development, with the events of the past linked to it functionally. The events of the past provide information about the influences and demands to which the person has been exposed and the manner in which they have consistently been managed. The emphasis is thus on the continuities between the past and present.

The process of obtaining a life history, either from an informant such as another member of the family, from objective records, or directly from the individual himself, raises the fundamental issue of the accuracy of the information which is provided. Even if such a history were obtained while the person is living it, so to speak, questions would arise about the objectivity and representativeness of the observations, questions we have discussed in the preceding section. However, since most life histories are obtained retrospectively, that is, they are based on the memory of the person or other informant about events long past, we should expect that there will be many inaccuracies. People forget details (sometimes even dates of birth or marriage) and embroider them (without necessarily realizing they are doing so) in order to present themselves or their loved ones in a particular light. More objective records, such as a birth document, a baby book, a school history, and police or military records sometimes provide useful checks on the factual data reported on by the informant.

There are two ways of looking at what the person reports about himself or others with whom he shares a close relationship: 1. The emphasis can be placed on the facts, on the grounds that we can best understand psychological development if we know the actual events which have shaped it. From this point of view, errors in reporting should be regarded as fatal to a correct understanding of the person. 2. In contrast, one may argue that it is not as important to know what actually happened, but rather how the person perceives the event. The reader will recall from Chapter 2 the distinction between personality theories such as that of Dollard and Miller (association-learning through reinforcement) which stressed the objective stimulus as the cause of behavior and development, and those of Rogers, Maslow, and Lewin (phenomenological) which stressed the role of the stimulus as it was subjectively apprehended by the person. Both points of view are important since discrepancies between the objective and subjective facts tell us much that is significant about the person, for example, the adequacy of his reality-testing, the reliance on reality distorting defenses which guide his decisions, etc.

Since the life history can be at most no more than a limited digest of the person's life, informed judgment about what is important in it is required. Different theoretical systems tend to emphasize somewhat different things and see the life events in different ways. It is no surprise, for example, when a Freudian is particularly interested in the events relevant to pregenital psychosexual stages, or when an Eriksonian seeks information about how the "identity crisis" of late adolescence has been experienced and handled. Personality theory provides an implicit roadmap by means of which the terrain of the life history is explored.

THE LIFE HISTORY AS A PERSONAL DOCUMENT

The life history is not only always a story about the person's life, but it is also often a personal document which has a special significance in assessment. A personal document, as defined by Gordon Allport, is "any self-revealing record that intentionally or unintentionally yields information regarding the structure, dynamics, and functioning of the author's mental life" (1965, p. xii). If a life history is obtained, as it so often is, by interviewing the person himself or by examining his writings or personal letters, it is also a personal document and subject to the principles applying to such documents.

Allport has enthusiastically supported the use of personal documents in psychological science in spite of the dangers of nonobjectivity and unrepresentativeness inherent in them. He argues that, "Since there are no facts in psychology that are divorced from personal lives, the human document is the most obvious place to find these facts in their raw state" (1942, pp. 143–44). By using such documents one can often observe longitudinal changes in the person which could almost never be observed directly. Moreover, the personal document, particularly when it is obtained with-

tained without solicitation, as in a person's personal letters or perhaps an autobiography, permits seeing the person in the context of his natural, whole life, rather than in an artificial laboratory setting. Although Allport recognizes the special problems inherent in the use of such documents in personality assessment, he considers the personal document to be a source of naturalistic information not usually available in any other way. Shortly before he died, Allport published an interesting book based on a series of letters written over a period of many years by a woman with the pseudonym of Jenny (1965), and in which he attempted to reconstruct Jenny's personality by examining these letters from the point of view of several different theoretical perspectives in personality theory.

Like any other method of assessment, the life history provides an observational base for constructing a picture of the individual's personality, for making inferences about his motives, the things which threaten or enhance him, the ways in which he characteristically goes about coping, how he has related to other people, or perceived himself in the world, depending on the qualities we regard as useful in conceptualizing a personality. Through descriptions of past life events, that is, the ways in which the person has lived his life, we get some sense of the traits of which his personality is comprised, and the continuities between such traits in the past, the present, and presumably the future.

THE INTERVIEW

The interview can be used in a number of different, but overlapping ways. For example, it can serve the purpose of assessment exclusively. Or, it can serve the function of psychotherapy. Or, it can be used to establish a working relationship with someone who is to be taught something, or to set the stage for providing him with information. Sometimes all of these functions may be combined in the same interview. It is notable, too, that the data of the life history is most often obtained by means of the interview technique, thus making the former somewhat dependent on the latter.

There is no technique of personality assessment more widely used than the interview, largely because it is the most flexible and revealing of human confrontations when performed skillfully and under appropriate conditions. On the other hand, this very flexibility creates a host of problems, all revolving mainly around the basic issues of reliability and the validity of the inferences drawn from the interview.

There are three key methodological problems.

1. Although the interviewer must get the person to *reveal himself candidly,* the interviewee is seldom fully prepared to do this, and commonly has little wish to expose himself fully to another person. Motivations for

undergoing an interview vary considerably with the individual and with the circumstances. Thus, the motivation to expose oneself is perhaps greatest in the case of the person seeking therapy. But even here, as Freud discovered, the patient comes with a prepared story that ironically is designed to present himself in a false light—he appears to resist exposing his vulnerabilities and defenses even though he has come for help. Perhaps the truth is not even known to himself, but has to be discovered in therapy. If revelation of one's own inner nature is so difficult even in the highly motivated situation of voluntary therapy, imagine the problem in the colder context of personality assessment! It is even more acute in severely hostile or evaluative contexts, such as when the person is being interrogated by an "enemy" or is being interviewed for employment.

There have been two basic solutions to this critical problem of motivating self-revelation. On the one hand, where it is feasible, efforts may be made to create an *atmosphere of acceptance* in contrast to evaluation, so that the individual need not feel so threatened by revealing himself Under these conditions, there should be less desire to conceal information about oneself, although the problem of lack of self-insight is not resolved by this solution. This has been the traditional approach of insight therapies as encouraged since the appearance of psychoanalysis, and its premises have been particularly well articulated by Carl Rogers (1942). The other solution is the *stress interview,* used for example where evaluation cannot be eliminated as the basic premise of the interview, as in the job interview or in interrogation of criminals or prisoners of war. The person is directly confronted with damaging material, either that he has opened up himself, or based on externally available evidence. The person is deliberately thrown off guard, caught in contradictions or insulted, and his reactions to this are carefully observed to test his "mettle," that is, to reveal his strengths and weaknesses. Used skillfully (and the problem of ethics aside) the stress interview can be a powerful source of assessment data under appropriate circumstances. It is another way of getting the person to reveal that which he might otherwise wish to remain hidden.

2. One of the most critical of the problems of the interview concerns the *representativeness* of the elicited sample of the person's behavior or thought. At the time of the interview, the person may be fatigued, apprehensive about something temporary in his life, happy, or unhappy, etc., states which are likely to change greatly from moment to moment. These moods and immediate preoccupations will influence the things a person talks about and the manner in which he does so. Unless he performs several interviews with that person, the interviewer has no way of knowing whether the interview's contents are representative or typical for that person. Interviews based on psychotherapy conducted over a long time provide one answer to this problem, but even here the

special relationship of treatment probably tends to shape the interaction in ways not necessarily typical of other social relationships.

3. Finally, the interview is a *two-way interaction,* with the interviewer having an effect on the interviewee, as well as vice-versa. These influences are likely to differ from one case to another, partly due to different skills and styles of the interviewer, but also because the interviewer is a person likely to respond differently to different people. One interviewer will stimulate talkativeness while another will inhibit it; similarly in the case of stimulating defensiveness or openness, liking or disliking, feeling threatened or at ease, etc. Interviewees will produce similar variations in the reactions of interviewers, reactions that feed back to the interviewee and influence the contents of the interaction. Therefore, if the same interviewer is assessing a number of persons and making comparisons among them, it is difficult to separate out of the mix the influence of particular personal qualities brought up to the situation by the two particular individuals who are party to the interaction. The solution in assessment research employing the interview is very costly, since it entails using more than one interviewer with the same subject in such a way as to determine the stimulus influence of the interviewer.

One of the unique features of the interview is that it permits two very diverse approaches to exploring personality structure and dynamics, each utilized simultaneously with one supplementing the other:

1. On the one hand, the person is asked to *introspect* about his life experiences, to present his own perceptions of them, to reveal his inner thoughts. One of the early schools of psychology, called "Structuralism," made systematic introspection its fundamental method for obtaining data on the nature of sensation and perception.

2. On the other hand, the person's words and acts serve as behavior to be *observed* and evaluated by the interviewer. In respect to the first, the subject is an active party to the exploration of his own mind, acting himself as an observer, as it were, as one who participates in life and also stands back and looks at himself. Existentialist psychologist Rollo May (1967) has suggested that this twofold and in a sense contradictory capability is man's most fundamental "dilemma," making him unique among the animal species.

Exclusive dependence on introspection poses some serious methodological problems in the search for knowledge about the mental life, problems which were touched on in Chapter I. And as was said, foremost among these is the possibility that a person will be unwilling or unable to reveal the nature of the important psychological processes which are taking place. A psychological approach which is entirely dependent on what the person says about himself is unable to differentiate between valid and confabulated constructions. This limitation led to the emphasis by modern psychology on the observation of behavior (what the person says is a form of behavior) from which the mediating psychological processes can be inferred. The behaviorally oriented psychologist does not take the contents of introspection literally to be true, but treats it as behavior to be interpreted. It is he who observes, rather than the person being studied.

Using both perspectives, the introspective and behavioral, the interviewer has access to what the person says about his experience and what he does behaviorally. One can be used as a check against the other. Thus, slips of the tongue, evidence of emotion, gestures, facial expressions, emphasis, characteristic styles of thinking—all these serve as additional information which can be evaluated when the interviewer makes his inferences, and he is right on the scene to detect these behavioral events, as well as to record the person's introspections about subjective states and processes.

In sum, used to its fullest advantage, the interview has qualities that set it apart from any other source of information. It can yield profound therapeutic consequences as well as information for assessment purposes. It provides a dynamic, two-person interaction in which the interviewer is both participant and observer. It has the tremendous advantage of enabling the interviewee to indulge in penetrating introspection, while at the same time, because of its face-to-face nature, permitting the interviewer to observe the subject's behavior as he introspects. These important qualities make the interview what is probably the most widely employed technique in personality assessment. More detailed general discussions of the interview may be found in Kahn and Cannell (1957) and Richardson, Dohrenwend, and Klein (1965).

THE PSYCHOLOGICAL TEST

Tests are ways of eliciting behaviors and introspections under standardized conditions. Much as in a laboratory experiment, in testing one attempts to control or exclude most of the irrelevant variables so as to focus on a limited number of conditions affecting the behavior in question. As much as possible subjects are presented with the same stimulus and similar background testing conditions.

There are many kinds of tests, but we shall consider only two main types here, structured tests and unstructured or projective tests. A more complete discussion of the topic of testing may be found in Cronbach (1960) and Tyler (1963).

Structured tests. These usually take the form of questionnaires. They are called "structured" by some assessment psychologists because they have limited and clearly designed alternative responses; for example the person must choose between a series of multiple choices, or answer each item as "yes," "no," or "cannot say." The task for the subject is thus

Table 6

Some Sample Items from the Woodworth Personal Data Sheet

PERSONAL DATA SHEET

Have you failed to get a square deal in life?
Is your speech free from stutter or stammer?
Does the sight of blood make you sick or dizzy?
Do people seem to overlook you, that is, fail to notice that you are about?
Do you sometimes wish that you had never been born?
Are you happy most of the time?
Do you find that people understand you and sympathize with you?
Would you rather be with those of your own age than with older people?
Do you nearly always feel that you have strength or energy enough for your work?
Do you feel that you are a little different from other people?
Do people find fault with you much?
Have your thoughts and dreams been free from bad sex stories which you have heard?
Do you feel tired and irritable after a day or evening of visiting and pleasure?
Do you suffer from headaches or dizziness?
Do you ever imagine stories to yourself so that you forget where you are?

From Woodworth (1918)

relatively limited and unambiguous, and observer reliability does not pose a problem.

Personality questionnaires first began to appear during World War I. The need to select emotionally stable men for military services led to the creation of a *Personal Data Sheet* by R. S. Woodworth (1918). Its 200 items dealt with the symptoms of neurosis, and this test became the father and the grandfather of a host of similar tests that later mushroomed. Examples of the items making up the Woodworth Personal Data Sheet are given in Table 6.

During the late 1940's, a wave of disillusionment about the usefulness of personality questionnaires built up, contributed to by critical reviews which raised doubts about the validity of these tests and the principles underlying them. Another factor contributing to this negative aura was the increasing impact on psychology (especially clinical psychology) of the Freudian and neo-Freudian concepts of dynamics. During this period projective techniques, seemingly more consistent with the "depth psychologies," became all the rage. Questionnaires, on the other hand, seemed superficial, easily "seen through," and incapable of tapping deeper layers of the personality. Not long after, a similar disillusionment spread to the projective techniques as well, as the claims about what they could do in assessment proved much overextended, and as clinical interest shifted from diagnosis to treatment.

Aside from a growing realism among professional workers about the uses and limitations of structured tests, and indeed about assessment in general, the most important developments over recent years have been

Table 7

Some Sample Items from the Minnesota Multiphasic Personality Inventory

SOME ITEMS CONTRIBUTING TOWARD A SCORE FOR HYPOCHONDRIASIS*

T   There seems to be a fullness in my head or nose most of the time.
T   Parts of my body often have feelings like burning, tingling, crawling, or like "going to sleep."
F   I have no difficulty in starting or holding my bowel movement.

SOME ITEMS CONTRIBUTING TOWARD A SCORE OF PSYCHASTHENIA

(OBSESSIVE-COMPULSIVE DISORDERS)

T   I usually have to stop and think before I act even in trifling matters.
T   I have a habit of counting things that are not important such as bulbs on electric signs, and so forth.
F   I have no dread of going into a room by myself where other people have already gathered and are talking.

SOME ITEMS CONTRIBUTING TOWARD A SCORE FOR PARANOIA

T   I believe I am being followed.
F   Most people inwardly dislike putting themselves out to help other people.
F   I have no enemies who really wish to harm me.

*Items labeled T and F are those which, when answered true or false respectively, contribute to a positive score in a particular diagnostic category. From Hathaway and McKinley (1943) by permission of University of Minnesota.

increased sophistication about underlying principles and the increased complexity of test design. Whereas Woodworth's (and most other questionnaires) had been a simple scale, designed to measure a single trait such as neuroticism, new scales came into being designed to measure a number of traits at the same time and provide a complex profile of the person. For example, in 1931, Bernreuter published a complex test with a number of subscales, and in 1943, one of the most important of this newer breed of personality questionnaires was introduced, the *Minnesota Multiphasic Personality Inventory* (MMPI) (Hathaway and McKinley, 1943).

In addition to having a number of subscales, the MMPI also made use of an important technique, first used by Hartshorne and May (1928), of having a series of subscales designed to detect attitudes tending to lower the validity of the subjects' answers. Efforts were made, for example, to measure the tendency of subjects to lie about socially unacceptable impulses and actions which most of us engage in from time to time, or to be excessively critical of one's shortcomings. The MMPI was also designed to distinguish between a variety of types of maladjustment, there being subscales differentiating persons tending to be hypochondriacal, hysterical, obsessional, paranoid, schizophrenic, psychopathic, depressive, etc. Examples of items from a few of the subscales are shown in Table 7.

One of the distinctive features of the MMPI is the manner in which it was constructed. Large numbers of questionnaire items were surveyed and reconstructed without explicit regard to theory concerning types of psychopathology. These items were then administered to many types of persons, known from their hospital diagnosis as hypochondriacs, obsessive-compulsive neurotics, paranoids, etc. Only those items were selected for the final scale that empirically differentiated one type of patient from another. For this reason, many of the items do not make obvious sense as bases for differentiating one form of psychopathology from another, although those shown in Table 7 were chosen as illustrations because they do make rational sense in connection with the three disorders represented there. In contrast, many other tests are designed more in the fashion of construct validity, by starting out with a conception of each type of disorder, or whatever property of personality is to be measured, and from this conception or theory, items are designed to tap the distinguishing traits. The MMPI is thus largely an empirically-derived, rather than theoretically-derived test, and as such represents a notable departure from the usual approach.

Other complex, structured tests have appeared since the MMPI, although the latter continues to be one of the most widely used in assessment research and clinical practice. Some of these newer scales, such as the California Psychological Inventory (Gough, 1957), or the Edwards' Personal Preference Schedule (1954), are designed to reveal personality traits not necessarily associated with psychopathology, as is the case with the MMPI. Each such test has its own theoretical background, standardization, and body of validation research.

There are some very new developments in the design theory of the unstructured test. While present tests such as the MMPI and the CPI attempt to measure broad personality traits, such as paranoid forms of thinking or degree of socialization, some assessment psychologists have argued that tests and test items should be focused on narrower, situationally defined traits. One influential thinker in this area, Donald Fiske (1963), has been quite critical of the adequacy of present-day personality tests, noting among other things that they have very limited predictive value or stability over time. He has blamed this, in part (cf. Turner and Fiske, 1968), on several problems.

For one thing, subjects taking tests interpret the meanings of the items quite differently, and use different strategies for going about the task of deciding whether an item describes him or not. The subject usually must indicate whether he "often" does something or other. Fiske asks, "How often is 'often'?" The process whereby the person arrives at his answer is not explicitly indicated. He writes, for example, "For instance, the question might be: do you find it difficult to give a speech before a large group? The subject can go about the process of answering it in several ways. He can compare this statement to his general picture of himself. He can recall one or several pertinent experiences and base his response on his memory of his feelings. He can also decide that an affirmative answer would be true for most people and therefore is true for him. (These are some of the processes discerned in reports from subjects responding to such an item.) Insofar as various subjects go about answering such a question in different ways, the task is not structured" (1966, p. 78). Such variations, says Fiske, decrease the adequacy of the test as a measure of some stable quality of personality.

Fiske recommends that the task of answering a questionnaire should be structured much more carefully and precisely, with specification in the item of the exact situation in which the behavioral reaction in question is presumed to occur. In effect, Fiske is saying that the so-called "structured tests" are really not structured enough. The reader will recall that Endler and Hunt (1968), cited earlier, were trying to do essentially this in their efforts to determine the contribution of situation, response modality, and person, to the variations in the subjects' questionnaire answers.

Present tests were designed to *ignore* as much as possible the situational context in which behavior occurs in order to tap broad personality dispositions to respond regardless of that context. Based on the line of reasoning advocated by Fiske, future tests would *emphasize* the situational context, their items tending to be specific to limited sets of situations and hence narrow in scope. Whether or not personality testing will move in the direction of greater specificity and narrowness, or remain oriented to broad traits or dispositions, is not yet evident. There is clearly a growing but unresolved controversy over the best model to use in creating structured tests of personality.

Projective or unstructured tests. These are tests designed to provide ambiguous stimulus situations to be interpreted by the person. The use of the term "projection" is related to, but has a slightly different meaning from "projection" as a defense mechanism where an unacceptable impulse is attributed to someone else. Since the projective task is ambiguous and wide latitude is permitted in the response, we may also call such tests "unstructured." The ambiguity of the stimulus and of the task set by the projective test decreases the extent to which the stimulus determines or constrains the nature of the response. Thus, for example, if a common, everyday object is presented to a person in full illumination, and he is asked to say what it is, little about his personality will be revealed by his answer. It is obviously a pencil, a book, a telephone, an egg, or what have you, and by and large everyone will agree on what it is. But if the illumination is reduced sharply, or the outlines of the object are disturbed, individual differences in interpretation will begin to emerge. With the usual cues missing, the stimulus will appear quite different to different individuals, and to give it meaning each individual must draw upon his own experience, preoccupations, and interests. He "projects" these things onto the ambiguous stimulus. This is why projective tests make use of materials such as inkblots, drawings, and photos of people in provocative but not entirely clear situations.

The projective test is particularly attractive to those who see psychopathology as the intrusion into rational life of primitive, unconscious forces. This is analogous to the way Freud (1938, 1953) viewed the dream and the slip of the tongue. Unconscious material was assumed to slip through the censorship of the ego to create the dream when the person was asleep, less vigilant than usual, or to appear as an unintended verbal slip revealing a hidden impulse or thought. The projective technique as it was originally conceived made use of the same principle. Interest in it was particularly stimulated by the importation from Europe in the late 1930's of the Rorschach Inkblot Test (e.g., Beck, 1930; Klopfer and Kelley, 1942), and the development in the United States of the Thematic Apperception Test by Henry Murray (1943). Three examples of projective techniques will be described here briefly, the Rorschach Test, the Thematic Apperception Test, and the Sentence Completion Test. These are among the most widely used projective techniques.

Ten inkblots comprise the stimulus materials of the *Rorschach Test,* originally selected out of many experimented with by its creator, a Swiss psychiatrist named Hermann Rorschach (1942). The subject looks at each of these blots one at a time, and indicates what they look like, resemble, or might be. The examiner writes down each response and later inquires about its location and its formal determinants, for example, whether the percept is seen as moving or stationary, the extent to which shape, color, or shading influenced it, etc. Interpretations of personality are made primarily from individual differences in the manner or *style* of going about the task, although the content of what is seen also plays a lesser role. Such interpretations are speculative, presumably based on normative data (some of it informal and part of the tradition of the test, and some of it formal) revealing how different kinds of people perform. An illustration of a Rorschach Inkblot is given in Figure 15.

Stylistic variations weigh heavily in the establishment of inferences about personality derived from performance on the Rorschach Test. For example, expressions of affect in response to objects that are seen, such as, "I despise them," or "How beautiful!", suggest repressive defensive modes, while qualifications, such as "It is not a very good version of a bat," or, "I can only see it if I stretch my imagination," suggest an obsessive-compulsive personality structure, someone who uses the defense mechanism of isolation or intellectualization. Such interpretations require research evidence of their validity, and much research effort has been devoted to this for every type of major interpretation Rorschach workers have suggested (with the consequent development of a very large literature).

A series of twenty ambiguous pictures and drawings comprises the

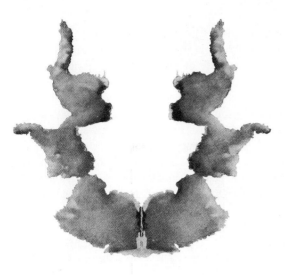

FIGURE 15. An example of a Rorschach inkblot. The picture that we project into inkblots like this one gives valuable clues to our thoughts and emotions. Hermann Rorschach, a Swiss psychiatrist, discovered that by carefully classifying responses to inkblots, he had a tool that could be used for the systematic study and appraisal of human personality (Rorschach, 1942).

Thematic Apperception Test (TAT), many taken from popular magazines, most of them dealing with men and women (sometimes the sex is not clear) in various settings and relationships. The subject is asked to tell a dramatic story, to spin a fantasy as it were, about some or all of the pictures. He is asked to indicate what the people are thinking and feeling, the events that have led up to the situation depicted, and the outcome. Although many of the pictures tend to stimulate particular types of story content (for example, some of the pictures are commonly seen as showing a father and a son, a mother and a son, a married couple, etc.), there is also great diversity in the story themes and details. It is assumed that the stories reflect the process of identification on the part of the subject with the characters depicted, thus revealing some things also about his own impulses, conflicts, sources of threat, etc.

Although the TAT is commonly used in the clinical setting in order better to plan a course of treatment, experimental versions have been created for purposes of measuring specific motivational characteristics of people. The best-known example is the research of David C. McClelland and his colleagues (1953) to measure *achievement motivation.* In their early studies, a set of pictures likely to elicit achievement-related story themes was created. Subjects were tested after they had been exposed to an experimental situation designed to induce achievement strivings, and after one designed to be neutral. In the achievement-arousing situation, some tests were given in an atmosphere of formality and seriousness, with

FIGURE 16.   One of the pictures used to elicit stories which are scored for achievement. From Fig: 3. 1. A. in *The Achievement Motive* by McClelland, Atkinson, Clark, and Lowell (1953). Reproduced by permission of Appleton-Century-Crofts, Educational Division Meredith Publishing Company.

the instructions that the subjects' performances would reveal their intelligence, capacity for leadership, and administrative ability. Subjects then wrote stories to pictures especially designed to be relevant to achievement themes. The same procedure was followed after the neutral situation in which the atmosphere was relaxed and unevaluative. The evaluative context produced more achievement-related imagery in the stories than did the relaxed, unevaluative context, and the difference was explained on the basis of the greater arousal of achievement motivation by the former context. A scoring system was developed to reflect this aroused achievement motivation, and later it was used for the purpose of differentiating persons with high and low dispositions toward achievement motivation, that is, achievement motivation as a personality trait.

This may be illustrated with two stories reported by Atkinson, the first reflecting a subject high in achievement imagery and presumably strong achievement motivation, the second low in achievement imagery. They were given to the specially designed picture displayed in Figure 16.

HIGH ACHIEVEMENT IMAGERY

This chap is doing some heavy meditating. He is a sophomore and has reached an intellectual crisis. He cannot make up his mind. He is troubled, worried.

He is trying to reconcile the philosophies of Descartes and Thomas Aquinas —and at his tender age of eighteen. He has read several books on philosophy and feels the weight of the world on his shoulders.

He wants to present a clear-cut synthesis of these two conflicting philosophies, to satisfy his ego and to gain academic recognition from his professor.

He will screw himself up royally. Too inexperienced and uninformed, he has tackled too great a problem. He will give up in despair, go down to the G—
—— and drown his sorrows in a bucket of beer (1958, p. 697).

LOW ACHIEVEMENT IMAGERY

The boy in the checkered shirt whose name is Ed is in a classroom. He is supposed to be listening to the teacher.

Ed has been troubled by his father's drunkenness and his maltreatment of Ed's mother. He thinks of this often and worries about it.

Ed is thinking of leaving home for a while in the hope that this might shock his parents into getting along.

He will leave home but will only meet further disillusionment away from home (1958, p. 697).

Both these stories contain considerable conflict. However, the first story is filled with evidence of intense striving against a standard of excellence (McClellan's definition of achievement motivation), expressed by the effort to tackle a difficult problem, gain recognition and ego satisfaction. The second story about the same picture contains no achievement theme; it is centered around a family conflict and a boy's efforts to patch it up. The differences in achievement-related content between these stories illustrate very well the use of the TAT type procedures in the assessment of personality variables.

It must be recognized that motives are not always directly expressed in storytelling as is implied above. Sometimes, particularly when such motives are proscribed in the culture or are unacceptable to the individual, they will be absent from the story content, although perhaps represented symbolically or indirectly (cf. Clark, 1952, 1955). The rules by which personality traits are expressed or inhibited from storytelling are themselves the subject of much research and theorizing by psychologists. This problem is particularly important to the psychologist adopting a Freudian approach to psychodynamics, because much of the impulse life which he seeks to explore is assumed to be unconscious or even repressed, and he can expect no simple direct expression of such mental content about which the person is deeply ashamed or threatened, as might be the case for socially acceptable motives such as achievement.

In the *sentence completion* projective technique, an incomplete stem of a sentence must be completed by the subject. The stem, for example, "I feel," "I get angry when," or "girls," suggests the basic theme of the sentence. It may be highly ambiguous as in the first example, or it may constrain to a high degree the kinds of responses that are possible, as in the second and third example above, that suggest aggressive and sexual ideation, respectively. This variation in the degree of structure or ambiguity is important, since in the more ambiguous items the subject can volunteer themes which are very pressing for him, while in the more unambiguous items the subject is confronted with certain themes which may disturb him, and he is forced to deal with them.

Sentence completion tests take many forms, depending on the interests of the assessment psychologist. They may be illustrated with one particular version employed by Michael Goldstein (1959) to differentiate forms of coping with threatening impulses. Goldstein has been concerned with two styles of coping which he refers to as avoidance and sensitization (or approach). *Avoidance* is reflected in sentence completions that consistently evade the content implied by the stem, while sensitization is reflected in an acceptance of the stem content and its further elaboration. An illustration of four items in the sentence completion test used by Goldstein, and the scoring of the items for avoidance and sensitization may be seen in Table 8.

Table 8

Sample Items and Responses (with their scoring) from Goldstein's Sentence-completion Test

1. *If I were struck:*
   - (2) I would hit back
     I would get mad
   - (1) I'd quit
     I would call for help
   - (0) by lightning, I would die
     I don't know

2. *The worst thing a girl can do:*
   - (2) sell herself or go willingly
     think about a male's sex
     have a baby before she is married
   - (1) lie
     slap a boy
     be stuck up
   - (0) go to a beauty parlor
     eat too much
     not be ladylike

3. *I hate:*
   - (2) my parents
     Mr. Jones
     my sister
   - (1) some people
     Democrats
     being called names
   - (0) snakes and wiggly worms
     pickles
     nothing

4. *A girl's figure:*
   - (2) is very important to me
     is to have fun with
     hard to keep your eyes off
   - (1) has a lot to do with friends
     should be feminine
     is pretty good
   - (0) is slim
     is not her personality
     I don't know

From Goldstein (1959).

In Table 8, low scores for each of the sentence completion stems are given for avoidance, while high scores are used for sensitization. Consider, for example, item 4, "A girl's figure." The obvious connotation is sex (heterosex if the subject is a male). The response, "Hard to keep your eyes off," accepts the sexual theme and elaborates it. The subject is saying in effect that he is attracted to a girl's body, in fact, so much so that effort is required to look away. This answer is given a high sensitization or approach score. Consider, however, the answer, "Is not their personality," or "I don't know." Here the sexual connotation is completely evaded, and this completion is given a low score implying an avoidance response. Research by Goldstein and his students on the two types of personalities, avoiders and sensitizers, has suggested that they behave in other ways consistent with his interpretation of these coping processes (construct validity). For example, avoiders dealt with threatening propaganda about dental decay by failing to remember the information given afterwards and failing to change their dental practices, while sensitizers behaved in the opposite fashion.

Before leaving projective techniques, we should mention the present day viewpoint of assessment psychologists toward them. In the early days of enthusiasm for this approach, projective tests like the dream were thought to be, in Freud's words, the "royal road to the unconscious." It has become increasingly evident however that projective test content, such as stories told to TAT cards, while conceivably influenced by unconscious, "primary process" mental activity, are mainly determined by "secondary process" thinking characteristic of mature and adaptive ego activity. In the TAT, for example, the subject is given stimulus pictures and told to tell stories about them. In the normal individual, the response is likely to be adaptive to the stimuli and to the social context—in general the stories match the stimulus objects to a high degree, the subject follows the instructions, and he is sensitive to the social limitations of the testing relationship. Thus, the analogy between primary process (primitive fantasy) and TAT storytelling is rather forced.

It is, of course, possible to score projective test content for primary process and secondary process activity, as Holt and Havel (1960) have done. However, it is no longer regarded as appropriate to regard the general productions of subjects to projective test stimuli as equivalent to primitive ideation or primary process thought as was once assumed. There has been a shift in viewpoint that coincides also with a change in emphasis in psychoanalytic thinking, too, from concern mainly with the motivational forces of the "id" to concern with the adaptive processes of the ego. Just as the views about structured tests have moved sharply from the oversimplified conceptions characteristic of their early beginnings, so have conceptions of projective techniques gradually evolved from naive and oversanguine early formulations, to a more realistic and modest set of notions about their value in assessment. As we shall see shortly, the chief criticism that can be leveled at such tests, and in fact all assessment devices, is that of extremely limited evidence of their validity.

TECHNIQUES FOR OBTAINING AND CODING DIRECT OBSERVATIONS OF BEHAVIOR

In the discussion of the life history and the interview it was pointed out that the assessment psychologist not only made use of the subjective contents reported by the subject or other informants, but that simultaneously the behavior of the person was observed as well in order to make sounder inferences about the psychological structures and processes in which he was interested. The same point should be made about the psychological test, particularly the projective test. Moreover, observations are sometimes made in the natural setting, as when we want to know how children act in school or with their families, or how men respond to captivity, or handle natural disasters, such as floods, tornadoes, bombings, etc. Other observations are derived by creating simulated life situations, that is, laboratory test situations, such as the use of simulated airplane or automobile controls which the person can operate to provide data on the learning of the basic skills involved in flying or driving.

In the usual laboratory testing situation, or in the naturalistic and simulated life setting from which behavior is elicited and interpreted for assessment, techniques are needed that will increase the reliability of the observations to be made, and that permit coding the complex behavior into manageable and theoretically useful analytic categories. Not all of the behavior that takes place is equally relevant or interpretable, so such techniques are necessary to aid the assessment psychologist in his observational and interpretive task.

Two procedures have become especially important in this regard, the rating scale and the Q-sort. The *rating scale* formalizes the interpretive judgments of observers, whether the behavior is obtained in interview, a psychological test, in a naturalistic or simulated life setting. It permits each of the observers to translate his impressions of the subject's personality, or of his behavior, into roughly similar quantitative terms. In this way, one person can be compared with another on a common scale, and the judgment of two different observers on the same subject can also be compared on the same scale.

Most commonly, rating scales consist of lists of traits or characteristics which observers must evaluate on the basis of the behavior they observe. Such scales are as variable as the kinds of behaviors and traits in which assessment psychologists are interested. Sometimes the subject himself does the rating, as for example when he is asked to describe the different feelings he experiences while watching a movie. An illustrative self-rating scale is shown in Table 9. Note that although these scales have been designed for the subject to rate his own feelings, they could equally well be used to enable several observers to estimate another's sociability, tranquility, impulsiveness, or energy.

The *Q-sort* is designed to make possible certain statistical treatments which are difficult to perform properly with most rating scales because the psychological distance between each of the numerical ratings is unknown. For example, in the scale illustrated in Table 9 it is impossible to say whether a rating of 5 on the subscale dealing with "energy versus fatigue" means that a person is half as energetic as one with a rating of 10. The numbers are not like those we use for weights and heights—these can be added, subtracted, multiplied, and divided without distortion of their meaning.

In the Q-sort, a person is given a set of statements describing himself or someone else, and he must sort these statements into consecutive piles, each pile varying (as in all rating scales) in the degree to which the statement is descriptive of the person. However, unlike the usual, simpler rating scales, the person is not free to place the statements anywhere he wishes. He must sort them into a limited number of piles, say nine, and in such a way that the frequency of statements in each pile creates a "normal" distribution, that is, a bell-shaped curve with very few items in the extreme categories and most in the middle categories. By doing so, and for reasons that we need not go into here, it is possible to do statistical operations on the rating data which ordinarily would not be justified, for example, to correlate one set of Q-sort ratings with another. Thus, the Q-sort method is really a fancy way of arranging rating scale data so that they are amenable to more precise quantification and statistical manipulation than is possible with the more casual type of rating scale. One way in which it has been used extensively is in the evaluation of the changes in persons undergoing psychotherapy, where, for example, Q-sorts of persons describing themselves are compared before and after the treatment process.

Personality Assessment—An Overview

We began this chapter by noting that assessment might be directed at the measurement of a single trait, say intelligence or impulse control, or the description and evaluation of the "whole" person. It is the latter for which the word assessment is technically most appropriate, but much more of the assessment activity in personality research nevertheless consists of the former. The task of specifying a single trait is far simpler than that of evaluating the "whole" individual, in which a multiplicity of individual

Table 9

Four Personal Feeling Scales Used by Wessman and Ricks

III. OWN SOCIABILITY VS. WITHDRAWAL
(how socially outgoing or withdrawn you felt today)

10. Immensely sociable and outgoing.
9. Highly outgoing, congenial, and friendly.
8. Very sociable and involved in things.
7. Companionable. Ready to mix with others.
6. Fairly sociable. More or less accessible.
5. Not particularly outgoing. Feel a little bit unsociable.
4. Retiring, would like to avoid people.
3. Feel detached and withdrawn. A great distance between myself and others.
2. Self-contained and solitary.
1. Completely withdrawn. Want no human contact.

IV. TRANQUILITY VS. ANXIETY
(how calm or troubled you felt)

10. Perfect and complete tranquility. Unshakably secure.
9. Exceptional calm, wonderfully secure and carefree.
8. Great sense of well-being. Essentially secure, and very much at ease.
7. Pretty generally secure and free from care.
6. Nothing particularly troubling me. More or less at ease.
5. Somewhat concerned with minor worries or problems. Slightly ill at ease, a bit troubled.
4. Experiencing some worry, fear, trouble, or uncertainty. Nervous, jittery, on edge.
3. Considerable insecurity. Very troubled by significant worries, fears, uncertainties.
2. Tremendous anxiety and concern. Harassed by major worries and fears.
1. Completely beside myself with dread, worry, fear. Overwhelmingly distraught and apprehensive. Obsessed or terrified by insoluble problems and fears.

V. IMPULSE EXPRESSION VS. SELF-RESTRAINT
(how expressive and impulsive, or internally restrained and controlled, you felt)

10. Wild and complete abandon. No impulse denied.
9. Exhilarating sense of release. Say whatever I feel, and do just as I want.
8. Quick to act on every immediate desire.
7. Allowing my impulses and desires a pretty free rein.
6. Moderate acceptance and expression of my own needs and desires.
5. Keep a check on most whims and impulses.
4. On the straight and narrow path. Keeping myself within strong bounds.
3. Obeying rigorous standards. Strict with myself.
2. Refuse to permit the slightest self-indulgence or impulsive action.
1. Complete renunciation of all desires. Needs and impulses totally conquered.

VI. ENERGY VS. FATIGUE
(how energetic, or tired and weary, you felt)

10. Limitless zeal. Surging with energy. Vitality spilling over.
9. Exuberant vitality, tremendous energy, great zest for activity.
8. Great energy and drive.
7. Very fresh, considerable energy.
6. Fairly fresh. Adequate energy.
5. Slightly tired, indolent. Somewhat lacking in energy.
4. Rather tired. Lethargic. Not much energy.
3. Great fatigue. Sluggish. Can hardly keep going. Meager resources.
2. Tremendously weary. Nearly worn out and practically at a standstill. Almost no resources.
1. Utterly exhausted. Entirely worn out. Completely incapable of even the slightest effort.

From Wessman and Ricks (1966)

traits are integrated into the organized system we call personality.

There are both applied and research contexts in which the assessment psychologist employs not one, but a battery of techniques and observational aids, and tries to draw an integrated psychological picture of the "whole" individual. One such context is the psychological or psychiatric clinic where the professional worker is concerned with planning a treatment program for a person suffering from an adjustive failure. Personality assessment in the clinical setting is often referred to as "psychodiagnosis," and its emphasis is on the conflicts which trouble the individual, the manner in which he copes with them, and the relations between these dynamics and his symptoms of adjustive failure. Such a psychodiagnosis does not consist of compiling a list of individual traits, but rather, it is a psychological portrait of a "whole" person.

One approach to such a psychological portrait that has been gaining increasing stature consists of the examination of patterns or profiles of traits in individuals. Thus, for example, on the MMPI questionnaire which has been described earlier, one can select all persons who share a profile in common, for example, high scores in hypochondriasis, hysteria, and depression, and low scores in paranoia, schizophrenia, and psychopathic deviate. These can be compared as a group with other types displaying a different profile. This kind of reasoning could be considerably complicated over the above example, thus approaching more closely a picture of a complex, organized personality system.

It might also be noted in this connection that when psychologists speak of the "whole" person, as distinguished from a collection of individual traits, they often mean something a bit different from a mere pattern or profile. The "whole" person can be conceived in terms of a set of organizing principles rather than a description of many diverse elements which go together. Such a principle, or set of principles, is an abstraction attempting to express the rule or rules by which the parts or structures of the system are organized, just as the term "internal combustion engine" connotes also a set of general rules for transforming energy in a particular way; other ways also exist. Presumably the organizing principles characterizing one person will be different from those characterizing another, and the touchstone of personality description would be to specify them in each case. This is not to say, as I have been at pains to make clear in earlier chapters, that the search for common organizing principles applying to all persons is not also an integral part of the science of personality.

Complex assessment programs for research purposes represent another context in which personality assessment of the "whole" person is undertaken. Such programs are rare because they are so costly of human and economic resources. Examples include the attempt during World War II by the Office of Strategic Services to assess the fitness of men for the role of undercover agents (OSS Assessment Staff, 1948), studies of clinical psychologists at Michigan (Kelly and Fiske, 1951; Kelly and Goldberg, 1959), a study of psychiatrists at the Menninger Foundation in Topeka, Kansas (Holt and Luborsky, 1958), and a continuing assessment program at the Institute of Personality Assessment and Research (IPAR) at the University of California, Berkeley (MacKinnon, 1966). This latter effort has included personality assessments of the American team that climbed Mt. Everest, creative and noncreative architects, a group of world-famous writers, and several other groups of persons.

In this IPAR assessment program, 10 subjects are typically studied at one time by 15 to 20 staff psychologists. The subjects usually live together and are studied intensively over a period of three days. Large numbers of observations, ratings, and descriptions are obtained on each subject. Some staff members interview, others use certain tests, etc., and ultimately each staff member must integrate his impressions by drawing portraits of each subject using personality-relevant adjectives, Q-sorts, and character sketches. The results of each assessment psychologist's efforts are compared for agreement and averaged to produce a composite account of each individual. This account can then be used in predicting other things about the person, this prediction being the test of the validity and usefulness of the assessment.

In both the limited assessment of single traits and the complex assessment of the "whole" person, the key problem, as might be anticipated, is the validity of the assessments. The knowledge and technology that would permit highly valid assessments is still quite limited. Personality assessment is also handicapped by limitations in personality theory and by problems related to the strong influence of situational factors on a person's behavior. Such situational influences, as we have seen, make the task of predicting behavior from assessment statements exceedingly difficult. Assessment as a field, like many other aspects of psychological science, is still in its infancy, a fact which is very discouraging to those who are impatient to solve practical problems that depend for solution on accurate assessment.

The task of personality assessment is of the utmost importance to the practical management of many human problems. There are two applied areas where assessment is of particular relevance, personnel selection and the clinical treatment of adjustive failure. With respect to personnel selection, it is often important to screen individuals who can function effectively in certain settings, for example, in military service, industry, school, special educational programs, various trades, etc. Surely it would be better for most individuals to be able to have the work tasks of their lives matched to their particular abilities and interests, and assessment is the potential means by which this might be done. Human satisfaction, efficiency, and justice all depend on such rational selection, as opposed, for example, to selection by family background, race, socioeconomic criteria, ethnic origin, etc.

With respect to clinical treatment, programs of treatment must be based on a knowledge of the nature of the disturbance, its etiology, and of the effective ways of dealing with each. The answers depend in part on personality assessment (or in this case, clinical diagnosis). Moreover, if we are to evaluate treatment programs, we must be able to determine the ways in which the person has changed (or not changed) as a consequence of some given treatment approach. In short, effective assessment is a prerequisite for the evaluation of psychotherapy.

The need for valid personality assessment is equally important if personality theory is to advance. Unless the individual constructs of personality theory can be assessed, empirical verification, rejection, or modification of theoretical principles about personality will be systematically impossible. Thus assessment is truly a fundamental aspect of the total field of personality. When the science of personality has finally evolved into a well-established and integrated body of knowledge, it will be in large measure through the creation of a technology of assessment superior to what it is today and on which the necessary research into the description, development, dynamics, and determinants of personality depends.

References

ADELSON, J., and O'NEIL, R. P. 1966. Growth of political ideas in adolescence: The sense of community. *Journal of Personality and Social Psychology,* 4:295–306.

ALLPORT, G. W. 1937a. *Personality.* New York: Holt, Rinehart and Winston, Inc.

———1937b. The functional autonomy of motives. *American Journal of Psychology,* 50:141–56.

———1942. The use of personal documents in psychological science. *Social Science Research Council Bulletin* 49.

———1955. *Becoming: Basic considerations for a psychology of personality.* New Haven: Yale University Press.

———1961. *Pattern and growth in personality.* New York: Holt, Rinehart and Winston, Inc.

———1962. The general and the unique in psychological science. *Journal of Personality* 30:405–22.

———1965. *Letters from Jenny.* New York: Harcourt, Brace & World, Inc.

———and ODBERT, H. S. 1936. Trait-names: A psycho-lexical study. *Psychological monographs* 47:1–171.

ALLPORT, G.W., and VERNON, P. E. 1933. *Studies in expressive movement.* New York: The Macmillan Company.

ANSBACHER, H. L., and ANSBACHER, ROWENA R. eds. 1956. *The individual-psychology of Alfred Adler.* New York: Basic Books, Inc., Publishers.

ARONFREED, J. 1968. *Conduct and conscience.* New York: Academic Press Inc.

ASCH, S. E. 1952. Effects of group pressure upon the modification and distortion of judgments. In *Readings in social psychology,* ed. G. E. Swanson, J. M. Newcomb, and E. L. Hartley. New York: Holt, Rinehart and Winston, Inc., pp. 2–11.

————1952. *Social psychology.* Englewood Cliffs, N. J.: Prentice-Hall, Inc.

————1956. Studies of independence and conformity: A minority of one against a unanimous majority. *Psychological Monographs: General and Applied* 70 (9): No. 416.

ATKINSON, J. W. ed. 1958. *Motives in fantasy, action and society.* Princeton, N. J.: D. Van Nostrand Co., Inc.

BANDURA, A., ROSS, DOROTHEA, and ROSS, SHEILA A. 1963. A comparative test of the status envy, social power, and the secondary reinforcement theories of identification learning. *Journal of Abnormal and Social Psychology* 67:527–34.

BARKER, R. G., and WRIGHT, H. F. 1951. *One boy's day.* New York: Harper & Row, Publishers.

BASS, B. M., and BERG, I. A. 1959. *Objective approaches to personality assessment.* Princeton, N. J.: D. Van Nostrand Co., Inc.

BAUMRIND, DIANA, and BLACK, A. E. 1967. Socialization practices associated with dimensions of competence in preschool boys and girls. *Child Development* 38 (No. 2):291–327.

BEACH, F. A. 1955. The descent of instinct. *Psychological Review* 62, 401–10.

BECK, S. J. 1930. Personality diagnosis by means of the Rorschach Test. *American Journal of Orthopsychiatry* 1:81–88.

BECKER, W. C. 1964. Consequences of different kinds of parental discipline. In *Review of Child Development Research,* ed. M. L. Hoffman and Lois W. Hoffman. New York: Russell Sage Foundation, pp. 169–208.

BETTELHEIM, B. 1960. *The informed heart.* New York: Free Press of Glencoe, Inc.

BINET, A., and SIMON, T. L. 1905. Application des methodes nouvelles au diagnostic du niveau intellectual chez des enfants normaux et anormaux d'hospice et d'école primaire. *Année Psychologique* 11:245–366.

BLUM, G. S. 1950. *The Blacky Pictures: A technique for the exploration of personality dynamics.* Ann Arbor, Mich.: Psychodynamic Instruments.

BORING, E. G. 1950. *A history of experimental psychology.* New York: Appleton Century-Crofts.

BREGER, L. 1963. Conformity as a function of the ability to express hostility. *Journal of Personality* 31:247–57.

BRONFENBRENNER, U. 1958. Socialization and social class through time and space. In *Readings in social psychology,* ed. Eleanor E. Maccoby, T. M. Newcomb, and E. L. Hartley. 3rd ed. New York: Holt, Rinehart and Winston, Inc.

BROWN, R. 1965. *Social psychology.* New York: Free Press of Glencoe, Inc.

CATTELL, R. B. 1950. *Personality: A systematic, theoretical and factual study.* New York: McGraw-Hill Book Company.

————1957. Handbook for the Sixteen Personality Factor Questionaire

————1965. *The scientific analysis of personality.* Baltimore: Penguin Books, Inc.

CAUDILL, W. 1959. Observations on the cultural context of Japanese psychiatry. In *Culture and Mental Health,* ed. M. K. Opler. New York: The Macmillan Company, pp. 213–42.

CHRISTIAN, J. J., and DAVIS, D. E. 1964. Endocrines, behavior, and population. *Science* 146:1550–60.

CLARK, G., and BIRCH, H. B. 1945. Hormonal modifications of social behavior. I. *Psychosomatic Medicine* 7:321–29.

———1946. Hormonal modifications of social behavior. II. *Psychosomatic Medicine* 8:320-31.

CLARK, R. A. 1952. The projective measurement of experimentally induced levels of sexual motivation. *Journal of Experimental Psychology* 44:391–99.

———1955. The effects of sexual motivation on phantasy. In *Studies in motivation,* ed. D. C. McClelland. New York: Appleton-Century-Crofts, pp. 132–38.

CRONBACH, L. J. 1960. *Essentials of psychological testing.* 2d ed. New York: Harper & Row, Publishers.

———and MEEHL, P. E. 1955. Construct validity in psychological tests. *Psychological Bulletin* 52:381–302.

DARWIN, C. 1859. *The origin of species.* London: John Murray Ltd.

———1873. *Expression of the emotions in man and animals.* New York: D. Appleton Company. (Reprinted by courtesy of Appleton-Century-Crofts, Inc.)

DAVIS, A., and HAVIGHURST, R. J. 1946. Social class and colour differences in childrearing. *American Sociological Review* 11:698–710.

DEMBER, W. N. 1960. *Psychology of Perception.* New York: Holt, Rinehart and Winston, Inc.

DEUTSCH, HELENE. 1944–1945. *The psychology of women.* 2 vols. New York: Grune & Stratton, Inc.

DOBZHANSKY, T. 1967. Changing man. *Science* 155:409–15.

———1967. Of flies and men. *American Psychologist* 22(No. 1):41–48.

DOLLARD, J., and MILLER, N. E. 1950. *Personality and psychotherapy: An analysis in terms of learning, thinking and culture.* New York: McGraw-Hill Book Company.

DUGDALE, R. W. 1877. *The Jukes.* New York: G. P. Putnam's Sons.

DUKES, W. F., N-1. 1965. *Psychological Bulletin* 64:74–79.

DUNDES, A. 1966. Here I sit—a study of American latrinalia. *Croeber Anthropological Society Papers* No. 34, pp. 91–105.

EDWARDS, A. L. 1954. *Edwards Personal Preference Schedule.* Manual. New York: Psychological Corporation.

EKMAN, P., and FRIESEN, W. V. 1967. Nonverbal behavior in psychotherapy research. In *Research on psychotherapy,* ed. J. Shlien. Vol. 3. Washington, D. C.: American Psychological Association.

ELKINS, S. 1961. Slavery and personality. In *Studying personality cross-culturally,* ed. B. Kaplan. New York: Harper & Row, Publishers, pp. 243–70.

ENDLER, N. S., and HUNT, J. McV. 1968. S-R inventories of hostility and comparisons of the proportions of variance from persons, responses, and situations for hostility and anxiousness. *Journal of Personality and Social Psychology* 9:309–15.

ERIKSON, E. H. 1959. Growth and crises of the healthy personality. *Psychological Issues* 1:5–-100. Also reprinted in *Personality,* ed. R. S. Lazarus and E. M. Opton, Jr. Middlesex, England: Penguin Books, Ltd., 1967, pp. 167–213.

———1963. *Childhood and society.* rev. ed. New York: W. W. Norton & Company, Inc.

EYSENCK, H. J. 1952. *The scientific study of personality.* London: Routledge & Kegan Paul Ltd.

FISKE, D. 1963. Homogeneity and variation in measuring personality. *American Psychologist* 18:643–52.

————1966. Some hypotheses concerning test adequacy. *Educational and Psychological Measurement* 26:69–88.

FLAVELL, J. H. 1963. *The developmental psychology of Jean Piaget.* New York: D. Van Nostrand Co., Inc.

FREUD, S. 1925. Instincts and their vicissitudes. In *Collected papers,* vol. 4. London: Hogarth Press. pp. 60–83. (First German edition, 1918).

————1933. Analysis of a phobia in a five-year old boy. In *Collected papers,* vol. 3. London: Hogarth, pp. 149–296. (First published in German, 1909).

————1933. *New introductory lectures on psychoanalysis.* New York: W. W. Norton & Company, Inc. (First German edition, 1933).

————1933. Psychoanalytic notes upon an autobiographical account of a case of paranoia (dementia paranoides). In *Collected papers,* vol. 3. London: Hogarth, pp. 390–472 (First published in German, 1911).

————1938. The psychopathology of everyday life. In *The basic writings of Sigmund Freud,* ed. A. A. Brill. New York: Modern Library, Inc.

————1949. *An outline of psychoanalysis.* New York: W. W. Norton & Company, Inc. (First German edition, 1940).

————1953. *The interpretation of dreams.* In Standard Edition, vols. 4 and 5. London: Hogarth (First German edition, 1900).

————1957. *Civilization and its discontents,* trans. Joan Riviere. London: Hogarth. (First German edition, 1930).

————1961. The ego and the id. In *The complete psychological works of Sigmund Freud,* vol. 21. Trans. James Strachey in collaboration with Anna Freud, vol. 21, London: Hogarth.

FROMM, E. 1941. *Escape from freedom.* New York: Holt, Rinehart and Winston, Inc.

————1947. *Man for himself.* New York: Holt, Rinehart and Winston, Inc.

————1949. Psychoanalytic characterology and its application to understanding of culture. In *Culture and personality,* ed. S. S. Sargent and Marian W. Smith. New York: Basic Books, Inc., Publishers, pp. 1–12.

————1955. *The sane society.* New York: Holt, Rinehart and Winston, Inc.

GALTON, F. 1869. *Hereditary Genius.* London: Macmillan & Co. Ltd.

GIBSON, J. J. 1966. *The senses considered as perceptual systems.* Boston: Houghton Mifflin Company.

GLUECK, S., and GLUECK, ELEANOR. 1950. *Unraveling juvenile delinquency.* New York: Commonwealth Fund.

GODDARD, H. H. 1912. *The Kallikak family.* New York: The Macmillan Company.

GOLDSTEIN, K. 1940. *Human nature in the light of psychopathology.* Cambridge: Harvard University Press.

GOLDSTEIN, M. J. 1959. The relationship between coping and avoiding behavior and response to fear-arousing propaganda. *Journal of Abnormal and Social Psychology* 58:247–52.

GOTTESMAN, I. 1966. Genetic variance in adaptive personality traits. *Journal of Child Psychology and Psychiatry* 7:199–208.

———1968. Genetics. In *Biology and behavior,* ed. D. C. Glass. New York: Rockefeller University Press and Russell Sage Foundation, pp. 59–68.

GOUGH, H. G. 1957. *Manual for the California Psychological Inventory.* Palo Alto, Calif : Consulting Psychologists Press.

———1960. Theory and measurement of socialization. *Journal of Consulting Psychology* 24:23–30.

HALL, C. S., and LINDZEY, G. 1957. *Theories of personality.* New York: John Wiley & Sons, Inc.

HALL, K. R. L. 1964. Aggression in monkey and ape societies. In *The natural history of aggression,* ed. J. D. Carthy, and F. J. Ebling. New York: Academic Press, Inc., pp. 51–64.

HARDIN, GARETT. 1949. *Biology: Its human implications.* San Francisco: W. H. Freeman and Co., Publishers.

HARLOW, H. F. 1953. Mice, monkeys, men and motives. *Psychological Review* 60:23–32.

HARTMANN, H. 1964. *Essays on ego psychology.* New York: International University Press.

HARTSHORNE, H., and MAY, M. A. 1928. *Studies in deceit.* In *Studies in the nature of character,* vol. I New York: The Macmillan Company.

HATHAWAY, S. R., and MCKINLEY, J. C. 1943. *The Minnesota Multiphasic Personality Inventory.* rev. ed. Minneapolis: University of Minnesota Press.

HEALY, W., BRONNER, AUGUSTA, F., and BOWERS, ANNA MAE. 1930. *The structure and meaning of psychoanalysis.* New York: Alfred A. Knopf, Inc.

HEMMENDINGER, L. 1960. Developmental theory and the Rorschach method. In *Rorschach Psychology,* ed. Maria A. Rickers-Ovsiankina. New York: John Wiley & Sons, Inc., pp. 58–79.

HETHERINGTON, E. M., and WRAY, NANCY P. 1964. Aggression, need for social approval, and humor preferences. *Journal of Abnormal and Social Psychology* 68:685–89.

HIRSCH, J. 1967. *Behavior genetic analysis.* New York: McGraw-Hill Book Company.

HOLLINGSHEAD, A. B. 1949. *Elmtown's youth.* New York: John Wiley & Sons, Inc.

HOLT, R. R. 1962. Individuality and generality in the psychology of personality. *Journal of Personality* 30:377–404.

HOLT, R. R., and LUBORSKY, L. 1958. Personality patterns of psychiatrists. New York: Basic Books, Inc., Publishers.

HOLT, R. R., and HAVEL, JOAN. 1960. A method for assessing primary and secondary process in the Rorschach. In *Rorschach Psychology,* ed. Maria A. Rickers-Ovsiankina. New York: John Wiley & Sons, Inc., pp. 263–315.

HOOKER, D. 1943. The reflex activities in the human fetus. In *Child behavior and development,* ed. R. S. Barker, J. S. Kounin, and H. F. Wright. New York: McGraw-Hill Book Company.

HORNEY, KAREN. 1937. *Neurotic personality of our times.* New York: W. W. Norton & Company, Inc.

HSU, FRANCIS L. K. 1961. *Psychological anthropology: Approaches to culture and personality.* Homewood, Ill.: Dorsey Press.

HULL, C. L. 1943. *Principles of behavior.* New York: Appleton-Century-Crofts.

HUXLEY, A. 1965. Human potentialities. In *Science and human affairs,* ed. R. E. Farson. California: Science and Behavior Books.

INHELDER, B., and PIAGET, J. 1958. *The growth of logical thinking from childhood to adolescence.* New York: Basic Books, Inc., Publishers.

————1947. Studies of phenylpyruvic oligophrenia. The position of the metabolic error. *Journal of Biological Chemistry* 169:651–56.

————1953. Phenylpyruvic oligophrenia: Deficiency of phenylalanine oxidizing system. *Proceedings of the Society for Experimental Biology* 82:514–15.

JENSEN, A. R. 1969. How much can we boost IQ and scholastic achievement? *Harvard Educational Review* 39 (No. 1).

JERVIS, G. A. 1937. Introductory study of fifty cases of mental deficiency associated with excretion of phenulpyruvic acid. *Archives of Neurology and Psychiatry* 38:944–63.

JUNG, C. G. 1916. *Analytical psychology.* New York: Moffat, Yard.

————1933. *Psychological types.* New York: Harcourt, Brace & World, Inc.

————1953. Two essays on analytical psychology. In *Collected works,* vol. 7. New York: Pantheon Books, Inc.

KAHL, J. A., and DAVIS, J. A. 1955. A comparison of indexes of socio-economic status. *American Sociological Review* 20:314–25.

KAHN, R. L., and CANNELL, C. F. 1957. *The dynamics of interviewing.* New York: John Wiley & Sons, Inc.

KALLMAN, F. J. 1953. *Heredity in health and mental disorder.* New York: W. W. Norton & Company, Inc.

KARDINER, A. 1939. *The individual and his society.* New York: Columbia University Press.

————1949. Psychodynamics and the social sciences. In *Culture and personality,* eds. S. S. Sargent and Marian W. Smith, New York: Basic Books, Inc., Publishers, pp. 59–74.

KELLY, E. L., and FISKE, D. W. 1951. *The prediction of performance in clinical psychology.* Ann Arbor: University of Michigan Press.

KELLY, E. L., and GOLDBERG, L. R. 1959. Correlates of later performance and specialization in psychology. *Psychological Monographs* 73: Whole No. 482.

KELLY, G. A. 1955. *The psychology of personal constructs,* vols. 1 and 2. New York: W. W. Norton & Company, Inc.

KELMAN, H. C. 1961. Processes of opinion change. *Public Opinion Quarterly* 25:57–58.

KENNISTON, K. 1965. *The uncommitted: Alienated youth in American society.* New York: Delta, Dell Publishing Co., Inc.

————1968. *The young radicals: Notes on committed youth.* New York: Harcourt, Brace & World, Inc.

KEYS, A. B.; BROZEK, J.; HEUSCHEL, A.: MICKELSON, O.: and TAYLOR, H. L. 1950. *The biology of human starvation.* Minneapolis: University of Minnesota Press.

KLINEBERG, O. 1935. *Negro intelligence and selective migration.* New York: Holt, Rinehart and Winston, Inc.

KLOPFER, B., and KELLEY, D. M. 1942. *The Rorschach Technique.* New York: World Publishing Co.

KOHLBERG, L. 1963. The development of children's orientations toward a moral order: 1. Sequence in the development of moral thought. *Vita Humana* 6:11–33.

KRECH, D., CRUTCHFIELD, R. S., and BALLACHEY, E. L. 1962. *Individual in society.* New York: McGraw-Hill Book Company.

KRETSCHMER, E. 1925. *Physique and character.* New York: Harcourt, Brace & World, Inc.

LAMBERT, W. W., and LAMBERT, W. E. 1963. *Social psychology.* Englewood Cliffs, N. J.: Prentice-Hall, Inc.

LANGER, J. 1969. *Theories of development.* New York: Holt, Rinehart and Winston, Inc.

LAZARUS, R. S. 1969. *Patterns of adjustment and human effectiveness.* New York: McGraw-Hill Book Company.

——— OPTON, E. M., JR, NOMIKOS, M. S., and RANKIN, N. O. 1965. The principle of short-circuiting of threat: Further evidence. *Journal of Personality* 33:622–35.

LAZARUS, R. S. and OPTON, E. M., JR., eds. 1967. *Personality,* part I. Middlesex, England: Penguin Books, Ltd.

LEAKEY, L. S. B. 1967. Development of aggression as a factor in early human and prehuman evolution. In *Aggression and defense,* ed. C. D. Clemente, and D. B. Lindsey. Berkeley and Los Angeles: University of California Press.

LEHRMAN, D. S. 1964. The reproductive behavior of ring doves. *Scientific American* 211:48–54.

LERNER, I. M. 1968. *Heredity, evolution, and society.* San Francisco: W. H. Freeman and Co., Publishers.

LEVINE, S. 1966. Sex differences in the brain. *Scientific American* 214:84–90.

———and MULLINS, R. F., JR. 1966. Hormonal influences on brain organization in infant rats. *Science* 152:1585–92.

LEVY, D. M. 1955. Oppositional syndromes and oppositional behavior. In *Psychopathology of childhood,* ed. P. H. Hoch and J. Zubin. New York: Grune & Stratton, Inc., pp. 204–26.

LEWIN, K. 1935. *A dynamic theory of personality,* trans. K. E. Zener and D. K. Adams. New York: McGraw-Hill Book Company

LIPSITT, P. D., and STRODTBECK, F. L. 1967. Defensiveness in decision making as a function of sex-role identification. *Journal of Personality and Social Psychology* 6:10–15.

MACKINNON, D. W. 1966. Some reflections on the current status of personality assessment. Paper presented at faculty symposium, Department of Psychology, University of California, Berkeley, 15 Nov. 1966.

MADDI, S. R. 1968. *Personality theories: A comparative analysis.* Homewood, Ill.: Dorsey Press.

MASLOW, A. H. 1954. *Motivation and personality.* New York: Harper & Row, Publishers.

————1964. Synergy in the society and in the individual. *Journal of Individual Psychology* 20:153-64.

MATTHEWS, L. H. 1964. Overt fighting in mammals. In *The natural history of aggression,* ed. J. D. Carthy and F. J. Ebling, New York: Academic Press, Inc., pp. 7–14.

MAY, R. 1967. *Psychology and the human dilemma.* Princeton, N. J.: D. Van Nostrand Co., Inc.

MCCLELLAND, D. C. 1951. *Personality.* New York: The Dryden Press.

————ATKINSON, J. W., CLARK, R. A., and LOWELL, E. L. 1953. *The achievement motive.* New York: Appleton-Century-Crofts.

MCCORD, W., and MCCORD, JOAN. 1958. The effects of parental role model on criminality. *Journal of Social Issues* 14:66–75.

————1956. *Psychopathy and delinquency.* New York: Grune & Stratton, Inc.

MCGAUGH, J. L., WEINBERGER, N. M., and WHALEN, R. E., eds. 1967. *Psychobiology.* San Francisco: W. H. Freeman and Co., Publishers.

MEAD, G. H. 1934. *Mind, self, and society,* ed. C. W. Morris. Chicago: University of Chicago Press.

MECHANIC, D. 1968. *Medical sociology.* New York: Free Press of Glencoe, Inc.

————1963. Religion, religiosity, and illness behavior: The special case of the Jews. *Human Organization* 22:202–8.

MILLER, N. E., and DOLLARD, J. 1941. *Social learning and imitation.* New Haven: Yale University Press.

MISCHEL, W. 1968. *Personality and assessment.* New York: John Wiley & Sons, Inc.

MOYER, K. E. 1967. *Kinds of aggression and their physiological basis.* Carnegie-Mellon University Report No. 67–12.

MURPHY, G. 1947. *Personality.* New York: Harper & Row, Publishers.

MURRAY, E. J. 1964. *Motivation and emotion.* Englewood Cliffs, N. J.: Prentice-Hall, Inc.

MURRAY, H. A. 1938. *Explorations in personality.* New York: Oxford University Press, Inc.

————1943. *Manual for the Thematic Apperception Test.* Cambridge, Mass.: Harvard University Press.

OPLER, M. K. ed. 1959. *Culture and mental health.* New York: The Macmillan Company.

OSS ASSESSMENT STAFF. 1948. *Assessment of men.* New York: Holt, Rinehart and Winston, Inc.

PETERSEN, W., and MATZA, D. 1963. *Social controversy.* Belmont, Calif.: Wadsworth.

PIAGET, J. 1948. *The moral judgment of the child.* New York: Free Press of Glencoe, Inc. (1st ed., 1932).

————1952. *The origins of intelligence in children.* New York: International University Press.

PRINCE, M. 1920. Miss Beauchamp—The theory of the psychogenesis of multiple personality. *Journal of Abnormal and Social Psychology* 15:82–85, 87–91, 96–98, 102–4, 135.

RANK, O. 1952. *The trauma of birth.* New York: Robert Brunner, Publishers.

RAPAPORT, D. 1967. *Collected papers,* ed. M. M. Gill. New York: Basic Books, Inc., Publishers.

REED, C. F., and CUADRA, C. A. 1957. The role-taking hypothesis in delinquency. *Journal of Consulting Psychology* 21:386–90.

RICHARDSON, S. A., DOHRENWEND, BARBARA S., and KLEIN, D. 1965. *Interviewing: Its forms and functions.* New York: Basic Books, Inc., Publishers.

ROGERS, C. R. 1942. *Counseling and psychotherapy.* Boston: Houghton Mifflin Company.

———1947. Some observations on the organization of personality. *American Psychologist* 2:358–68.

———1951. *Client-centered therapy.* Boston: Houghton Mifflin Company.

——— and ROETHLISBERGER, F. J. 1952. Barriers and gateways to communication. *Harvard Business Review* 30 (July–August): 46–52.

RORSCHACH, H. 1942. *Psychodiagnostics,* trans. P. Lemkau and B. Kronenberg. New York: Grune & Stratton, Inc. (First German edition 1932).

ROSENFELD, H. M. 1966. Instrumental affiliation functions of facial and gestural expressions. *Journal of Personality and Social Psychology* 4:65–72.

ROTHBALLER, A. G. 1967. Aggression, defense, and neurohumors. In *Aggression and defense: Neural mechanisms and social patterns,* ed. C. D. Clemente, and D. B. Lindsley. Los Angeles: University of California Press, pp. 135–70.

SAHAKIAN, W. S., ed. 1965. *Psychology of personality: Readings in theory.* Chicago: Rand McNally & Co.

SARBIN, T. R. 1954. Role theory. In *Handbook of social psychology,* ed. G. Lindzey. Reading, Mass.: Addison-Wesley, p. 223–58.

SCHACHTER, S. 1951. Deviation, rejection, and communication. *Journal of Abnormal and Social Psychology* 46:190–207.

SEARS, R. R., MACCOBY, ELEANOR E., and LEVIN, H. 1957. *Patterns of child rearing.* New York: Harper & Row, Publishers.

SELYÉ, H. 1956. *The stress of life.* New York: McGraw-Hill Book Company.

SHELDON, W. H. (with S. S. Stevens and W. B. Tucker). 1940. *The varieties of human physique: An introduction to constitutional psychology.* New York: Harper & Row, Publishers.

SHELDON, W. H. (with S. S. Stevens). 1942. *The varieties of temperament: A psychology of constitutional differences.* New York: Harper & Row, Publishers.

SHERIFF, M. 1935. A study of some social factors in perception. *Archives of Psychology,* no. 187.

———and CANTRIL, H. 1947. *The psychology of ego-involvements.* New York: John Wiley & Sons, Inc.

SINGER, J. L., and OPLER, M. K. 1956. Contrasting patterns of fantasy and motility in Irish and Italian schizophrenics. *Journal of Abnormal and Social Psychology* 53: 42–47.

SINGER, M. 1961. A survey of culture and personality theory and research. In *Studying personality cross-culturally,* ed. B. Kaplan. New York: Harper & Row, Publishers, pp. 9–90.

SKEELS, H. M. 1940. Some Iowa studies of the mental growth of children in relation to differentials in the environment: A summary. In *Intelligence: Its nature and nurture*. Thirty-ninth Yearbook, Part II. National Society for the Study of Education, pp. 281–308.

————1942. A study of the effects of differential stimulation on mentally retarded children: A follow up report. *American Journal of Mental Deficiency* 46:340–50.

————1966. Adult status of children with contrasting early life experiences. *Monographs of the Society for Research in Child Development* 31 (Serial No. 105).

SMELSER, N. J., and SMELSER, W. T. 1963. Introduction: Analyzing personality and social systems. In *Personality and social systems,* ed. N. J. and W. T. Smelser. New York: John Wiley & Sons, Inc., pp. 1–18.

SPOCK, B. 1957. *Baby and child care.* New York: Pocket Books.

STONE, A. A., and STONE, SUE SMART. 1966. *The abnormal personality through literature.* Englewood Cliffs, N. J.: Prentice-Hall, Inc.

TEITELBAUM, P. 1967. *Physiological psychology.* Englewood Cliffs, N. J.: Prentice-Hall, Inc.

TERMAN, L. M. 1916. *The measurement of intelligence.* Boston: Houghton Mifflin Company.

THIGPEN, C. H., and KLECKLEY, H. M. 1957. *The three faces of Eve.* New York: McGraw-Hill Book Company.

THOMPSON, W. R. 1965. Behavior genetics. In *McGraw-Hill Yearbook of Science and Technology.* New York: McGraw-Hill Book Company, pp. 27–35.

TIMMONS, E. O., and NOBLIN, C. D. 1963. The differential performance of orals and anals in a verbal conditioning paradigm. *Journal of Consulting Psychology* 27: 383–86.

TINBERGEN, N. 1951. *The study of instincts.* London: Oxford University Press.

TRYON, R. C. 1940. Genetic differences in maze-learning ability in rats. *Yearbook of the National Society for the Study of Education* 39 (Part I): 111–19.

————1955. Identification of social areas by cluster analysis: A general method with an application to the San Francisco Bay Area. *Univ. of California Publications in Psychology* 8: (No. 1).

————1955. Biosocial constancy of urban social areas. Paper read before American Psychological Association.

————1959. The social dimensions of metropolitan man (revised title). Paper read before American Psychological Association.

TURNER, C. B., and FISKE, D. W. 1968. Item quality and appropriateness of response processes. *Educational and Psychological Measurement* 28:297–315.

TYLER, LEONA E. 1963. *Tests and measurements.* Englewood Cliffs, N. J.: Prentice-Hall, Inc.

ULLMANN, L. P., and KRASNER, L. 1969. *A psychological approach to abnormal behavior.* Englewood Cliffs, N. J.: Prentice-Hall, Inc.

VERNON, P. E. 1964. *Personality assessment: A critical survey.* London: Methuen & Co. Ltd.

WALLACH, M. A., GREEN, L. R., LIPSETT, L., and MINEHART, JEAN B. 1962. Contradiction between overt and projective personality indicators as a function of defensiveness. *Psychological Monographs* 76:23.

WARNER, W. L., and LUNT, P. S. 1941. *The social life of a modern community.* New Haven, Conn.: Yale University Press.

WEINSTEIN, J., AVERILL, J. R., OPTON, E. M., Jr., and LAZARUS, R. S. 1968. Defensive style and discrepancy between self-report and physiological indexes of stress. *Journal of Personality and Social Psychology* 10:406–13.

WERNER, H. 1954. Developmental approaches to general and clinical psychology. Paper read as part of a symposium, "Developmental Approach to Problems of General and Clinical Psychology," at a meeting of the Massachusetts Psychological Association, March 1954.

WESSMAN, A. E., and RICKS, D. F. 1966. *Mood and personality.* New York: Holt, Rinehart and Winston, Inc.

WHALEN, R. E. 1967. *Hormones and behavior.* Princeton, N. J.: D. Van Nostrand Co., Inc.

WHITE, R. W. 1956. *The abnormal personality.* 2d ed. New York: The Ronald Press Company.

————1960. Competence and the psychosexual stages of development. In *Nebraska Symposium on Motivation,* ed. M. R. Jones. Lincoln-University of Nebraska Press, pp. 97–141.

WISSLER, C. 1901. The correlation of mental and physical tests. *Psychological Review* 3(No. 6). Monograph Supplement.

WITKIN, H. A., DYK, R. B., FATERSON, H. F., GOODENOUGH, D. R., and KARP, S. A. 1962. *Psychological differentiation.* New York: John Wiley & Sons, Inc.

WOLFENSTEIN, MARTHA, 1953. Trends in infant care. *American Journal of Orthopsychiatry* 23:120–30.

WOLFF, H., ed. 1950. Life stress and bodily disease. *Proceedings of the Association for Research in Nervous and Mental Diseases.* Baltimore: The Williams & Wilkins Co.

WOLFF, P. H. 1960. The developmental psychologies of Jean Piaget and psychoanalysis. *Psychological Issues* 2 (1): No. 5.

WOODWORTH, R. S. 1918. *Personal Data Sheet.* Chicago: Stoelting.

ZBOROWSKY, M. 1958. Cultural components in response to pain. In *Patients, physicians, and illness,* ed. E. G. Jaco. New York: Free Press of Glencoe, Inc., pp. 256–68.

ZIGLER, E. 1967. Familial mental retardation: A continuing dilemma. *Science* 155: 292–98.

ZOLA, I. K. 1966. Culture and symptoms—An analysis of patients' presenting complaints. *American Sociological Review* 31: 615–30.

Suggested Readings

Chapter 1

ALLPORT, G. W. *Personality.* New York: Henry Holt & Co., Inc., 1937. *Pattern and Growth in Personality.* New York: Holt, Rinehart & Winston, Inc., 1961.

CATTELL, R. B. *The scientific analysis of personality.* Baltimore, Md.: Penguin Books, Inc., 1965.

LAZARUS, R. S., and OPTON, E. M., JR., eds., *Personality.* Middlesex, England: Penguin Books, Ltd. 1967.

MURPHY, G. *Personality.* New York: Harper & Row, Publishers, 1947.

Chapter 2

CATTELL, R. B. *The scientific analysis of personality.* Baltimore, Md.: Penguin Books, Inc., 1965.

EYSENCK, H. J. *The scientific study of personality.* London: Routledge & Kegan Paul, Ltd., 1952.

HALL, C. S., and LINDZEY, G. *Theories of personality.* New York: John Wiley & Sons, Inc., 1957.

LAZARUS, R. S., and OPTON, E. M., JR. *Personality.* Middlesex, England: Penguin Books, Ltd. 1967. Part I.

SAHAKIAN, W. S., ed. *Psychology of personality: Readings in theory.* Chicago: Rand McNally & Co. 1965.

Chapter 3

ERIKSON, E. H. "Growth and crisis of the healthy personality." *Psychological Issues,* I (1959): 50–100. "Eight ages of man," In *Childhood and society.* 2d ed. New York: W. W. Norton, 1963, Ch. 7, pp. 247–74.

FLAVELL, J. H. *The developmental psychology of Jean Piaget.* New York: D. Van Nostrand Co., Inc., 1963.

FREUD, S. *A general introduction to psychoanalysis.* Garden City, N. Y.: Garden City Books, 1943. (First German edition 1917).

HEALY, W., BRONNER, AUGUSTA F., and BOWERS, ANNA MAE. *The structure and meaning of psychoanalysis.* New York: Alfred A. Knopf, Inc., 1930, Section II.

LANGER, J. *Theories of development.* New York: Holt, Rinehart and Winston, Inc., 1969.

Chapter 4

ANSBACHER, H. L., and ANSBACHER, ROWENA R., eds. *The individual-psychology of Alfred Adler.* New York: Basic Books Inc., Publishers 1956.

FREUD, S. "The development of the libido and the sexual organizations." In Introductory lectures on psychoanalysis, *The complete works of Sigmund Freud.* London: Hogarth Press, 1962, Vol. 16, Lecture 21, pp. 320–38.
———*A general introduction to psychoanalysis.* Garden City, N. Y.: Garden City Books, 1943. (First German edition 1917).

FROMM, E. *The sane society.* New York: Holt, Rinehart and Winston, Inc., 1955.

DOLLARD, J., and MILLER, N. E. *Personality and psychotherapy.* New York: McGraw-Hill Book Company, 1950.

MASLOW, A. H. *Motivation and personality.* New York: Harper & Row Publishers, 1954.

RANK, O. *The trauma of birth.* New York: Robert Brunner, Publishers. 1952.

ROGERS, C. R. *Client-centered therapy.* Boston: Houghton Mifflin Company, 1951.

WHITE, R. "Competence and the psychosexual stages of development." In *Nebraska Symposium on Motivation,* ed. M. R. Jones. Lincoln: Univ. of Nebraska Press, 1960, pp. 97–141.

Chapter 5

HIRSCH, J. *Behavior genetic analysis.* New York: McGraw-Hill Book Company, 1967.

LERNER, I. M. *Heredity, evolution, and society.* San Francisco, Calif.: W. H. Freeman and Co., Publishers, 1968.

MCGAUGH, J. L. WINBERGER, N. M., and WHALEN, R. E., eds. *Psychobiology.* San Francisco, Calif.: W. H. Freeman and Co., Publishers, 1967.

MURRAY, E. J. *Motivation and emotion.* Englewood Cliffs, N. J.: Prentice-Hall, Inc., 1964.

TEITELBAUM, P. *Physiological psychology.* Englewood Cliffs, N. J.: Prentice-Hall, Inc., 1967.

WHALEN, R. E. *Hormones and behavior.* Princeton, N. J.: D. Van Nostrand Co., Inc.,

1967.

Chapter 6

BROWN, R. *Social psychology.* New York: Free Press of Glencoe, Inc., 1965.

HSU, FRANCIS L. K. *Psychological anthropology: Approaches to culture and personality.* Homewood, Ill.: Dorsey Press, 1961.

KRECH, D., CRUTCHFIELD, R. S., and BALLACHEY, E. L. *Individual in society.* New York: McGraw-Hill Book Company, 1964.

LAMBERT, W. W., and LAMBERT, W. E. *Social psychology.* Englewood Cliffs, N. J.: Prentice-Hall, Inc., 1963.

SINGER, M. "A survey of culture and personality theory and research." In *Studying personality cross-culturally,* ed. B. Kaplan. New York: Harper & Row, Publishers, 1961, pp. 9–90.

Chapter 7

BASS, B. M., and BERG, I. A. *Objective approaches to personality assessment.* Princeton, New Jersey: D. Van Nostrand Co., Inc., 1959.

CRONBACH, L. J. *Essentials of psychological testing.* 2d ed. New York: Harper & Row, Publishers, 1960.

MISCHEL, W. *Personality and assessment.* New York: John Wiley & Sons, Inc., 1968.

TYLER, LEONA E. *Tests and measurements.* Englewood Cliffs, N. J.: Prentice-Hall, Inc., 1963.

VERNON, P. E. *Personality assessment: A critical survey.* London: Methuen & Co., Ltd., 1964.

Index